'This extraordinary book illuminates in a coherent manner, imaginatively combining data with formal modelling, that dark corner of development economics called the 'nonfarm' informal economy. Although India is the primary focus, many developing countries and regions across the globe find their place in the comparative analysis. It is an extremely valuable addition to the development literature and should be on the essential reading list of students, researchers, and practitioners concerned with development studies and problems.'

—Amit Bhaduri, Retired Professor, Centre for Economic Studies and Planning, Jawaharlal Nehru University

'This ground-breaking book is a must-read for anyone concerned about the persistence and even the rise of the informal sector. Based on an extended structuralist model, the authors use in-depth case studies of selected Indian regions, econometric analysis, and international comparisons to provide empirical evidence of the counterintuitive effect of formal sector growth: the squeezing out of the agricultural sector and the consequent expansion of petty, non-agricultural, informal activities in rural areas. It is up to date with an analysis of the impact of the COVID-19 pandemic and offers thoughtful policy recommendations.'

—Christoph Scherrer, Kassel Institute for Sustainability

'Mainstream development literature maintains that economic dualism will gradually disappear in the poorer countries as, under the guidance of free market forces, they converge to a unified capitalistic modern economy with full participation of the labour force. This has not happened. Not only has the old industry–agriculture dualism persisted, but also, even within non-agriculture, a significant type of neo-dualism has emerged, comprising a modernizing nonfarm sector and petty informal activities. As a result, poverty, unemployment, economic exclusion, and insecurity refuse to vanish despite impressive overall aggregative growth. Using an elegant analytical framework well supported by Indian data, the authors have succeeded in providing very important insights into this disturbing puzzle of neo-dualism. This is a truly impressive intellectual achievement'.

—Soumyen Sikdar, Retired Professor,
Indian Institute of Management, Calcutta

'The authors of *The Nonfarm Economy* combine considerable analytical expertise, deep knowledge of data, keen understanding of policymaking, and clear, effective writing to explore a key question in India's ongoing economic transformation: how does capitalist growth impact rural economic structures?'

—Tirthankar Roy, Professor of Economic History,
London School of Economics

The Nonfarm Economy

The Nonfarm Economy

Continuity and Change in Rural India

MANOJIT BHATTACHARJEE
SAUMYA CHAKRABARTI
MEENAKSHI RAJEEV

OXFORD
UNIVERSITY PRESS

OXFORD
UNIVERSITY PRESS

Great Clarendon Street, Oxford, OX2 6DP,
United Kingdom

Oxford University Press is a department of the University of Oxford. It furthers the University's objective of excellence in research, scholarship, and education by publishing worldwide. Oxford is a registered trade mark of Oxford University Press in the UK and in certain other countries.

Published in the United States of America by Oxford University Press
198 Madison Avenue, New York, NY 10016, United States of America.

British Library Cataloguing in Publication Data
Data available

Library of Congress Control Number: 2025944870

ISBN 9780198972020

DOI: 10.1093/9780198972013.001.0001

Printed in India by
Replika Press Pvt. Ltd.

The manufacturer's authorised representative in the EU for product safety is Oxford University Press España S.A. of Parque Empresarial San Fernando de Henares, Avenida de Castilla, 2 – 28830 Madrid (www.oup.es/en or product.safety@oup.com). OUP España S.A. also acts as importer into Spain of products made by the manufacturer.

This book is dedicated to our spouses, parents, and children, whose enormous sacrifices have made it possible.

Preface and Acknowledgements

The Indian economy, previously perceived as stagnant or sluggish for several decades following the independence of the country, has now been projected in the mainstream literature for the past few decades as transforming towards a grand, unified, and dynamic market economy. This book questions this dominant narrative. Based on theoretical and empirical analyses, carried out using data from diverse sources, we propose that rather than converging into an integrated capitalistic economy, in India, various types of dualism are intensifying over time. Further, we demonstrate that this feature of persistence and deepening of dualism, as observed in the case of the Indian economy, is not confined to a localized context. Many regions or countries in the Global South observe similar patterns of dualistic development, though the causes may not be the same.

This book examines the origin of this dualistic developmental pattern. In this context, it is important to emphasize that dualism in developing nations is not a new phenomenon, and mainstream development economics literature has extensively examined the persistence of this problem. These studies mostly assert that excess population and insufficient accumulation contribute to the perpetuation of dualism. Although the book acknowledges that excess population growth can contribute to dualism in many less developed economies, it challenges the dominant claim that posits a deep positive association between growth, structural transformation, capitalist consolidation, and development.

Contrarily, our book's examination of the Indian rural economy and segments of the rural Global South indicates the presence of a profound positive correlation between growth and persistence, and even intensification, of structural dualism. In the context of the Indian economy, our analysis specifically demonstrates that as the economy has expanded, individuals have predominantly transitioned away from traditional/petty agriculture owing to various shocks and incentives generated by the accumulation process in the modern capitalistic or formal sector.

However, it is found that, mostly, individuals are not getting absorbed into the formal nonfarm sector or the remunerative formal-sector-linked nonfarm informal activities. A significant part of the diversifying or dispossessed mass actually gets attached to the petty informal nonfarm sector (as mainly self-employed and/or wage workers), owing to several constraints. Thus, we contend that the rise of the formal sector not only means an expansion of the rural capitalist circuit and the modernization and inclusion of some segments of the rural informal sector but it may also generate a push effect that significantly promotes or expands petty, nonfarm informal activities—the sites of exclusion.

Apart from capturing the impact of capital accumulation on rural development, our book also captures the impact of the recent COVID-19 pandemic, which jeopardized the whole capital accumulation process. The analysis of the available data shows that the phenomenon of dualism that we theorized and tested in this study can become stronger in both the COVID-19 and post-COVID-19 situations. The implications drawn in this book with respect to the shocks generated by COVID-19 can have wider applications in contexts or situations in which the economy experiences a slowdown.

The book concludes with constructive but critical policy recommendations for achieving inclusive growth. The recommendations extend beyond current dominant prescriptions that are obsessed with formal sector growth and with policies associated with the extension of government support. This book, on the contrary, posits a labour-focused, cluster-based development model, along with the immediate management of underdevelopment.

The completion of this book was made possible by the support and assistance of various individuals and institutions. We would like to acknowledge and express our deep gratitude to each one of them. First, we wish to acknowledge the financial help from the Indian Council of Social Science Research (ICSSR) through two major projects funded at the Institute for Social and Economic Change (ISEC), Bangalore, and Visva-Bharati (University), Santiniketan. These projects have aided us in conducting numerous field visits in different states, which eventually helped us strengthen our understanding of the rural economy of India. Second, the unit-level secondary data sets used in Chapters 5 and 7 were largely downloaded free of cost from the National Data Archive of the Ministry of Statistics and Program Implementation, Government of India. We express our gratitude in this regard.

We collectively express our gratefulness for the support we received from our respective institutions, including the Indian Institute of Technology Jammu, Visva-Bharati, Santiniketan (especially the faculty and staff members of the Department of Economics and Politics); Mahatma Gandhi Government Arts College in Mahe, ISEC, Bangalore; and the Reserve Bank of India at ISEC.

We would also like to thank Amit Bhaduri, Deepankar Basu, Debarshi Das, Rajesh Bhattacharya, Snehashish Bhattacharya, Pratip Kumar Datta, Anirban Dasgupta, Anirban Kundu, and Kasturi Sadhu for numerous discussions and very important suggestions. Furthermore, we are extremely grateful to the OUP editors, especially Dhiraj Pandey, Senior Project Editor at OUP, Amrita Brahmo, and the anonymous referees, for their crucial support and valuable suggestions. We also express our heartfelt thanks to the large mass of informal workers, who have helped by providing valuable information and by giving vital household, technical, and logistics support. Finally, we thank our extended family members, friends, and former students for their support in times of need. Views expressed in this book are those of the authors.

Contents

Figures

Tables

Abbreviations

1D1F	One District One Factory Initiative
1-H	Simpson's Index
3SLS model	Three-state least squares model
AGR	Agricultural sector
AGR_m	Modern agricultural sector
AGR_t	Traditional agricultural sector
AIDIS	All India Debt and Investment Survey
ASI	Annual Survey of Industries
CDI	Crop Diversification Index
CMIE	Centre for Monitoring Indian Economy
'Const.'	Construction
CPI	Consumer Price Index
CSA	Central Statistical Agency
CSO	Central Statistical Organisation
Est.	Informal establishment, i.e. firms using hired workers
FAO	Food and Agriculture Organization
FGLS	Feasible generalized least squares
F. Manuf.	Formal manufacturing
FS	Formal sector
FSU	First-stage sampling unit
GDP	Gross domestic product
GLS	Generalized least squares
GLSS	Ghana Living Standards Survey
GST	Goods and services tax
GVA	Gross value added
H	Herfindahl index
HIES	Household Integrated Economic Survey
H–T method	Harris–Todaro method
HVC	High-value crop
IFPRI	International Food Policy Research Institute
IHDS	India Human Development Survey
ILO	International Labour Organization
IMF	International Monetary Fund
IOI	Incidence of indebtedness
LARR 2013	The Right to Fair Compensation and Transparency in Land Acquisition, Rehabilitation and Resettlement Act 2013

LFS	Labour Force Survey
LSLA	Large-scale land acquisition
METASIP	Medium-Term Agriculture Sector Investment Plan
MNREGA	Mahatma Gandhi National Rural Employment Guarantee Act
MPCE	Monthly per capita consumption expenditure
MPI	Multidimensional Poverty Index
NAS	National Account Statistics
NEIP	National Entrepreneurship and Innovation Plan
NFSA	National Food Security Act
NSSO	National Sample Survey Office
NVA	Net value added
OAE	Own account enterprise, i.e. informal self-employment unit that does not have any hired workers
OLS	Ordinary least squares
PCE	Per capita expenditure
PIB	Press Information Bureau
PLFS	Periodic Labour Force Survey
PMGKAY	Pradhan Mantri Garib Kalyan Anna Yojana
RBI	Reserve Bank of India
RNF	Rural nonfarm
RNFE	Rural nonfarm economy
RNFS	Rural nonfarm sector
$RNFS_m$	Modern rural nonfarm sector
$RNFS_t$	Traditional nonfarm sector
SAS	Situation Assessment Survey
SME	Small and medium-sized enterprise
SUR	Seemingly unrelated regression
UNDP	United Nations Development Programme
UNPD	United Nations Population Division
VND	Vietnam Dongs
VTCS	Village Tank Cascade System
WDR	World Development Report
WPI	Wholesale Price Index

1
Introduction

The Indian economy is transforming. Not only the urban growth poles but also the vast rural hinterland is changing. The dominant discourses consider this transformation as a protracted capitalistic transition or, at least, a movement, albeit a tortuous and slow one, towards a grand, unified, and dynamic market economy (Reddy et al., 2014; Himanshu et al., 2018; Invest India, 2024; World Bank, n.d.). Further, according to both the official and critical strands of the narrative, contemporary political regimes are playing an important role in building this supposedly monolithic structure, having a single market for all exchangeable goods and services—from labour to means of labour, from entertainment to education.[1] The intentions of these efforts are often critiqued as an endeavour to forcefully convert and converge disparate parts of the economy into a grand, uniform whole.[2] This economic process of consolidation is argued to be complemented by the political and ideological discourses on identity, which try to push the socio-economic dynamics towards a homogeneous structure (Bhambhri, 2016; Chakrabarti et al., 2020). This is because the construction of a cohesive political-economic-social and cultural space across the whole country is considered a necessary condition to support the supposedly homogeneous economic entities to interact in a seemingly standardized environment with allegedly uniform objectives and thereby produce a purportedly homogenizing economic process of growth and development.

[1] For instance, see Narendra Modi (n.d.). Further, one of the goals of the recently introduced goods and services tax is to create one common market in the entire country (The Economic Times, 2014, 2015). For critical analyses, see Chakrabarti et al. (2015); Jha (2019).

[2] Patnaik (2017) argued that some of the recent policies in India, such as introduction of the goods and services tax (GST) or demonetization are the ways of pursuing centralization of capital at the cost of the smaller, dispersed, and widely diverse informal producers.

The Nonfarm Economy. Manojit Bhattacharjee, Saumya Chakrabarti, and Meenakshi Rajeev,
Oxford University Press.
DOI: 10.1093/9780198972013.003.0001

Contrarily, the Indian economic space in particular, and the Global South to some extent, as conceptualized and presented in this book, is starkly different from what is stated above (mainly by the mainstream discourses). Through our theoretical and empirical analyses, not only do we point out the persistence of widespread heterogeneities and deep fissures, but we also demonstrate how these dichotomies are being intensified and, in addition to the old unevenness (Sen, 2012), how newer forms of dualism are being generated. Further, for the Indian economy in particular, we show how the ongoing (private-accumulation-centric and market-centric) growth process by its very nature is inducing this dualism; this is just the opposite of the claim of the dominant discourse, which considers economic growth as the main driver for convergence and comprehensive capitalistic transition.

Thus, we too acknowledge that the Indian economy, and even its vast rural space, are changing. But we present a much more nuanced picture—a more complex dynamic. Even the supposedly homogeneous rural India (and the rural Global South to some extent) is creating acute dichotomies with simultaneous processes of growth, persistence, and sometimes even immiseration; concurrent processes of continuity and change are operating together. Of course, politically, there is a deliberate push to make India a homogeneous entity; however, in reality, in the socio-economic space, there is growing unevenness—old occupations are persisting, new dynamic segments are emerging, and even newer forms of petty production are being generated. This growing unevenness is not only an intensification of socio-economic inequality but also a proliferation of dichotomous/heterogeneous economic systems/structures existing simultaneously and having conflicts and complementarities among themselves.

Further, and most importantly, we also show theoretically as well as empirically that, for India, the ongoing (capital-centric and market-centric) growth process itself is spreading and deepening dualism. The very pattern of progress is reproducing a heterogeneous structure instead of the projected path of convergence and a comprehensive transition.

Thus, the contributions of the present work are the following:

1. Moving away from the mainstream projection of convergence, homogenization, and capitalistic transition (albeit slow and tortuous),

we show empirically that rural India (and also the rural Global South, to some extent) is producing a variety of heterogeneities across both the farm and (particularly) the nonfarm segments. To be precise, we demonstrate that there is a spreading and deepening of the phenomenon of dualism across rural India, contrary to the dominant claims or, at least, expectations. Not only the farm–nonfarm duality but also, more importantly, the intra-nonfarm dichotomy is accentuating; even a variety of (distinctly different) economic structures/systems are conjectured to evolve. There are found to be simultaneous processes of evolution, persistence, and even involution.

2. Further, most importantly, we analyse theoretically and empirically that this deepening of dualism in rural India is correlated with the overall capital-centric growth process of the economy. The accumulative (modern sector-based) growth mechanism generates a variety of shocks (especially the price/cost shocks, in the short and medium term)[3] for the rural traditional (farm–nonfarm) economy and thereby immiserates and/or dispossesses a large segment of the population. Only a small part of this immiserated and/or dispossessed mass can be accommodated into the growing circuits (of capital) due to their endowments, abilities, and networks. But a much larger part is pushed into inferior and relatively under-remunerative activities; such activities are undertaken essentially to supplement household income from traditional occupations. Thus, the ongoing growth process itself is reproducing dualism even within the (apparently homogeneous) rural economy of India (and particularly within its nonfarm segment) instead of its mitigation, through mostly diversification and sometimes shifts of jobs. Old structures/systems/sectors/activities are being replaced and/or complemented/supplemented by the new ones. Thus, a very complex (and in fact, a fractured) economic structure is emerging across India and in some segments of the rural Global South. This

[3] A process of accumulation by dispossession (Harvey, 2003) could also operate in the longer run.

raises critical questions about the very claim of having or, at least, expecting a process of 'inclusive growth'.

In this context, it is worth pointing out that the presence of dualism in the developing countries is not a new phenomenon, and mainstream development economics literature has accommodated the existence/sustenance of duality/heterogeneity from the very beginning (Lewis, 1954; Ranis and Fei, 1961; Fei and Ranis, 1964).[4] Such studies on development have largely considered excess population, along with a lack of sufficient growth or lack of expansion of the capitalist circuit in developing countries, as the primary reason behind the persistence of such duality. However, the problem is that this viewpoint has not changed much over the years (Fields, 2004; La Porta and Shleifer, 2014). In fact, this position has been sustained (particularly among the policymakers), even though in the past few decades, many erstwhile overpopulated countries, such as China and India, have observed a slowdown of the population growth rate accompanied by a rise in the economic growth rate. This period has also witnessed an expansion of the formal sector in the rural areas (World Bank, 2009; Ghani et al., 2012) and an increase in inequality in these countries (Bardhan, 2010; Chancel and Piketty, 2019).[5] Thus, this literature has failed to recognize that despite economic growth and population control, the Global South has not been able to resolve the old problem of dualism fundamentally; understandably, it has also failed to recognize the newer forms of dualism across the Global South.

Contrary to these conventional claims on the deep association between growth, structural transformation, capitalist consolidation, and development (Chakravarty, 2014), our analysis of the Indian rural economy (and parts of the rural Global South) suggests proliferation and deepening of dualism with growth. Along with the widely discussed rural–urban,

[4] However, contrarily, mainstream studies have also questioned the existence of duality and argued that the informal (the supposedly dual of the formal) segment of the economy is essentially a continuum of the formal segment (Guha-Khasnobis and Kanbur, 2006; Guha-Khasnobis et al., 2006).

[5] Few recent studies have emphasized the increase in inequality with the growth of the Indian economy (Chancel and Piketty, 2019). However, it is important to note that the concept of duality is different in comparison to the concept of inequality. Dualism implies prevalence of two or more sets of structures or mode of production within the same society. Further, while prevalence of dualism leads to inequality, presence of inequality may not automatically signify duality (Sadhu and Chakrabarti, 2021).

sub-national/regional, modern–traditional, accumulation–need, and agriculture–industry or farm–nonfarm dichotomies/dualities and dynamics (Bernstein, 1996, 2006; Sanyal, 2007; Haggblade et al., 2008; McMichael, 2008; Mookherjee and White, 2011; Binswanger-Mkhize, 2012, 2013; Kathuria et al., 2013; Lerche, 2013, 2021; Lagakos, 2020), in our subsequent explorations, within-farm and especially intra-rural–nonfarm fissures have been found to be spreading in India (and across a major part of the Global South). This analysis shows that only a part of the farm and the rural (informal) nonfarm sectors are becoming modernized (along with the rural, formal nonfarm sector), with a much larger (and even growing) part persisting in misery. With the growth of the economy, barring sudden frictions (such as the COVID-19 pandemic, Indian demonetization of 2016, etc.), people have generally been moving out of agriculture due to a variety of shocks or incentives, induced primarily by the modern capitalist sector.[6] However, not all of them are getting absorbed into the formal nonfarm sector or the remunerative formal sector-linked nonfarm informal activities. A large part of the diversifying or dispossessed mass also throngs the petty/informal nonfarm sector (as mostly self-employed and/or wage-worker). Thus, formal sector growth is not only associated with a pulled expansion of the circuit of capital and/or modernization of some parts of the rural nonfarm informal sector, as it has been generally presumed by Fields (2004), but is also pushing the traditional/petty nonfarm informal activities to proliferate or multiply (Harriss-White, 2023), fuelled through the process of dispossession.

In this work, we not only wish to illustrate in detail this peculiar phenomenon of growth-induced intensification of dualism but also to provide a theoretical explanation of this process. However, before going into our own theoretical explanations, empirical expositions, and subsequently, the post-COVID-19 analytical projections, let us first present some of the dominant arguments of the existing literature on the nature of the transformation of the Global South in general and that of the Indian economy in particular.

[6] In Chapter 6, we have delineated in detail how the expansion of the formal sector, along with other factors, has been reducing the size of the agricultural workforce until recently.

1.1 Literature

During the early decades of the twentieth century, when development economics evolved as a separate discipline, it was thought that the problem of underdevelopment of the newly emerging (post-colonial) independent countries could be mitigated through a process of growth based on (mainly market-centric) capital accumulation-led modern industrialization. This capitalistic growth process would not only expand the modern sectors of the then underdeveloped countries but also transform the traditional sectors by drawing in their surplus labour and other resources and thereby reducing the burden of backwardness (Lewis, 1954). Thus, it was argued that not only traditional agriculture but also primitive/pre-capitalistic/traditional non-agriculture would either wither away or be incorporated into the expanding modern economic spaces or would, at least, transform into vibrant segments.[7] This idea of development was essentially borrowed from the prolonged European experience of Industrial Revolution and its subsequent changes. It was thought that a much quicker process could be introduced in the then underdeveloped Global South if a well-orchestrated, market-based, and capital accumulation-driven path is followed. It was also acknowledged, following the then Soviet experience, that if private capital accumulation and market were not capable of undertaking this gigantic task, government intervention in allocation, production, and distribution would be necessary. Accordingly, the mixed economy models of development and economic transformation were introduced.

However, the experience turned out to be starkly different. Although during the mid-twentieth century, in the then underdeveloped countries, the modern industrial base expanded, a sizable accumulation of capital took place, surplus labour was mobilized, and considerable improvement

[7] In fact, this happens to be a dominant discourse even today: it conjectures that, with the growth of the modern capitalistic (formal) sector, the petty/non-capitalistic (informal) sector would either wither away, or be incorporated, or get linked with the formal sector, or at least be able to enter into a phase of tortuous transition (Hymer and Resnick, 1969; Ranis and Stewart, 1993; Fields, 2004; Bardhan, 2009; La Porta and Shleifer, 2014).

> (W)e have seen that modern sector enlargement has two beneficial effects on poverty. One is that poverty falls among those workers who are able to move from the informal sector to the formal sector. The other is that poverty falls among the workers who remain informal. [...] wages do rise in [...] (Lewis) [...] model via these two mechanisms, and poverty is correspondingly reduced as Lewis-type growth takes place.
>
> (Fields, 2004, pp. 13)

in state and market functioning was achieved, large-scale quality employment generation within (and around) the growing modern sectors remained a distant dream (Harris and Todaro, 1970; Sen, 1983). Despite modernization through capital accumulation, with the support of state and market institutions, a large part of the population could not be incorporated into the growth process. Not only did the centuries-old farm and nonfarm practices continue to persist but also a variety of activities, especially in the non-agricultural sector, evolved beyond the core of the capitalistic growth process. Thus, instead of the targeted/expected structural transformation of the underdeveloped economies and, hence, transition of the traditional segments, ironically, the 'outside' (beyond the centre of modernization) kept on expanding steadily (Sanyal, 2007; Sanyal and Bhattacharya, 2009).

Not only did urban unemployment and underemployment expand considerably (Harris and Todaro, 1970), but also there was very little transformation of the traditional rural economy (Breman and Mundle, 1991; Rajeev and Bhattacharjee, 2018; Breman, 2019). Akin to the projections of the initial development models, with the growth of the formal sector, a sizable part of the workforce moved out of agriculture; however, they have taken refuge largely as self-employed in the traditional nonfarm or newly forming petty informal sectors or, at best, they got engaged as casual/contract/part-time/'*badli*' workers in the rural modern nonfarm segments (Jatav and Sen, 2013); only a minority could get remunerative jobs within the ambit of the rural–urban modern sectors. The process of transformation has become stunted (Binswanger-Mkhize, 2013).

Thus, despite an occupational transformation (shift or diversification) within the rural space, very little has happened so far as modernization and the uplift of the overall economy are concerned. A sizeable number of people have left traditional agriculture to be engaged either in the rural age-old traditional or newly emerging informal nonfarm activities or in the periphery of modern industry and services. Only a fortunate few could find a place in the urban and rural modernizing segments (Bhattacharya et al., 2013; Breman, 2013, 2019; Standing, 2014; Chakrabarti, 2016; Raj and Sen, 2016; Bhattacharya and Kesar, 2018; Harriss, 2020; Kesar and Bhattacharya, 2020; Kesar, 2023).

Thus, the transformations of the Global South in general, India in particular, and rural India specifically have been marked as stunted/truncated/fractured/ruptured. The efficacy of urbanization-driven transformation has been questioned even by a section of the mainstream (World Resources Institute, n.d.). And it is now being recognized by both mainstream (although tangentially) and its critics that the Indian scenario is pretty complex and volatile (Kalaiyarasan, 2022; Yadu and Mehra, 2023). The ongoing processes of (so-called) rural transformation of India are increasingly being critiqued by the heterodoxy (Abraham, 2016, 2023, 2024; Binswanger-Mkhize, 2013; Lerche, 2013; Dasgupta, 2021; Basole, 2022; Harriss-White, 2023). In fact, the very claim of capitalist transition and mitigation of dualism is put under scrutiny.

This peculiar feature of the Global South in general and India in particular grabs our attention. We contemplate whether a study of this scenario could generate some novel as well as generalizable insights on the proliferation of precarious jobs (and thereby on the reproduction of dualism), going beyond some recent standard mainstream positions, which propose the proliferation of petty jobs just as a product of surplus labour and lack of sufficient growth and expansion of the capitalist circuit (modern industry, services, and infrastructure), lack of sufficient education and skill, lack of well-defined property right, lack of flexibility of labour market, and lack of governance and sufficient safeguard against global competition and crisis pushing firms towards informalization, etc. (Portes and Jensen, 1989; De Soto and Diaz, 2002; Bardhan, 2009; Haggblade et al., 2010; La Porta and Shleifer, 2014; Pattayat and Parida, 2024).

Given the varied theoretical positions (orthodox as well as heterodox), as mentioned above, the question is posited of understanding the processes operating in the rural Global South in general and rural India in particular. Essentially, while the orthodox discourse (barring a few apprehensions) is still optimistic about the issue of dualism and expects that, with accelerated growth and institutional manoeuvring, this problem of duality could be mitigated, the heterodox discourse critiques this view and conjectures that the very process and pattern of growth itself is the cause of the proliferation and intensification of dualism. Thus, while the dominant literature focuses on the 'pull factors', the critical analysis emphasizes the 'push factors'. This dichotomy across discourses obviously makes this issue an object of more rigorous study.

Thus the questions that arise through a critical reading of the literature are whether, following the mainstream arguments, the growth pull is working for the rural economy of India and what could be the sources and mechanisms of this pull; whether, following some of the heterodox positions, growth push is a significant force (beyond the standard push factors like population explosion, land fragmentation, policy-driven farmers' income squeeze, global price-shocks, etc.) and how this works through intersectoral mobility and linkages; whether both pull and push forces (mainly driven by the ongoing growth process, going beyond the institutional, demographic, natural, and policy factors) are working simultaneously (instead of their dichotomous operations); and finally, and most importantly, whether these very simultaneous processes are spreading and deepening dualism in rural India instead of the projected, or at least expected, process of convergence (albeit a prolonged one).

These questions need to be studied together, instead of focusing on any one or two separately, if we want to understand the economic dynamics properly.

1.2 Some stylized facts

Such a comprehensive study demands a closer look at the overall structure of Indian employment and its trends over time, especially when the economy has grown fast. But, before going into these Indian data, let us have a look at the global scenario to understand whether India happens to be an outlier or a representative case and hence, a researchable, large-country example.

Table 1.1 presents the changing nature of rural employment and overall urban employment in Asian, Latin American, and African regions. The data show that the share of rural jobs in overall employment has declined in most regions of the world. However, the share of employment in the rural nonfarm sector has increased over the years. We see that, with an increase in the share of urban employment, there is also an increase in rural nonfarm employment. In fact, the percentage change in employment in the rural nonfarm sector is higher in most regions than that in urban areas. This might have happened either because of a variety of positive linkages between the rural nonfarm and formal sectors[8]

[8] Positive interlinkages operating through market integration (Ranis and Stewart, 1993), urban sector subcontracting job to the rural nonfarm sector (Lanjouw and Lanjouw, 2001), capital flow and technology transfer from the urban sector to the rural nonfarm sector (Marjit and Kar, 2011), etc.

Table 1.1 Share of employment across sectors and rural–urban regions and over time (%)

Region	Year	Rural agricultural	Rural non-agricultural	Rural total	Urban total	Total
South Asia	2005	50.9	23.4	74.4	25.6	100
	2010	47.1	26	73.1	26.9	100
	2015	42.1	28.3	70.4	29.6	100
East Asia	2005	35.7	22.5	58.2	41.8	100
	2010	29	22.7	51.7	48.3	100
	2015	22.4	23.5	45.9	54.1	100
West Asia	2005	19.4	14.7	34.1	65.9	100
	2010	17.6	16.2	33.8	66.2	100
	2015	15.4	18.3	33.7	66.3	100
South Eastern Asia	2005	40	22.1	62.1	37.9	100
	2010	36.5	25.2	61.7	38.3	100
	2015	30	24.4	54.3	45.7	100
Northern Africa	2005	27.7	23.5	51.2	48.8	100
	2010	24.8	26.9	51.7	48.3	100
	2015	22.9	28.6	51.4	48.6	100
Sub-Saharan Africa	2005	54	15.2	69.1	30.9	100
	2010	51.6	16.6	68.2	31.8	100
	2015	48.3	18.1	66.4	33.6	100
Latin America and the Caribbean	2005	13.5	10.1	23.6	76.4	100
	2010	11.4	10.8	22.2	77.8	100
	2015	10.1	11.3	21.4	78.6	100

Source: Computed from International Labour Organization (ILO) database.

or due to the fact that the growth of the capitalist sector has induced some crucial agrarian changes[9] that, in turn, have pushed out farmers and farm workers from agriculture towards the nonfarm sector, or because of both these factors.

[9] Induced agrarian changes such as (i) increased mechanization and increased use of modern costly inputs raising the costs of production and thereby *reducing the net income of the farmers* because of their inability to increase the output prices commensurately in the presence of intermediaries and also uncontrolled exposure to the global market (Himanshu, 2019), (ii) land conversion for urbanization and industrial expansion *squeezing traditional agriculture* (Chakrabarti and Kundu, 2009a), and (iii) large-scale crop diversification to match the growing urban demand for high-value crops as inputs for processing as well as outputs for consumption; this large-scale crop diversification makes agriculture and the associated supply chain *more capital intensive* (World Bank, 2007).

From Table 1.1, one gets only an outline of the changes that are happening across different regions of the globe. The table does not provide detailed information about the movement of the workforce across different sectors within the farm and nonfarm economies, primarily due to data limitation. To get a comprehensive picture, we now take up the employment dynamics in the rural and urban areas of India, where data is available across different sectors.

Table 1.2 presents the share of different sectors in total employment in India over time. The table clearly shows that there is a movement of the workforce away from agriculture, mostly towards the informal segment within the nonfarm sector and construction. Further, if we segregate these movements across rural–urban locations, intriguingly, the rural nonfarm sector (RNFS) is found to grow at a faster rate as compared to its urban counterpart (excluding the category 'Others'). For instance, from Table 1.2, one finds that agricultural employment has declined from 61 per cent in 1999–2000 to around 45.7 per cent in 2015–2016. This decline is associated with an increase in jobs in the rural informal (nonfarm) sector (which includes employment in the rural establishments hiring labour and rural own account enterprises (OAEs), i.e. self-employment), the rural formal manufacturing sector, and the rural construction sector by 1.47, 0.65, and 5.67 per cent, respectively (i.e. 7.79 per cent in total). On the other hand, if we consider the increase in the urban informal sector and formal manufacturing jobs, it is only 4.99 per cent. The category 'Others' has expanded by around 2 per cent, and it includes both rural and urban employment.

Such changes in employment patterns (especially rural) might have happened because of two fundamental contributors: the Mahatma Gandhi National Rural Employment Guarantee Programme and other construction-related rural programmes (e.g. rural housing, rural infrastructure development, etc.), creating jobs at the minimum wage and ruralization of erstwhile urban jobs, mainly via peri-urbanization and subcontracting, contractualization, casualization, informalization, etc. (Jatav and Sen, 2013).

Thus, a large part of the agrarian population seems to have moved/diversified en masse (be it locally, regionally, or even nationally), mostly towards poorer quality nonfarm jobs, and this is corroborated by the findings of Table 1.3.

Table 1.2 Share of different sectors in total employment in India over time

Year		Rural		Urban		Total	Rural	Urban	Rural	Urban	Others	Total
	(1) Agriculture	(2) OAE	(3) Est.	(4) OAE	(5) Est.	(6) Informal nonfarm enterprises 1 + 2+3 + 4	(7) F. Manuf.	(8) F. Manuf.	(9) Const.	(10) Const.	(11)	(12) 1 + 6+7 + 8 + 9 + 10 +11
1999–2000	61.0	8.28	1.34	5.39	4.37	19.38	0.75	1.30	2.29	1.56	13.72	100
2015–2016	45.7	8.48	2.61	6.88	6.77	24.74	1.40	1.78	7.96	2.66	15.78	100

Note: 'OAE' stands for 'own account enterprise' or informal self-employment without any hired worker on a fairly regular basis. 'Est.' stands for informal establishment with hired workers on a fairly regular basis. OAE and Est. employment were computed using the unit-level enterprise survey, NSSO (Government of India) data. F. Manuf. stands for 'Formal manufacturing'. Annual Survey of Industries data was used for its computation. 'Const.' stands for 'Construction'. We obtained construction data from employment and unemployment surveys of the NSSO. 'Others' primarily includes formal services and is computed by subtracting employment in agriculture, informal sector, formal manufacturing, and construction sector from total employment obtained from the ILO.

Source: Authors' computation based on various databases (ILO), Annual Survey of Industries (ASI), National Sample Survey Office (NSSO).

Table 1.3 Percentage distribution of rural households by household type within each asset ownership decile in India (taken from an International Labour Organization report)

Asset class	Agriculture		Non-Agriculture	
	2002–2003	2012–2013	2002–2003	2012–2013
0–10	42.1	34.8	57.9	65.2
10–20	60.5	47.9	39.5	52.1
20–30	59.8	52.3	40.2	47.7
30–40	62	49.8	38	50.2
40–50	61.5	58.3	38.5	41.7
50–60	63.2	62.2	36.8	37.8
60–70	66.1	66.2	33.9	33.8
70–80	70.6	69.1	29.4	30.9
80–90	71.6	70.5	28.4	29.5
90–100	76.4	72	23.6	28

Source: All India Debt and Investment Survey (NSSO), 2002–2003 and 2012–2013.

Table 1.3 shows that workers, mainly from the poorer economic classes, have shifted from agriculture to non-agriculture in rural areas. This table primarily indicates horizontal mobility rather than upward mobility (be it local or regional, or even national) of workers; hence, it may mean that a push-driven sectoral transformation is happening rather than a pulled one. This apparent dominance of push over pull is further explicated in Table 1.4.

Table 1.4 presents gross value added (GVA) per worker across different sectors of India (which partially captures labour productivity levels, particularly for the informal sector in which capital intensity is low). It is observed that the GVA per worker of formal manufacturing and services are overwhelmingly higher compared to those of agriculture and the informal sector, and these absolute differences have been increasing over time. Not only that, but the absolute differences in GVA per worker across informal segments (rural/urban, self-employment/establishment) have also been increasing.

A few more striking observations in Table 1.4 are the following:

1. The GVA per worker of the rural self-employment segment (OAE) is markedly lower than that of all other sectors (even agriculture),

Table 1.4 Gross value added per worker (in Indian rupees) at 2017–2018 prices

Year	Agriculture	Informal rural OAE	Informal rural Est.	Informal urban OAE	Informal urban Est.	Informal sector	Rural formal manufac. sector	Urban formal manufac. sector	Const.	Others
1999–2000	56,410	38,073	70,898	76,294	135,110	57,457	725,435	700,856	187,385	331,618
2015–2016	115,398	59,029	121,364	103,622	179,592	87,538	1,125,593	819,562	221,834	1,036,524

Note: Agriculture and construction sector gross value-added data are taken from the National Account Statistics (NAS) and the Central Statistics Office (CSO), Government of India; informal sector gross value added (GVA) data is taken from the NSSO's Enterprise Survey as mentioned in Table 1.2; and data on organized manufacturing's GVA is taken from the ASI. 'Others' data are obtained as residual. OAE stands for informal self-employment as before; Est. stands for the informal establishment with hired labour as before; Const. stands for the construction sector; 'Others' stands for mainly formal services. The construction sector's GVA for 1999–2000 is obtained from the 55th round of the NSSO; for 2010–2011, the GVA of this sector is computed based on the average sectoral GVA of the NSSO's Employment–Unemployment Survey; and the same for 2015–2016 is taken from India Employment Report (IMA). GVA for the rest of the sectors is taken from the Reserve Bank of India database. The Consumer Price Index (CPI) for agricultural workers (2017–2018 base price) is used to deflate the GVA of the agriculture and rural informal sector. The CPI for industrial workers (2017–2018 base price) is used to deflate the GVA of the urban informal sector. The Wholesale Price Index (WPI) for all commodities (2017–2018 base price) is used to deflate the GVA of formal manufacturing and other sectors.

Source: Authors' computation based on various databases.

although the share of the workforce in this segment is large, and it is still increasing (Table 1.2);

2. the GVA per worker of rural informal firms with hired labour (Establishment) is just above that of agriculture, and this gap is reducing considerably over time;
3. although, initially, the labour productivity of urban OAE was higher than that of agriculture, lately, the latter has become lower, maybe due to migration and employment diversification leading to urban congestion;
4. however, urban informal establishments with hired labour (Establishment) are in a better position;
5. although, initially, the condition of the construction sector (rural–urban combined) was much better than that of agriculture and the informal sector, recently, these differences have reduced, possibly due to migration-induced congestion; and finally,
6. rural–urban formal manufacturing and services are hugely better off, and their relative position is still improving.

Thus, fundamentally, it is clear that not only the rural–urban dichotomy is deepening but also the intra-rural and especially the intra-rural nonfarm dualities are proliferating. Instead of a process of structural transformation and (inter- and intra-sectoral) convergence, the Indian economy, in general, and rural India, in particular, is becoming more heterogeneous and uneven. This unevenness is accentuated through rural–urban and especially intra-rural employment diversification and/or migration from farm to nonfarm. Not only are the local and regional level fissures widening, but also the national-level divergence is deepening. This country-wide heterogeneity has been identified in our own fieldwork as well. We have found that, depending on the general economic condition, the RNFS has assumed a variety of patterns across different places in India.[10]

Further, apparently, it seems that, in this process of movement of the workforce away from agriculture, both pull and push factors are working. A part of the agricultural workforce (and of the increased population, too) moves into high productivity (rural–urban) formal manufacturing

[10] See Appendix A.1.1 for a glimpse of the heterogeneities within the rural nonfarm sector across different locations in India.

and services and into construction and urban informal establishments as well, maybe due to the pull factors (Harris and Todaro, 1970). On the other hand, perhaps, the push factors (such as overcrowding in agriculture, fall in relative income of agriculture, absolute income deflation, and forced dissociation of small farmers from means of farming through a variety of political-economic processes, etc.) (Sanyal 2007; Patnaik 2008) force the agricultural labourers and petty farmers (as well as fresh entrants into the labour force) to get engaged in the less productive rural OAE and Establishment segments and in urban OAE too. Thus, dualism is found to be proliferating and deepening across the rural economy through the simultaneous operations of push-and-pull forces.

1.3 The plan of the work and its broad outcomes

With this crucial backdrop of probable operations of the push and pull forces reallocating labour and thereby multiplying the nonfarm sector along with its deepening (intra- and inter-sectoral) divides, strikingly, in a period of high growth, we posit our basic questions: is it just a coincidence for India that growth and fragmentation are moving hand in hand? Or, contrary to the orthodox optimism about growth annihilating, or absorbing, or transforming petty farm and nonfarm (La Porta and Shleifer, 2014), is it actually a product of growth pull and associated institutional features (Harris and Todaro, 1970; Fields, 1975; Thakur and Guha, 2019)? Or is it an outcome of a variety of push factors broadly classified as the growth–accumulation–dispossession–informalization nexus (Harvey, 2003; Sanyal, 2007; Patnaik, 2008; Munck, 2013; Standing, 2011; Bhaduri, 2018)? Or, something more nuanced (deviating from both orthodoxy and heterodoxy and, at the same time, deriving from both), producing a complex economic structure?

To deal with these issues, first, in Chapter 2, we introduce a theoretical model along structuralist lines (Kalecki, 1934/1971, 1954/1993; Bhaduri, 1986; Sadhu and Chakrabarti, 2021). The static model and its extensions (comparative static analysis) succinctly present a process of accumulation engendering income deflation, resource expropriation, and also demand pull, spreading a heterogeneous (rural) nonfarm sector and, thereby, reproducing a new form of dualism. The specific contributions of this theoretical framework are the following:

1. It discusses the (sectoral and sub-sectoral) structural specificities and inter-sectoral relationships considering the heterogeneous, rural non-capitalistic nonfarm (henceforth RNF) and agricultural (henceforth AGR) sectors along with the (rural) modern capitalistic formal sector (henceforth, FS). This considerably concretizes our understanding of the complex RNF sector going beyond the standard location–size–industry-based categorization, which happens to be mostly vague (Haggblade et al., 2002, 2008). Thus, characterization of the RNF and its different segments in terms of structural features is a major contribution of the model.
2. Contrary to the dominant literature (Ranis and Stewart, 1993; Marjit, 2003; Fields, 2004; Bardhan, 2009, 2018), which presents a variety of mechanisms through which the FS triggers a transition within the heterogeneous RNF, bringing it close to the FS itself and also making it a comprehensive and dynamic whole, our model explicates how the FS (rural, in particular) could, in fact, create a division within the farm and nonfarm sectors (across modern and traditional segments) and thereby, accentuate the intra-RNF and intra-agriculture structural dualities. Thus, our framework could be a critique of the deterministic narrative of (all-inclusive) transition from the traditional to the modern.
3. Going beyond the dichotomous doctrines of growth-pulled (Harris and Todaro, 1970; Haggblade et al., 2002, 2010; Thakur and Guha, 2019) and growth-pushed (Sanyal, 2007; Bhaduri, 2018) migrations/evictions away from the traditional farm and nonfarm, and thereby creations or expansions of the new rural–urban nonfarm, we present a more comprehensive framework combining both the dynamics—pull and also push. Thus, we deviate from both orthodoxy and heterodoxy but, simultaneously, draw from both the genres.
4. While a large part of the orthodox, as well as heterodox literature, considers the RNF as an integral segment of the broad capitalistic network, of course, having widely diverse loci, relationships, and impacts (Moser, 1978; Portes and Jenson, 1989; Basole and Basu, 2011a, 2011b; Breman, 2013; Munck, 2013; Thakur and Guha, 2019), an important strand of heterodox literature considers it as a vast sea of surplus humanity that is redundant for the

capitalist economic system (Nun, 2000; Davis, 2004; Sanyal, 2007; Chatterjee, 2008a, 2008b). We, on the contrary, deal with a dichotomous RNF; the two sub-segments having two distinctly different loci vis-à-vis capital: while a relatively advanced but smaller segment is close to capital (and serving it), the remaining vast petty segment is separated (and redundant).

5. Both the sub-segments of our RNF behave in a non-capitalistic way (be it self-employment or establishments hiring labour), survival and/or decent living being the primary objective of production (and hence, deeply associated with basic resources). Thus, our FS–RNF and intra-RNF dualities are not just quantitative differences (in terms of the size of an enterprise). For some of such micro-foundations, we have consulted with a very recent empirical literature (Bhattacharya et al., 2013; Basole et al., 2015; Chakrabarti, 2013, 2016; Bhattacharya and Keshar, 2018; Kesar and Bhattacharya, 2020) along with some of the analytical and theoretical writings mentioned earlier.
6. To the best of our knowledge, no other theoretical framework simultaneously discusses the process of creation of the RNF, its heterogeneity at the micro-level, its heterogeneous loci vis-à-vis modern capital, and its macro-political-economic implications. Ours is a first attempt in this regard.
7. We have extended our theoretical framework to understand the impact of the COVID-19 pandemic, which led to a setback in the capital accumulation process of the FS.

Next, we test empirically (both statistically and econometrically) the propositions derived from this model. The empirical analysis is presented in five chapters. Chapter 3 presents some glimpses of the changing nature of the global rural economy over the past few decades (prior to the COVID-19 pandemic). The main objective of presenting an analysis using global data is to show that our main contentions (i.e. the spreading and intensification of dualism and the fact that growth augments duality) are not location-specific; in fact, they are global phenomena. Due to the presence of limited data, we could not establish all our propositions in this chapter. Therefore, we present selected country-specific evidence in Chapter 4 and a more rigorous analysis using Indian data in Chapter 5.

This is followed by a chapter on agriculture (Chapter 6), which identifies the factors that are causing a decline in agricultural employment and also focuses on the nature of dualism propounded within the agricultural sector. Chapter 7 presents the impact of the COVID-19 pandemic on the complex economic structure of rural India. A chapter on the pandemic is pertinent, since Chapters 3–6 primarily delve into the impact of modern capital accumulation on the rural economy. The pandemic, on the contrary, halted this accumulation process. Thus, Chapter 7's primary objective is to help us understand what happens to this developmental trajectory when there is a cessation of the process of general capital accumulation. We present the concluding observations in Chapter 8, along with certain alternative policy implications.

1.4 The fundamental empirical results

Our book comes up with certain intriguing empirical results. These are as follows.

1. There is a clear indication of movement and diversification of the workforce from the surplus labour pool and from traditional agriculture into both the advanced segments of agriculture and the advanced and petty segments of the RNF.
2. The FS has a noteworthy impact on this dual movement/diversification process, most probably triggering both the push and pull effects.
3. Apart from the FS, land fragmentation also triggers migration.
4. The FS productivity improvement increases the productivity gap across advanced-petty segments of the farm and nonfarm sectors.

1.5 Some political-economic and policy implications

Finally, while concluding the book, certain general macro-political-economic implications of this study are discussed, which are encapsulated in the following points:

1. Modernity itself is creating its own other (outside), reversing or, at least, constraining and distorting the so-called process of transition towards comprehensive capitalism. Hence, one needs to acknowledge that either there is an impossibility of emergence of a comprehensive/complete capitalistic structure in the Global South in the near future or, at least, the contemporary capitalism is a fractured entity and a complete capitalistic transition seems to be extremely difficult. Contemporary capitalism, with a very high degree of concentration of capital, capital–labour ratio, resource expropriation, and technological advancement, must recognize and learn to deal with a growing outside.
2. Thus, the creation of a new form of dualism in India is a particularity of a general global phenomenon: accumulation by dispossession (ABD) (Harvey, 2003) without proletarianization; this makes political-economic 'management' of the outside an imperative. Contemporary capital goes on creating/proliferating its outside and hence, it needs to negotiate with this 'other' for maintaining the socio-economic conditions/stability for its existence and reproduction (although it may not always be functionally dependent on this outside for its existence and expanded reproduction).
3. Although a part of the farm and nonfarm is utilized by (global) capital, a much larger part struggles to procreate itself in limbo. This calls for a dual political–economic response. While the former part of the farm and nonfarm composite could directly bargain with modern capital, the latter has to organize (cluster) itself for its fast-evaporating spaces—economic-geographic-social-cultural-political. While the first group of firms and farms could bargain for better contracts, the second set could realize a variety of scale and synergic effects beyond the economic circuits of modern capitalism and thereby could negotiate with it (despite being tiny in size and organized on the basis of private property rights principle and not collective rights).
4. Thus, two types of policy support are needed. For the first group, institutional support (such as legal support, support for the marketing networks, etc.) and support on the supply side (such as technology, skill, loan, cheap and quality inputs, electricity, space, supply chain, etc.) are crucial so that they could reap the benefits

> of their linkages with the modern sector. For the second group, institutional (such as access to space, financial system, skill development, etc.) and demand–supply side supports (such as access to input and output markets) assume critical importance; these are essential for a cluster-based development framework. Furthermore, especially for this second group, development programmes (such as Bolsa Familia of Brazil or the Mahatma Gandhi National Rural Employment Guarantee Act—MNREGA—of India) and development financing (such as self-help group-based micro-credit) become very important. Such programmes and financing mechanisms could help capital in managing its outside. Although, to a large extent, modern capital could be functionally independent of this outside, for its own socio-political existence and for the stability of capitalism as a system, this 'development management' or 'developmentalism' could be of enormous value.

Our empirical analysis on the COVID-19 pandemic indicated further intensification of the agrarian crisis (especially for the petty farmers), deepening of duality within the RNFS; and squeezing of the urban petty nonfarm sector, triggering either reverse (urban–rural) migration, or creating resistance for rural–urban migration, or both. In fact, the devastating pandemic has made the problem of the existence of the vast rural nonfarm labour force a central question in the discourse of the political economy of development of the Global South, necessitating the ideology of 'developmentalism', as mentioned above, to proliferate across the Global South. It is increasingly recognized that the mainstream accumulation and market-centric development path is not generating anticipated results, and 'development management' is an essentiality.

Thus, we recognize the need for direct state support to the individuals engaged in the rural nonfarm sector (RNFS) in the short and medium term (via the cash and commodity transfer programmes). On the other hand, in the long run, we identify the need for the path of cluster-based development of the (almost) ostracized RNFS (especially its traditional and emerging petty production segments) as a dire necessity, in order to ensure a balanced development of its traditional/petty and modern sectors.

A.1 Appendix

A.1.1 The rural nonfarm sector in India: Three case studies

The process of interstate/inter-regional intensification of dualism in India is explained in detail using secondary data in Chapter 5. In addition, we also observed the presence of the wide heterogeneity and prevalence of dualism within the nonfarm sector in the field visits we made before the COVID-19 pandemic to some purposively chosen heterogeneous rural regions of India. This included Assam (a less developed sub-national state in terms of FS growth and per capita income), West Bengal (a middle-performing sub-national state in terms of both the above-mentioned criteria), and Karnataka (a better-performing sub-national state). During the field visits, personal interviews and focus group discussions were carried out with villagers. Our objectives were two-fold, namely, to explore or map the current state of the occupational patterns (and standards) and to understand the changes that have happened within the farm and nonfarm segments in these places over the years.

The field survey covered sixty households in Sonapur, Sansari, and Moirgaon villages in Assam, which depend on traditional agriculture (such as paddy cultivation) and do not have strong links to the FS or any big urban centre. In West Bengal, an otherwise middle-income state but agriculturally developed, we interviewed fifty households from Balagarh village of the prosperous Hooghly district, seventy-five firm units of the traditional handloom hub Dhaniakhali (of the same Hooghly district), and seventy-five firm units from Tantipara (an ancient handloom hub) of Birbhum district. Finally, in Karnataka, 100 sample households were interviewed from the villages of Mandya, Ramnagara, Kolar, Bangalore Rural, and Tumkur districts, which surround and have close links to the large urban area of the state capital city, Bengaluru. Our observations are as follows.

In the villages we visited in Assam, we found that, though the land is fertile, farmers are engaged in rain-fed traditional crops due to the absence of infrastructure, such as irrigation facilities. This results in low income from farming and, hence, low levels of surplus and demand for the local RNFS. The nonfarm sector mainly consists of petty handloom and handicraft activities. However, these activities have remained traditional, with a low capital base, and cannot reach high-value urban markets. The urban FS is not developed either to create demand for the RNFS. Thus, these regions are characterized by the predominance of traditional agriculture and traditional nonfarm sector, generating meagre surpluses and demand for each other.

In West Bengal (notably, Dhaniakhali of Hooghly district and Tantipara of Birbhum district), we observed the dominance of traditional agriculture (such as high-yielding paddy cultivation for self-consumption and local markets) and traditional nonfarm activities (such as centuries-old handloom clusters, making cotton and Tasar (coarse silk) clothes and garments, respectively). On the other hand, in Balagarh, we observed a section of the farmers practising modern agriculture (such as mango cultivation on a large scale). In this region, the erstwhile traditional nonfarm sector that used to produce minor implements (such as sickles) and farm-related petty services (storing, processing, packaging, and so on) for conventional crops such as rice declined, and a modern nonfarm segment, closely linked with modern agriculture developed. The formal sector (FS) also created jobs and brought surplus to the villages, which helped develop the modern nonfarm sector; the FS–RNFS linkage has also helped the latter to access the high-value urban market.

Regions we visited in Karnataka, a more developed sub-national state, have moved towards high-value cash crops. Surplus from diversified agriculture has been used to develop the modern nonfarm sector; remunerative agriculture also created a larger demand base for sophisticated nonfarm goods and services. This advanced rural nonfarm segment has benefited from urban FS growth too.

Thus, our field visits in different parts of India, having a variety of general economic conditions, have shown that there are stark heterogeneities within the RNFS. In some places, we have relatively advanced activities, while in others, we have the persistence of the age-old production system. Further, in some areas, we have a mixture of both—modern firms as well as traditional units. Importantly, this farm–nonfarm heterogeneity has been found to be somewhat correlated with the overall development of the localities and the development of the formal/modern sectors.

2

Capitalist Growth and the Proliferation of Dualism

A Theoretical Framework

We have seen in Chapter 1 that India's farm and nonfarm sectors have experienced a deepening of the intra- and inter-sectoral divide with the economy's growth. This chapter, in this background, addresses a fundamental question: is it just a coincidence that growth and divergence are moving hand in hand, or can there be some explanations that can relate growth with the observed phenomena of the generation, spreading, and deepening of duality?

In this chapter, we try to look at this issue theoretically. To this end, we construct a theoretical model along the structuralist lines (Kalecki, 1934/1971, 1955/1993; Bhaduri, 1986; Chakrabarti, 2013, 2016; Sadhu and Chakrabarti, 2021).[11] Our model uses the Harris–Todaro (H–T) method (Harris and Todaro, 1970; see also Ray, 1998, pp. 374–386) and places it within an essentially structuralist theoretical frame. This is a novel approach as far as the transition debate concerning the Global South is concerned. Regarding our model, we need to discuss the following fundamental properties setting up the background:

1. We try to understand the macro-phenomenon of deepening structural dualism across rural India in particular and the Global South in general. Hence, we need to specify the nature of this dualism. Ours is not just a technology-, productivity-, income-,

[11] Many of the structural features of our framework have been derived from the field-based study by Mukherjee et al. (2019); see also Kesar and Bhattacharya (2020) and especially Sadhu and Chakrabarti (2021) in this regard. For this framework, we are indebted to Amit Bhaduri, Deepankar Basu, and Debarshi Das.

The Nonfarm Economy. Manojit Bhattacharjee, Saumya Chakrabarti, and Meenakshi Rajeev,
Oxford University Press.
DOI: 10.1093/9780198972013.003.0002

size-, location-, product-, input-intensity-, etc.-based dualism, which could be mitigated mostly through market forces with flexibility, mobility, and accumulation-led dynamism complemented by certain institutional manoeuvring. Contrarily, we are trying to explain the existence and spread of the starkly different economic structures/systems with distinctly different movements and linkages, which cannot be homogenized through the market mechanism. Hence, we prefer a structuralist framework for our analysis on dualism, which understands an economy as a collection of distinct substructures having distinct properties and dynamics.

2. Further, we ask why and how, across the rural economy, both the processes of evolution and involution—pull and push—operate simultaneously, and instead of homogenization, heterogeneity is reproduced. Thus, we wish to study not only the different structures but also qualitatively different processes. Hence, a structuralist framework suits our purpose.
3. Our theoretical framework tries to capture the above-mentioned macro-phenomenon from a micro perspective where an individual's decision-making and the resultant process is taken as a method to explain the macro-dynamics of deepening dualism. Hence, we use an H–T method of analysis.
4. However, instead of assuming a representative rational, neoclassical agent (as in the H–T framework), we consider that our individuals are structurally different having distinctly different socio-economic identities, endowments, abilities, networks, constraints, and motives. Accordingly, their distinctive behaviours are set, and (given the varied socio-economic processes, inducements, and constraints) outcomes are determined. Further, we extend the H–T method by incorporating push effect/process in addition to pull/demand effect.
5. Thus, our model, having a specific micro-foundation, explains the macro-phenomenon of deepening dualism and relates it to the ongoing market-centric–capital-centric growth process. However, methodologically, the model uses a mainstream method but applies it in a set-up where—from the micro-agents to the macroeconomy—all have distinct structural characteristics and dynamics. Further, it extends the mainstream method qualitatively by

introducing a heterodox phenomenon arising out of accumulation-driven immiseration.

6. This should be a novelty of our approach and, hence, a contribution to the literature. Thus, we combine both orthodox and heterodox elements and build our theoretical model explaining how capitalistic growth could accentuate dualism.
7. Specifically, the theoretical model begins with an equilibrium condition in line with the standard H–T model, in which there is no worker migration between traditional agriculture and the remaining sectors of the rural economy, that is, informal (traditional or newly emerging) petty nonfarm, informal modern farm and nonfarm, and formal sectors. Our comparative static analyses succinctly capture a process of formal sector accumulation that generates two effects in the rural informal nonfarm sectors: a push effect (mainly due to income deflation and sometimes resource expropriation as well) and a pull effect (due to demand boost). We show how these effects reproduce dualism in the farm and the nonfarm sectors.

The chapter proceeds as follows. In section 2.1, we briefly review existing perspectives on the rural nonfarm economy and define our stand among these perspectives. This is followed by section 2.2, which explains the assumptions and basic structure of our model representing a rural economy, consisting of the formal sector and modern and traditional segments of the informal farm and nonfarm economies. The assumptions in this section comprise the production and consumption structures/patterns and linkages among the formal sector, informal modern farm and nonfarm sectors, and informal traditional farm and nonfarm segments. A figure is also presented to explain the sectoral characteristics and intersectoral linkages. A theoretical model is constructed subsequently, based on the assumptions. The model has the following parts.

As already mentioned, the model begins with the no-migration equilibrium of an H–T (Harris and Todaro 1970) framework. The no-migration equilibrium in our model is characterized by the equalization of actual per capita real income from traditional agriculture and expected per capita real income from all other sectors. The equilibrium condition is then explained graphically with the help of two functions/

graphs: the per capita real income of the traditional agriculture schedule and the contour for the expected per capita real income of the combined residual sectors. These curves are shown as the functions of workforce in the traditional informal nonfarm sector. The equilibrium is shown diagrammatically using the intersection of both these schedules. A comparative static exercise is then conducted to capture the effect of formal sector investment on the migration equilibrium. We show that an increase in formal sector investment generates demand for goods and services (and expands employment) in the modern informal nonfarm sector; however, it also causes an expansion of traditional informal nonfarm employment. In other words, we show how the expansion of the modern formal sector itself creates new forms of dualism through the conjoint operations of individual decision-making and socio-economic processes. The formal proof of the proposition is presented in two forms. Graphical analysis is carried out in the chapter, and an algebraic proof of the main propositions is presented in Appendix A.2.1.

Our model is novel in several respects. First, unlike the H–T model, we not only explicate a demand-pull expansion of the modern sector, in which rational individuals engaged in the traditional sector migrate/diversify, being guided by their own preference (in the presence of information asymmetry) towards the modern sector, but also we highlight the push-driven process initiated by the formal sector.[12] The push effect in our framework is a consequence of real income deflation in the traditional agricultural sector, which results from inflation generated by the formal sector's accumulation, thus limiting the workforce's ability to sustain itself in that sector. This is a significant addition to the existing dominant literature.

Essentially, although we use the H–T method, we incorporate the issue of push-driven migration/employment diversification. This is done by recognizing the specificities of different sectors and the

[12] Studies have modified or extended the standard H–T model in different dimensions. Works have assumed capital mobility between the urban and the rural sectors; introduced the presence of trade unions in the urban sector; reformulated the standard H–T model with endogenous wages; and incorporated the presence of duality within the rural space, risk aversion, land rent, and many other issues (Corden and Findlay, 1975; Calvo, 1978; Moene, 1988; Fields, 1989; 2005; Grinols, 1991; Bandyopadhyay and Gupta, 1995; Basu, 1997; Brueckner and Zenou, 1999; Issah et al., 2005). However, to the best of our knowledge, incorporation of a push effect owing to capital accumulation is a significant addition to the existing dominant literature.

particularities of the inter-sectoral linkages. Thus, an extended H–T method (incorporating the push dynamics) is used in a structuralist framework. Next, section 2.6 incorporates the effect of the COVID-19 pandemic in the model, which has an adverse impact on capital accumulation. Finally, section 2.7 concludes.

2.1 Existing perspectives on the rural nonfarm economy

Existing literature has examined the rural nonfarm economy (RNFE) from four different perspectives. These are the farm–nonfarm linkage view, the firm perspective, the household livelihood point of view, and the regional development viewpoint (Haggblade, 2007).[13]

The farm–nonfarm linkage viewpoint, or the perspective of the farm–nonfarm interaction, examines the dynamics of the rural nonfarm sector through the lens of its linkage with the farm sector (Mellor and Lele, 1973; Hazell and Haggblade, 1990; Lanjouw and Lanjouw, 2001; Chakrabarti et al., 2011). A variant of this literature has also considered the role of the urban/formal sector (in conjunction with the farm sector) in understanding the growth or transformation of the nonfarm sector (Ranis and Stewart, 1993; Chakrabarti and Kundu, 2009b).

In contrast, the literature focusing solely on the rural nonfarm sector (i.e. the firm perspective) considers only the individual nonfarm enterprise and examines the supply, demand, and institutional factors that promote or inhibit its expansion (Haggblade, 2007; Ahmed et al., 2007; Kundu and Chakrabarti, 2008).

The household livelihood literature considers the existence of nonfarm activity as a result of the household decision-making process in which resources (such as time or capital) are allocated across various activities or ends based on the preferences of the households (Lee, 1965; Hymer and Resnick, 1969; Singh et al., 1986; Abdulai and Delgado, 1999; Hitayezu et al., 2014).

[13] Reardon et al. (1998) and Coppard (2001) have provided a very detailed review of the literature on India.

The regional development perspective examines the role of spatial or location-specific factors (such as infrastructure, labour supply, presence/absence of skills, etc.) in determining the output and employment in the rural nonfarm sector (Chatterjee et al., 2021).

In this book, we primarily focus on the nature, and especially dynamics, of the nonfarm sector from the point of view of its characteristics and linkages with the formal sector and agricultural economies. Thus, we engage with the first two perspectives as mentioned above. We now elaborate on our model in sections 2.2 and 2.3.

2.2 Assumptions and basic features of our model rural economy

In this model, we confine ourselves to the rural economy. Based on existing literature, we have segregated the rural economy into three broad sectors:

1. The modern capitalistic formal sector (FS) of the rural economy, driving growth through capital accumulation;
2. the non-capitalistic informal rural nonfarm sector (RNFS) with two segments: (a) petty/traditional informal RNFS ($RNFS_t$) with small, self-employment-based firms, devoid of surplus over subsistence and (b) advanced/modern informal RNFS ($RNFS_m$) with relatively large, labour-hiring units, producing surplus for future consumption over subsistence (although not for accumulation);
3. the vast non-capitalistic agricultural sector (AGR) also has two segments: (a) petty/traditional AGR (AGR_t) with small, self-employment-based firms, devoid of surplus over subsistence and (b) advanced/modern AGR (AGR_m) with relatively large, labour-hiring units, producing surplus for future consumption over subsistence (although not for accumulation).

A detailed description of the structural features and linkages of each one of these sectors is provided below.

The capitalistic FS produces consumer goods, investment goods, and intermediate inputs for itself as well as for other sectors of the economy.

The FS is dominated by large capitalistic producers and uses permanent workers as well as contract/temporary/casual labourers. Based on existing literature, we assume the presence of excess capacity and surplus labour ('reserve army') in this sector (Kalecki, 1934/1971; Bhaduri, 1986; Rakshit, 1989). Thus, this sector has an elastic supply. Aggregate real investment in the FS is exogenously set by the capitalist (I_f^0, say) based on their perceptions about the demand-side conditions and depending on their access to the financial system. Change in the investment of the FS affects the output and employment of the FS and the related sector/s (explained below). The price of this (mostly oligopolistic) sector consists of the cost component per unit of production and a mark-up (Bhaduri, 1986; Chakrabarti, 2016). If the average costs and/or mark-up rise, the price rises accordingly.

The non-capitalistic AGR, which consists of a traditional and a modern segment, produces food and agro-inputs for itself and the non-agricultural sectors. Petty farmers dominate the AGR_t. They produce food primarily for self-consumption and sell the surplus output, in the local markets, for the AGR_m and the rural nonfarm sectors ($RNFS_m$ and $RNFS_t$), where powerful traders (of the $RNFS_m$) dominate. Due to the presence of resource, institutional and technological constraints (Kalecki, 1955/1993), per capita marketable surplus is assumed to be rigid in the AGR_t. Specifically, we assume that per capita marketed output of the AGR_t (i.e. A, say) to be inflexible (A^0, say) in the absence of any exogenous shocks.[14] Since the output market of AGR_t is dominated by

[14] This is a standard assumption. We also assume that the per capita self-consumption of AGR_t is constant (in the presence of resource, technological, and institutional constraints). Hence, the per capita aggregate output (marketed surplus plus self-consumption) is assumed to be constant. This is like the constancy of average output (or real income, at the subsistence level) of the 'traditional sector' of Lewis (1954). Thus, the total output (marketed surplus plus self-consumption) of AGR_t is 'shared' by the corresponding population. This population consists of the productively employed people, the open and disguisedly unemployed mass, and the dependent segment as well. Further, when anyone moves/diversifies out of this AGR_t to any other sector, they draw their share from this AGR_t as well (in addition to their income from the new/diversified occupation). Actually, what happens is that the additional income from the other sector/occupation is added to the aggregate output/income from AGR_t. Hence, per capita aggregate output/real income from AGR_t remains the same, despite occupational movement/diversification. It resembles the Lewisian process of transfer of surplus labour and resource away from the traditional sector, keeping the residual per capita output intact. The underlying assumption is that, even if someone moves/diversifies away from the AGR_t to any other sector, the aggregate AGR_t output does not fall due to the presence/movement/diversification of surplus labour (for details, we could refer to Mukherjee and Chakrabarti, 2016).

powerful traders/intermediaries (of the $RNFS_m$) who set the price, the petty farmers are largely price takers. Thus, we assume that the price the traditional farmers receive (for AGR_t output) from AGR_m, $RNFS_m$, and $RNFS_t$ (via the powerful traders of $RNFS_m$) tends to be sticky and that the farmers get a fixed price (P_a^0, say). Even if, in the open markets (within the FS, AGR_m, $RNFS_m$, and $RNFS_t$), the AGR_t output price rises, the farm-gate price remains rigid for the petty farmers of the AGR_t.[15]

The income earned by the traditional farmers of the AGR_t by selling their surplus products (to $RNFS_t$–$RNFS_m$–AGR_m) is used for purchasing nonfarm goods. We assume that the expenditure basket of a farmer consists of both modern sector output (of the FS and $RNFS_m$) and output from the $RNFS_t$. The weights for the modern sector (FS and $RNFS_m$ combined) and $RNFS_t$ output in the expenditure basket are, respectively, w_1 and w_2.

Now, turning to the AGR_m, it includes the better-off cultivators (i.e. larger farmers). Farmers in the AGR_m generally sell their marketable surplus of food and non-food agro products to the $RNFS_m$ and the FS. For owning larger-sized land, the better-off farmers of the AGR_m have the option of diversifying production (towards high-value crops—HVCs—such as fruits, flowers, vegetables, agro-fuel, and feedstock) as per the requirements of the modern nonfarm sector and the FS. The companies/traders (of the FS and $RNFS_m$) linking AGR_m with its buyers also gain from this process of diversification. Owing to economies of scale, the companies experience a reduction in transaction costs when they procure high-value farm products in bulk from larger farmers in comparison to multiple small and marginal farmers (Bhattacharya and Mazumdar, 2020).

[15] The Dalwai Committee on Doubling Farmers' Income (Government of India) has pointed out that the share of farmers in the consumer's price is very low; it generally varies between 15 and 40 per cent. Studies conducted by the International Food Policy Research Institute and the World Bank have confirmed this. The dominant role of middlemen, among others, is primarily responsible for farmers not realizing a reasonable price for their produce, lowering farm income and profitability. This was recognized by the 12th Plan's Working Group on Agriculture Marketing (Government of India, 2011) and The Hindu Business Line (2015). Further, the distortionary market power of the rural commercial interests, controlling and depressing the farm-gate price in particular, is elaborated by Harriss-White (2013) and Rakshit (2014). The National Sample Survey Organization (NSSO) reports based on the Situation Assessment Survey of Agricultural Households data of 2002–2013, 2012–2013, and 2018–2019 show that a large section of the farmers, especially for paddy, sell their produce at a price lower than the government-stipulated minimum support price to the informal traders and in local markets.

Finally, the informally organized RNFS produces consumer goods, tools, and intermediate inputs mainly for itself and also for other sectors. This sector is overwhelmingly dominated by non-capitalistic producers (who participate in the production process mainly for survival or to uplift the standard of living). In general, they accumulate limited capital (sometimes having surplus for future consumption, especially for the $RNFS_m$, although not for the $RNFS_t$, which we have presumed as zero). In the RNFS (both segments), production takes place largely using indigenously acquired/produced nonfarm consumer goods and tools, using agro-based food and raw materials (from AGR: $RNFS_m$ from both AGR_m and AGR_t and $RNFS_t$ from AGR_t only) and by using labour (surplus and/or locally available diversifying/migrant). Further, output and employment and price are flexible in RNFS segments (both $RNFS_m$ and $RNFS_t$). This is because the RNFS primarily includes unregulated informal firms having family workers and few hired workers. Individuals (self-employed and hired workers both) engaged in these firms can shift to other activities, since the size of sunk cost is less. These firms have no regulatory obligation to pay a fixed salary to their hired workers and/or provide other formal benefits, while reducing the size of the workforce through retrenchment. The overall price of the RNFS has less rental component as well, and therefore it has higher flexibility in changing the price as compared to the formal segment. As already mentioned, this sector also has two types of firms: traditional and modern.

The $RNFS_t$ primarily includes petty producers, petty input–output traders, and small retail/service outlets in villages. The petty producers (for instance, a traditional weaver, a blacksmith, a village confectioner) produce goods using family workers for the local markets (i.e. specifically for the AGR_t). On the other hand, small retail outlets sell local products (such as a local kirana store selling traditional village inputs–outputs such as rice, puffed rice, cooking oil from village-produced oil mills, bidi (indigenously produced raw cigar), petty tools, local raw materials, etc.). In this sector, there is no entry and exit problem. Next, the aggregate output or aggregate real income (Y_t) of the $RNFS_t$ is assumed to be an increasing function of its workforce (L_t). This is because labour is the only (major) input, as mentioned above. However, the per capita real income of the workers in the $RNFS_t$ (y_t) is negatively influenced by the volume of the workforce (L_t); thus, there is diminishing real productivity of labour. As the volume of the workforce increases, there is congestion, which leads to higher demand for resources, raising the cost of production in the $RNFS_t$. The price of $RNFS_t$ output (P_t) is also negatively influenced by the volume of the workforce in the $RNFS_t$ (L_t). The $RNFS_t$ consists of a large number of self-employed enterprises. As the L_t expands, it leads to increased production/supply. Increased supply reduces the price of $RNFS_t$ output. Hence, P_t falls with a rise in L_t, ceteris paribus. Consequently, combining all these effects, y_t (the per capita real income of the workers in $RNFS_t$) falls with a rise in L_t, ceteris paribus. One can write the above argument in terms of two equations as provided below:

$$\frac{Y_t}{L_t} = y_t(L_t);\ y_t'(L_t) < 0.\ P_t = f(L_t);\ P_t'(L_t) < 0.$$

The modern segment of the RNFS, on the other hand, comprises firms that have a close association with the FS for output market. Examples of such firms include village weavers or papad (Indian wafer) manufacturers getting a contract from formal firms or a village automobile repair shop or restaurant located near a highway in a prime location. This segment also includes non-capitalistic locally powerful traders who buy food and agro raw materials from the AGR_m and AGR_t. The $RNFS_m$ is dominated by firms that produce or sell relatively larger volumes of output and thus require hired labour. For producing a relatively larger volume of output and for establishing linkage with the FS (say, for instance, getting public land in a prime location in front of a formal manufacturing unit), firms in the $RNFS_m$ may require specific skills and access to credit as well as social and/or political networks. Hence, although there is a free exit in the case of the $RNFS_m$, there is some form of entry restriction for the new firms (due to level of skill, assets, access to credit, and network specificities). We assume away any direct interactions between the $RNFS_t$ and $RNFS_m$.[16]

[16] As already stated, the $RNFS_t$ generally are smaller manufacturing or service units in villages. They make products having local demand such as earthen pot sold to villagers, iron sickle/hammers produced by blacksmiths for local farmers and nonfarm sectors, or sellers in a village selling local foods (such as puffed rice). These firms are less likely to have links with the modern nonfarm sector selling goods or services to formal sector as inputs. However, essentially, for our model, this is a simplifying assumption.

Our model allows a specific type of interaction between the FS, $RNFS_m$, and AGR_m. We propose that the FS (such as a registered cloth factory) purchases finished products and various types of inputs (such as cotton and stitched clothes), including (better-quality high-value) food from the $RNFS_m$ and AGR_m, via the open market exchanges as well as subcontracting, primarily to reduce costs and avoid labour resistance.[17] We assume away the reverse flow of commodities from the FS to the $RNFS_m$ and AGR_m to keep our model simple. Though the $RNFS_m$ and AGR_m use some essential FS commodities, in reality, the inter-sectoral trade balances of the $RNFS_m$ and AGR_m with the FS remain generally biased against the FS. This is because modern RNFS and AGR firms/farms generate income mainly from their trade with the FS. This means that modern RNFS and AGR firms/farms are selling more than the amount they are purchasing from formal firms. In our model, thus, an expansion of the FS induces an expansion of output, employment, price, and income in the AGR_m and $RNFS_m$. In other words, aggregate employment and output in the FS, $RNFS_m$, and AGR_m combined are positively dependent on the aggregate FS investment (I_f), ceteris paribus. The price (P_m) of the combined modern sector (i.e. the FS, $RNFS_m$, and AGR_m) is assumed to be flexible and varies with aggregate FS investment (I_f). As the FS investment rises, aggregate demand for this combined modern sector output rises, raising its price, ceteris paribus. Table A.2.2 of the Appendix provides support for some of these assumptions.

Finally, we have also made an assumption on the per capita income of these sectors. Based on existing empirical evidence, we assume that the average real per capita income in the FS, $RNFS_m$, and AGR_m combined is greater than the per capita real income of AGR_t. The per capita income of the AGR_t is higher than that of the $RNFS_t$. In this context, one can also refer to the data provided in Chapter 1 (see Table 1.4) pertaining to the value added per worker in different sectors of the economy. Specifically, Table 1.4 shows that the value added per worker is higher in rural establishments (firms using hired workers) compared to that of the AGR,

[17] The FS acquires cheap resources, wage goods, and even labour from the $RNFS_m$ and cheap resources and food from the AGR_m to maintain/increase its profit (Basole and Basu, 2011a, 2011b; Breman, 2013). This is also referred to in Harvey (2003), ch. 4, in a much broader context. Thus, the capitalistic FS, instead of endogenously producing many of the resources and foods, depends on the non-capitalistic AGR_m and $RNFS_m$.

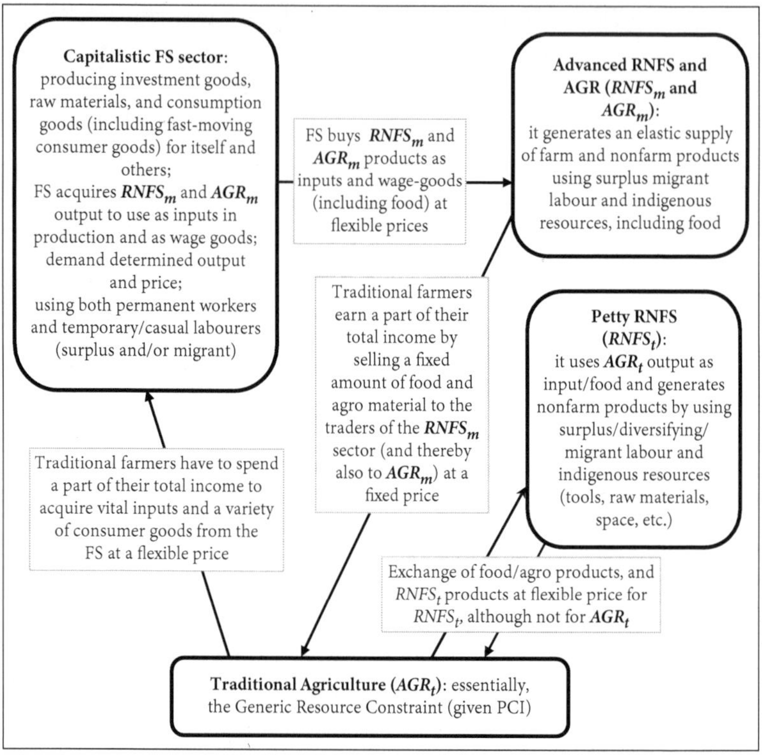

Figure 2.1 A flowchart on rural formal sector–rural nonfarm sector–agricultural sector income/expenditure linkages
Source: Constructed by the authors.

which in turn is higher than that of rural own account enterprises (OAEs or firms using family labour). These OAEs/$RNFS_t$ in our model can be thought of as a 'sink' or 'sponge' where the impoverished rural surplus labour force crowds in.

Based on the above-mentioned structures and linkages, a comprehensive macroeconomic framework of FS–RNFS–AGR interactions in our model rural economy is expressed via a flowchart (Figure 2.1).[18]

Figure 2.1 gives us a broad structure of the model macroeconomy and the pattern of linkages among the different sectors of the rural economy of

[18] There are different types of interactions among the sectors, but here we consider only the dominant streams.

a developing country. Using this structure, our main target is to explain the process of deepening intra- and inter-sectoral dualism. Therefore, we now focus on our theoretical model that starts with the issue of inter-sectoral labour mobility and the corresponding migration equilibrium.

A table of the notations used in our model is presented for the convenience of readers in Table 2.1.

2.3 A model of formal sector–rural nonfarm sector–agricultural sector migrations and/or employment diversifications

In the rural economy, following our structure as above, an individual could (potentially) find six job options (ruling out rural–urban migration): a permanent job in the rural FS (local or distant), a temporary job in the rural FS (local or distant), $RNFS_m$ employment (local or distant), $RNFS_t$ employment (mostly local), and employment in AGR_t (mostly local) and in AGR_m (local or distant).[19] Thus, if this individual is currently engaged in the AGR_t, theoretically, they could have five alternative rural options left (local or distant—ruling out rural–urban migration as mentioned earlier), given the fact that, in India, there are large rural–rural intra- and inter- (sub-national) state and district migrations (or employment diversifications), as is found in our empirical analysis of subsequent chapters.[20] Further, of course, there is the possibility of remaining unemployed.

[19] At the very outset, for simplification of analysis and, more importantly, for focusing on the issue of intensification of dualism in the rural economy, we presume that there is rural–urban migration equilibrium. Thus, the assumption is that, for a potential labourer, urban expected income = rural expected income. Consequently, the rural–urban (in or out) migration possibilities are ruled out so that we could focus only on the intra-rural migration and/or employment diversification flows.

[20] During 2006–2011 (approximately), 2.5 per cent of the Indian rural population migrated (to rural as well as urban areas) and during 2010–2011 alone (approximately), this percentage is 1.5 (computed using Indian Human Development Survey (IHDS)–II data of 2011–2012)! Out of the total rural-to-rural migration (during 2006–2011), 38.5 per cent migrated to other sub-national states, and this is quite substantial (IHDS–II data, 2011–2012). Finally, out of this rural-to-other states' rural migration, 61.4 per cent migrated to the nonfarm sector (IHDS–II data, 2011–2012). If we look at the rural males' out-migration flows (during approximately 2006–2011), the following tendencies emerge: first, exactly one-third of it was to rural (33.8 per cent); second, out of this one-third, 43.5 per cent was to another state, 54.2 per cent intra-state, and 2.4 per cent to foreign land (IHDS–II data, 2011–2012). Finally, we note that, compared to rural-to-rural migration, urban-to-rural migration is small (IHDS–II data, 2011–2012) and, hence, ignored in this theoretical framework.

Table 2.1 Notations and description of variables used in the model and their behaviours

Notations	Variable description
FS	Formal sector (effectively, *rural* formal sector, given the assumption, as delineated below, that rural–urban migration is closed)
AGR	Agricultural sector
RNFS	Rural nonfarm sector
$RNFS_t$	Traditional rural nonfarm sector
$RNFS_m$	Modern rural nonfarm sector
AGR_t	Traditional rural agricultural sector
AGR_m	Modern rural agricultural sector
I_f	Aggregate real investment in the FS
$L_m(I_f)$	Employment in the modern nonfarm sector (FS, $RNFS_m$, and AGR_m combined). It is an increasing function of the aggregate real investment in the FS (I_f).
L_t	Employment in the traditional rural nonfarm sector. Essentially, this sector acts as a 'sink' or 'sponge' where the rural surplus labour force crowds in.
$y_m(I_f)$	Per capita, real income in the FS, $RNFS_m$, and AGR_m combined. Akin to L_m, it is also an increasing function of I_f.
y_t	Per capita real income of the workers (mostly self-employed) in the $RNFS_t$ sector. This is negatively influenced by the volume of the workforce in the $RNFS_t$ (L_t).
P_a	Price per unit of AGR_t output received by the farmers. Due to the presence of intermediaries, farmers get only a fixed price (Pa^0, say).
A	Per capita marketed output that is produced in AGR_t, mostly by petty farmers. This is also assumed to be fixed in the absence of any exogenous shocks.
$P_m(I_f)$	The price of output of the FS, $RNFS_m$, and AGR_m combined. It is flexible and varies with aggregate FS investment (I_f).
$P_t(L_t)$	The price of $RNFS_t$ output. This is negatively influenced by the volume of the workforce in the $RNFS_t$ (L_t).
w_1	Weight of the modern sector (FS, $RNFS_m$, and AGR_m combined) output in the expenditure basket of a farmer. It is a constant.
w_2	Weight of $RNFS_t$ output in the expenditure basket of a farmer. It is constant.
Y_a	Per capita real income in AGR_t.
Y_{na}	Actual per capita real income in the non-agricultural sector.

The functions P_m, L_m and y_m, P_t and y_t are assumed to be linear in the algebraic analysis.

Source: Prepared by the authors.

However, for simplicity of analysis, we are ignoring that option for the time being (although it could be incorporated into the model easily). In our comparative static analysis, we will bring in the issue analytically.

Now, considering such a situation where an agent is currently engaged in the AGR_t and faces the other five rural options, as mentioned above, an intra-rural inter-sectoral (AGR_t to rural non-AGR_t, including AGR_m) migration equilibrium condition should be

> *Expected per capita real income from local or distant rural non AGR_t (including AGR_m) = Actual per capita real income (from marketable surplus) of local AGR_t.* (2.1)

This could be elaborated further as[21]

> [*Probability of getting a job in local or distant rural non AGR_t (including AGR_m)*] × [*average per capita real income in non AGR_t (including AGR_m) combining all the five options as mentioned above*] = *Actual per capita real income (from marketed surplus) of local AGR_t.* (2.2)

This implies, considering all the six intra-rural migration options, that the migration[22] equilibrium condition is

> [{(*Probability of getting a local/distant job in the rural* FS *as a permanent worker*) × (*average real income of a permanent worker in rural* FS)} + {(*Probability of getting a local/distant job in rural* FS *as a temporary worker*) × (*average real income of a temporary worker in rural* FS)} + {(*Probability of getting a local/distant job in $RNFS_m$*) × (*average real income of a worker in $RNFS_m$*)} + {(*Probability of getting a local job in $RNFS_t$*) × (*average real income of a worker in $RNFS_t$*)} + {(*Probability of getting a local/distant job in AGR_m*) × (*average real income of a worker in AGR_m*)}] = [*Actual per capita real income (from marketable surplus) of local AGR_t*]. (2.3)

[21] This is subject to the fulfilment of the grand migration equilibrium condition: expected per capita urban real income = Expected per capita real income from local or distant rural non-AGR_t (including AGR_m) = Actual per capita real income (from marketed surplus) in local AGR_t. However, we are assuming away the issue of urban in-migration, as mentioned earlier.

[22] Here by migration, we refer to occupational migration rather than spatial migration.

As, from section 2.2 and Figure 2.1 above, an expansion of the FS also induces the $RNFS_m$ and AGR_m, equation (2.3) can be rewritten succinctly as

[{(*Probability of getting a local/distant job in the rural* FS, $RNFS_m$, *and* AGR_m *combined*) × (*real per capita income in this rural FS*, $RNFS_m$, *and* AGR_m *combined*)} + {(*Probability of getting a local job in* $RNFS_t$) × (*real per capita income in this* $RNFS_t$)}] = [*Actual per capita real income* (*from marketed surplus*) *of local* AGR_t]. (2.4)

Here, in order to have the migration equilibrium condition, we need to assume the following:

[*real per capita income in the rural* FS, $RNFS_m$, *and* AGR_m *combined*] > [*per capita real income* (*from marketed surplus*) *of local* AGR_t] > [*real per capita income in* $RNFS_t$]. (2.5)

Using notations, as mentioned earlier, equation (2.4) (i.e. the intra-rural migration equilibrium condition) could be written as

$$\frac{L_m(I_f)}{L_m(I_f)+L_t}y_m(I_f)+\frac{L_t}{L_m(I_f)+L_t}y_t(L_t)=\frac{(P_a.A)}{w_1P_m(I_f)+w_2P_t(L_t)}. \tag{2.6}$$

Now, using the notations stated in Table 2.1 and the assumptions of our model rural economy, the following set of conditions are derived:

Aggregate rural modern sector employment $= L_m(I_f)$, with $\delta L_m/\delta I_f > 0$,

Per capita income in the rural modern sector $= y_m(I_f)$, with $\delta y_m/\delta I_f > 0$,

Per capita income in the traditional RNFS $= y_t(L_t)$, with $\delta y_t/\delta L_t < 0$, and

$$w_1P_m(I_f)+w_2P_t(L_t) = \text{price index faced by the farmers}$$
$$= P(I_f, L_t),\ \text{with}\ \frac{\delta P}{\delta I_f} > 0\ \text{and}\ \frac{\delta P}{\delta L_t} < 0. \tag{2.6'}$$

Using the above notations and behavioural conditions and also using the set of conditions (2.6′), equation (2.6) can be reorganized as

$$\frac{L_m(I_f)}{L_m(I_f)+L_t}y_m(I_f)+\frac{L_t}{L_m(I_f)+L_t}y_t(L_t)$$
$$=\frac{(P_a.A)}{P(I_f,L_t)} \text{ with } \frac{\delta L_m}{\delta I_f}>0;\frac{\delta y_m}{\delta I_f}>0;\frac{\delta y_t}{\delta L_t}<0;\frac{\delta P}{\delta I_f}>0 \text{ and } \frac{\delta P}{\delta L_t}<0. \quad (2.7)$$

Now, given the earlier discussion, with $I_f = I_f^0$, $P_a = P_a^0$ and $A = A^0$, equation (2.7) becomes

$$\frac{L_m^0(I_f^0)}{L_m^0(I_f^0)+L_t}y_m^0(I_f^0)+\frac{L_t}{L_m^0(I_f^0)+L_t}y_t(L_t)=\frac{(P_a^0.A^0)}{P^0(I_f^0,L_t)} \quad (2.8)$$

Let us denote expected per capita real income from local/distant rural non-AGR_t (combining all segments): $\frac{L_m^0(I_f^0)}{L_m^0(I_f^0)+L_t}y_m^0(I_f^0)+\frac{L_t}{L_m^0(I_f^0)+L_t}y_t(L_t)=y_{na}{}^0(I_f^0,L_t)$; And actual per capita real income (from marketable surplus) in local AGR_t:

$$\frac{(P_a^0.A^0)}{P^0(I_f^0,L_t)}=y_a{}^0(P_a^0,A^0,I_f^0,L_t). \quad (2.8')$$

Now, using these new notations, equation (2.8) can be rewritten as

$$y_{na}{}^0(I_f^0,L_t)=y_a{}^0(P_a^0,A^0,I_f^0,L_t) \quad (2.9)$$

The exogenously set 'I_f' determines L_m, y_m, and P_m, following equations and assumptions presented above. Next, given 'I_f' (= I_f^0), equation (2.9) solves for L_t and hence, for P_t, y_t, y_{na}, and y_a (following equations (2.6) and (2.9)). The whole system gets determined.

This migration equilibrium condition (2.9) could generate Figure 2.2 below where e^0 gives us, the initial equilibrium obtained from the

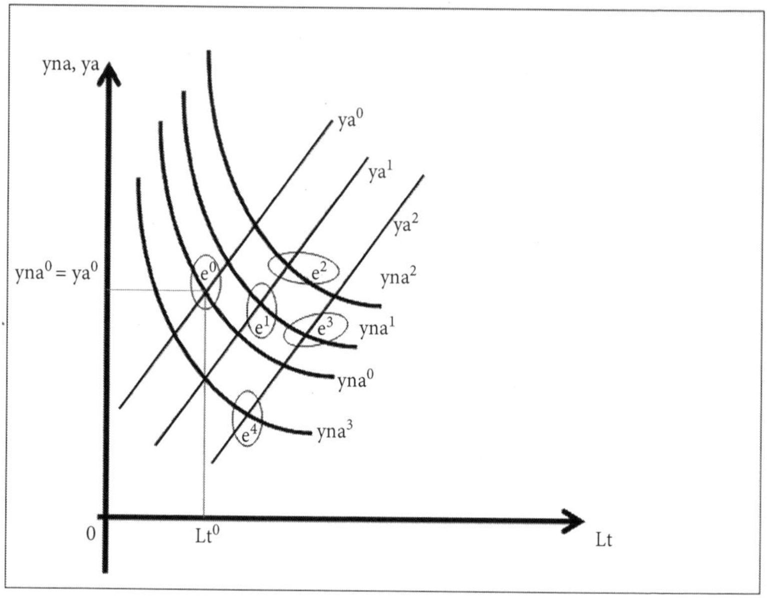

Figure 2.2 Migration equilibrium and a few comparative static outcomes
Source: Constructed by the authors.

intersection of y_a^0 and y_{na}^0 curves. The y_a^0 curve is upward rising and the y_{na}^0 curve is downward sloping due to the following reasons. From equation (2.7), one can see that as L_t rises, ceteris paribus, the probability of getting the modern rural job (in the FS, $RNFS_m$, and AGR_m combined) and per capita income in the $RNFS_t$ fall, along with an increased probability of getting traditional and non-remunerative $RNFS_t$ employment. Consequently, the expected per capita real income from local or distant rural non-AGR_t (i.e. the left-hand side of equation (2.7)), falls, reducing y_{na} in equation (2.9). Hence, we have a downward-sloping y_{na} curve (see Appendix A.2.1 for an algebraic derivation of the slope); although it could touch the ordinate, it cannot touch the abscissa. On the other hand, as L_t rises, the $RNFS_t$ output rises, reducing the $RNFS_t$ price. So, farmers' real income (from marketed surplus) rises (following the set of conditions (2.6′) and equation (2.7)), raising y_a in equation (2.9). Consequently, we have an upward-rising y_a curve; it could touch the ordinate (see Appendix A.2.1). Now, the y_{na} and y_a curves intersect to generate the migration equilibrium e^0.

2.4 Expansion of the formal sector and immiseration, accommodation, exclusion: A process of reproduction of dualism

Let us first discuss the impacts of a once-and-for-all increase in FS investment on the sectoral volumes, prices, and incomes across the different segments of the rural economy.

If the level of FS investment (in real terms) rises, the FS expands, being demand-driven, raising the level of demand for $RNFS_m$ and AGR_m outputs too. Consequently, in the rural FS, $RNFS_m$, and AGR_m combined, employment (be it permanent or temporary: L_m), product price (P_m) and per capita income (y_m) increase, once and for all, and the surplus/unemployed/'reserve' (skilled/semi-skilled) labour pool gets reduced (although not modelled explicitly).

Therefore, in the context of the migration equilibrium conditions (2.8) and (2.9), the expected per capita real income in local/distant rural non-AGR_t (i.e. y_{na}) rises, with an increased probability of getting a job in the modern rural sector (i.e. FS, $RNFS_m$, and AGR_m combined) as well as their increased per capita income, while the actual per capita real income (from marketed surplus) in $AGR_t(y_a)$ falls (with increased prices of FS, $RNFS_m$, and AGR_m products). This disturbs the migration equilibrium, immiserates the AGR_t population, and triggers off local/distant diversification/migration from local AGR_t towards the expanded rural modern non-AGR_t. However, this (pushed-out) migrating/diversifying (mostly unskilled) labour (although pulled by the anticipated new opportunities in the rural FS, $RNFS_m$, and AGR_m combined) cannot find any space in these modern segments, as the initial scope for additional employment (in these FS, $RNFS_m$, and AGR_m combined) has already been filled up by the local surplus/'reserve' labour (surrounding the FS–$RNFS_m$–AGR_m). There are also restrictions on the entry of newer firms in the modern nonfarm segment (FS–$RNFS_m$–AGR_m) that cannot generate new employment for want of credit access, network, skill, etc.

Consequently, this impoverished population of the AGR_t finds its refuge mostly in the localized $RNFS_t$; and another minor part (presumed as zero in our model) of this immiserated mass, a relatively more endowed/resilient section, manages to remain unemployed and thereby adds to the reserve army for the rural FS, $RNFS_m$, and AGR_m combined.

Thus, L_t rises (and there is a slight rise in unemployment, too) with a fall in per capita $RNFS_t$ income (y_t). These second-round changes reduce y_{na} and increase y_a (in comparison to their transitional values attained through the first round of changes), following equations (2.7) and (2.9), and thereby regain the migration equilibrium.[23]

Combining all these processes, we could say that, as a result of an expansion of the FS, on the one hand, new jobs are created in the rural FS, $RNFS_m$, and AGR_m combined (and per capita income, too, is increased in these modern segments); on the other, the backward $RNFS_t$ proliferates, and painfully, its price (P_t) and hence, per capita income (y_t) depress further owing to overcrowding and congestion. Moreover, from the sets of assumptions (2.6′) and (2.8′) and the equations (2.7) and (2.9), as the prices of FS, $RNFS_m$, and AGR_m combined outputs (P_m) increase, it is quite likely that the real per capita income in AGR_t(y_a) ultimately falls, even if the price of $RNFS_t$ output (P_t) falls, as seen just above. This is because, most probably, the combined weight of FS and $RNFS_m$ commodities in the expenditure basket of a petty farmer of the AGR_t (i.e. w_1) is larger than the corresponding weight for the $RNFS_t$ commodities (w_2). However, if it happens that, $w_1 < w_2$, y_a ultimately increases.

Many of these effects could be understood succinctly by analysing Figure 2.2. We know the initial equilibrium position is e^0 (point of intersection between y^0_{na} and y^0_a). As FS investment increases, following the above discussion, the y_{na} curve shifts up, and the y_a curve shifts down. Consequently, the equilibrium position shifts either to e^1 (intersection point of y^1_{na} and y^1_a) or to e^2 (intersection point of y^2_{na} and y^1_a), depending on the relative changes in y_{na} and y_a. However, it is clear that $RNFS_t$ aggregate employment (L_t) undoubtedly increases.

If y_a fall is stronger than y_{na} rise, we have e^1; otherwise, it is e^2. If AGR farmers are dependent more on FS and $RNFS_m$ as compared to $RNFS_t$ (i.e. $w_1 > w_2$), y_a ultimately falls, as analysed above, and the new equilibrium position becomes e^1. Otherwise, it is e^2. Whatever happens, however, there is a clear case of deepening dualism within the rural economy.

[23] When people migrate/diversify away from AGR_t to $RNFS_t$, they use the same amount of AGR_t output they were using before this movement/diversification. Hence, as mentioned earlier, the residual per capita output in AGR_t remains the same (i.e. A^0).

While, on the one hand, the FS, $RNFS_m$, and AGR_m prosper both in terms of sectoral size and income, the inferior $RNFS_t$ expands, engendering congestion and immiseration, on the other. Along with this, there is a real possibility of the impoverishment of the AGR_t too.

2.5 Accumulation by dispossession: A process of reproduction of dualism

Following Harvey (2003), we now consider a (longer-run) situation where the rural FS expands by extracting resources from the AGR_t.[24] Thus, the FS expropriates water resources, forest resources, land, etc., for peri-urbanization, rural infrastructure development, and large-scale rural industrialization.[25] Such a dual process of expansion of the modern sectors engendering immiseration has the following consequences:

1. As the rural FS expands, similar to the previous case, the y_{na} increases, and there is a shift of the y_{na} curve from y_{na}^0 to y_{na}^1 (Figure 2.2).
2. With this FS expansion, as in the previous case, there is a real income deflation in the AGR_t due to an increase in the prices of the FS, $RNFS_m$, and AGR_m. Consequently, the y_a curve shifts from y_a^0 to y_a^1 (Figure 2.2). One should note that individuals engaged in the traditional segment also purchase goods produced by the modern segment.
3. As the FS expands by expropriating resources from the AGR_t, and thereby adversely affecting the per capita output produced there (i.e. A), following equation (2.9), there is a fall in y_a. Consequently, the y_a curve shifts further to y_a^2, beyond y_a^1 (Figure 2.2).
4. All these combined together, we have AGR_t—non-AGR_t migration/diversification, and the new migration equilibrium is attained at e^3 (the intersection between y_a^2 and y_{na}^1). Thus, although the FS,

[24] In order to understand the impact of land acquisition on the informal sector in greater detail by incorporating several other factors such as connectivity between rural and urban areas, one can refer to Bhaduri and Banerjee (2025).

[25] Large-scale crop diversification, induced by the general process of modernization of the economy, plays a similar exclusionary role. However, we will elaborate this crucial but complex issue in the subsequent chapters (see also Chakrabarti and Kundu, 2009a).

$RNFS_m$, and AGR_m prosper, the $RNFS_t$ expands and immiserates too, and, most probably, AGR_t impoverishes due to cost escalation as well as resource expropriation.

Thus, starkly contrary to a so-called inclusive growth process (and a comprehensive capitalist transformation) driven by the modern sector's insertion into the rural space, we have a phenomenon of reproduction of dualism, the creation of a dual structure that is much more complex than the traditional industry–agriculture dichotomy. Instead of a comprehensive transition of the traditionally heterogeneous rural economy towards a homogeneous capitalist structure, we have a phenomenon of the evolution of a fractured rural space.

2.6 COVID-19 and lockdown: Intensification of dualism

Let us now consider the probable impacts of COVID-19-induced lockdowns on the rural economy. In analysing this, once again, we use Figure 2.2.

As the FS reduces operations and implements work from home for permanent employees or begins to stagger the workforce across shifts, the temporary, contractual, casual, and outsourced workers are laid off. Further, the overall wage rate in the FS decreases due to factors such as wage cuts, salary freezes, and allowance reductions. The sectors that are linked with the FS within the informal space (i.e. the $RNFS_m$ and AGR_m segments) are also adversely affected, leading to reductions in employment and per capita income in these segments. The laid-off workers of the modern sector (FS, $RNFS_m$, and AGR_m) trigger off reverse migration and move primarily towards the traditional sector, particularly (local/distant) $RNFS_t$, creating congestion and hence, income deflation; some others become and remain unemployed in/voluntarily and search for a new job. Consequently, as per Figure 2.2, the per capita income schedule of the sector outside non-traditional agriculture (i.e. the y_{na} curve) shifts back from y^0_{na} to y^3_{na}.

The aggregate price of the modern sector (P_m) rise considerably due to the adverse supply shocks (as mentioned above), including hoarding activities by powerful intermediaries (all along the production and supply chains) done in search of a windfall gain.

Next, as the COVID-19 lockdown is implemented, the AGR_t sector is severely affected. In terms of equation (2.6) (right-hand side in particular), a rise in $RNFS_t$ employment (L_t) reduces P_t, but P_m rises considerably, as mentioned above. More importantly, however, 'A' falls significantly due to COVID-19 and lockdown,[26] but the AGR_t price P_a cannot rise much due to intermediary dominance (although the open-market price of the AGR_t output rises substantially). Consequently, y_a falls noticeably and hence, the y_a curve shifts, say, from y_a^0 to y_a^2. As a result, there is an exodus of the labour force from the AGR_t too, and given the contractions in the FS, $RNFS_m$, and AGR_m, this immiserated mass is compelled to take refuge in the $RNFS_t$. This is captured by a shift of migration equilibrium position from e^0 to e^4.

Thus, we have the final outcomes, where, in the FS, the contract workers are adversely affected, the $RNFS_m$ and AGR_m workers become jobless, and the AGR_t too suffers significantly from the output (and input) price shocks. As a result of all these processes, the $RNFS_t$ expands, leading to congestion and income depression. However, in this whole phenomenon, both y_{na} and y_a are falling, and finally, what happens to the $RNFS_t$ depends on the relative impacts on y_{na} and y_a. It may so happen that not even the $RNFS_t$ (and, of course, the overcrowded AGR_t) is capable of absorbing the dispossessed destitute. Hence, under such a situation, only open unemployment rises. These tendencies could be captured by Figure 2.3.

First of all,

S^0 and D^0 curves of the first quadrant are the initial supply and demand contours, respectively, for the rural FS–$RNFS_m$–AGR_m outputs combined, with e^0 being the initial equilibrium (determining the initial output (Q^0), employment (L^0, assuming labour–output ratio to be '1', to simplify), and price P_m^0).

$S_a^{\,0}$, D_a^{m0}, and D_a^{f0} of the fourth quadrant are the initial supply, market-demand, and farm-gate-price (in the presence of intermediaries)

[26] This was assumed as constant in the pre-COVID-19 situation. However, here we assume a fall because of the exogenous shock resulting from the pandemic.

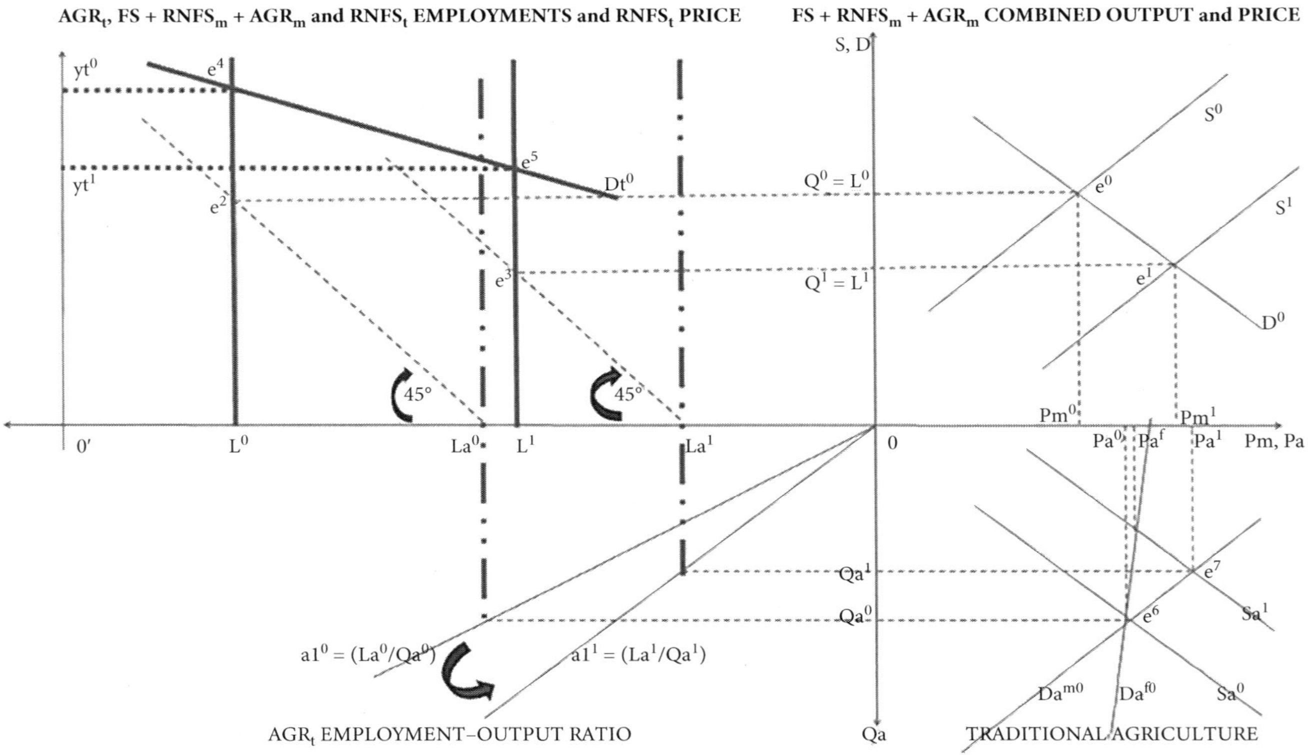

Figure 2.3 COVID-19 pandemic: Lockdown and employment in different sectors

contours,[27] respectively, for AGR_t, with e^6 being the initial equilibrium (determining the initial output (Q_a^0), employment (L_a^0, derived via the third quadrant's ray through the origin, as elaborated below), and the initial price P_a^0).

The rays through the origin in the third quadrant give us the actual employment–output ratio, given the ability of AGR_t (income) to absorb/accommodate surplus labour, with al^0 being the initial ray (determining AGR_t employment L_a^0, given Q_a^0).

And finally, in the second quadrant, we have the initial employment in AGR_t ($0L_a^0$), the initial employment in rural FS–$RNFS_m$–AGR_m combined ($L_a^0L^0 = L^0e^2$, using the 45^0 ray through L_a^0) and the initial employment in $RNFS_t$ ($00' - (0L_a^0 + L_a^0L^0) = 0'L^0$) and also the price and, hence, initial per capita income in the $RNFS_t$ (y_t^0 at e^4, derived through the interactions of initial labour supply $0'L^0$ and labour demand D_t^0).

Next, with COVID-19 and lockdown, we have the following changes:

Due to the supply shock, the S^1 curve of the first quadrant is the new supply contour for the rural FS–$RNFS_m$–AGR_m outputs combined, with e^1 being the new equilibrium (with a reduced output (Q^1), reduced employment (L^1, assuming labour–output ratio to be one) and an increased price P_m^1)

As the cost of production rises in the AGR_t (due to the increase in P_m to P_m^1), S_a^1 becomes its new supply contour, with e^7 being the new equilibrium (determining new output (Q_a^1), new employment (L_a^1, via the third quadrant's rotated new ray al^1, as elaborated next), and increased market price (P_a^1, although the farmers are receiving only P_a^f due to intermediary presence). As the cost of production rises substantially in the AGR_t, but the farm-gate price rises only marginally to P_a^f (due to intermediary control), there is a net income depression, and hence, the ability of the AGR_t to accommodate surplus labour diminishes. Consequently, the ray, through the origin in the third quadrant, rotates anticlockwise to al^1 (determining the AGR_t employment L_a^1, given Q_a^1). Thus, in the second quadrant, we have reduced employment in the AGR_t ($0L_a^1$), reduced employment in the rural FS–$RNFS_m$–AGR_m combined ($L_a^1L^1 = L^1e^3$, using

[27] The contour of the farm-gate price is steep in comparison to the market demand curve because powerful traders/intermediaries set the farm-gate price, and the farmers are largely price takers. Even if the market price increases, the farm-gate price shows a minor change.

the 45° ray through L_a^1), and increased employment in the $RNFS_t$ ($00' - (0L_a^1 + L_a^1L^1) = 0'L^1$), along with its reduced price and, hence, reduced per capita income (y_t^1 at e^5, derived through the interactions of the new labour supply $0'L^1$ and the old labour demand contour D_t^0).

Thus, COVID-19 and lockdown spread the $RNFS_t$, and its income plummets, while the other sectors of the economy contract; we have a phenomenon of deepening dualism.

2.7 Conclusion

This chapter provides a theoretical explanation of how growth causes the generation, persistence, and spread of duality across the rural Global South and, in particular, across rural India. Our model starts with the migration/diversification equilibrium akin to the H–T model. However, it has several novelties, which are listed below.

First, we consider a multifaceted process of labour migration/diversification, where apart from the pull-driven progression, push-driven migration or diversification happen as well, generating certain macroeconomic impacts, intensifying structural heterogeneities. Moreover, in our analysis, both these processes happen simultaneously.

Second, while explaining these pull- and push-driven processes and their macroeconomic outcomes, we consider certain distinct micro traits and behaviours, which are structurally different for different groups/'class' of people. Thus, our framework is uniquely eclectic, where we draw from the orthodox H–T method of analysis, the heterodox Kaleckian macro-analysis, and the heterodox political-economy discourse of Harvey (2003). Using such an eclectic framework, we thus explain a complex process of reproduction of dualism in rural India, contrary to the orthodox claim of (or policy push for) a phenomenon of tortuous transition towards a comprehensive capitalistic economic structure.

Next, we have captured/pointed out the internal duality existing within the rural informal sectors (both agriculture and nonfarm). In our model, agriculture (a part of the informal segment) is not considered as a homogenous sector; rather, we have categorized agriculture into traditional and modern in terms of kind of crops grown (high-value cash crops versus basic cereals, etc.), technology utilized, inputs and assets used, and infrastructure and market accessed. The informal RNFS is similarly categorized as a heterogeneous sector and consists of both traditional and modern segments, based on mainly surplus producing in/ability.

One should note that existing dominant literature has largely considered the informal sector as a homogenous sector in which marginal productivity is either zero or constant (Lewis, 1954; Fields, 1975, 1989; Harris and Todaro, 1970; Kar and Marjit, 2001; Chaudhuri and Mukhopadhyay, 2002).[28] It has been assumed that people get engaged in the informal sector because of a lack of opportunity in the FS, and also, it is considered to be better than remaining unemployed. An opposite view of the informal sector also exists in the mainstream literature. These studies consider that those working in the informal sector are there voluntarily, since the sector provides a higher return as compared to the FS contractual employment (Maloney, 2003, 2004). Some studies have also considered an internal duality within the informal sector by combining these two polar views (Fields, 1990; Ranis and Stewart, 1999). However, such studies are relatively fewer, and also the structures and linkages of the different segments of the informal economy have been defined loosely. On the other hand, important critical literature too considers the informal sector as somewhat homogeneous (Sanyal, 2007; Breman, 2019; Harris-White, 2023). We fill this gap in our above theoretical analysis. We deviate from both the mainstream and critical literature, but we derive from both as well and build our own eclectic framework. Thus, we contemplate an economic structure that is much more complex and perhaps more comprehensive and realistic. We show how the economy consists of differentiated segments and, at the same time, how the various sectors are interconnected or, at least, interdependent (directly and/or indirectly) and how this composite structure gets reproduced and proliferated.

Finally, in this framework, we have tried to explain the effect of a pandemic such as the COVID-19 pandemic of 2020/2021 on the persistence and generation of duality. We have shown that a pandemic expands the traditional/petty informality, and its income plummets, while the other sectors of the economy contract, contrarily. Even though our model was extended to explain the impact of the pandemic per se on the rural nonfarm sector, the same model can be used to explain any situation in which external shocks affect the accumulation process adversely.

[28] See also Elsevier (n.d.) for an overview.

In the next few chapters, we present empirical support for the propositions we have laid down in this chapter using both global and Indian data.

A.2 Appendix

A.2.1 Algebra of model

In this section, we illustrate the basic theoretical model in algebraic form. This exercise is a supplement to the analytical and graphical analysis provided in the chapter. We present here three results that are important in establishing our argument.

First, akin to Figure 2.2, we show that the slope of the per capita real income schedule of the traditional AGR (y_a) is positive, and the per capita real income schedule of the sector outside traditional AGR (y_{na}) is negatively sloped.

Second, we show the directions in which per capita real income schedules of both these sectors shift with respect to an increase in FS investment (I_f). The directions of the shift are important for the comparative static analysis. It is shown that, owing to FS investment, the y_{na} function shifts to the right and the y_a schedule shifts to the left.

Third, we show how employment in the $RNFS_t$ changes with respect to changes in the FS investment. We have shown that an expansion of the FS expands traditional employment. In other words, FS expansion aggravates the already existing duality. This is the fundamental proposition of our theoretical analysis.

A.2.1.1 The algebraic analysis

We have two rural sectors, namely, traditional agriculture and the sector outside it. The per capita real income schedule of both these sectors is provided below. The notations used have already been explained in the chapter.

$$y_a = \frac{P_a A}{w_1.P_m(I_f) + w_2.P_t(L_t)} \tag{A.2.1}$$

$$y_{na} = \frac{L_m(I_f)}{L_m(I_f)+L_t} y_m(I_f) + \frac{L_t}{L_m(I_f)+L_t} y_t(L_t). \tag{A.2.2}$$

In order to get the slope of the schedules or to map the shift of the functions owing to FS investment, one needs to find out the total derivative of both these schedules. We assume that $dP_a = dA = dw_1 = dw_2 = 0$. We start with the non-agricultural sector first.

Total differentiation of equation (A.2.2) gives us the following:

$$dy_{na} = \frac{\begin{array}{c}\{L_m'(I_f).y_m(I_f)+y_m'(I_f).L_m(I_f)\}\{L_m(I_f)+L_t\}\\ -L_m'(I_f)L_m(I_f)y_m(I_f)-L_m'(I_f)L_ty_t(l_t)\end{array}}{\{L_m(I_f)+L_t\}^2}.dI_f + \frac{-L_m(I_f)y_m(I_f)+\{y_t(L_t)+y_t'(L_t)L_t\}\{L_m(I_f)+L_t\}-L_ty_t(L_t)}{\{L_m(I_f)+L_t\}^2}.dL_t.$$

Rearranging, we get

$$dy_{na} = \frac{L_m'(I_f)L_t\{y_m(I_f)-y_t(L_t)\}+y_m'(I_f)L_m(I_f)\{L_m(I_f)+L_t\}}{\{L_m(I_f)+L_t\}^2}dI_f + \frac{L_m(I_f)\{y_t(L_t)-y_m(I_f)\}+y_t'(L_t)L_t\{L_m(I_f)+L_t\}}{\{L_m(I_f)+L_t\}^2}dL_t. \quad \text{(A.2.3)}$$

Total differentiation of equation (A.2.1) gives us the following:

$$dy_a = -\frac{w_1P_m'(I_f).P_aA}{\{w_1.P_m(I_f)+w_2.P_t(L_t)\}^2}dI_f - \frac{w_2P_t'(L_t).P_aA}{\{w_1.P_m(I_f)+w_2.P_t(L_t)\}^2}dL_t. \quad \text{(A.2.4)}$$

A.2.1.2 The slope of the per capita real income schedules

The slope of per capita real income of both these sectors can be obtained by assuming dI_f as zero in equations (A.2.3) and (A.2.4). Alternatively, one can also get it by partially differentiating equations (A.2.1) and (A.2.2) with respect to I_f.

The slope of per capita real income schedule of the sector outside traditional agriculture is

$$\frac{\delta y_{na}}{\delta L_t} = \frac{L_m(I_f)\{y_t(L_t)-y_m(I_f)\}+y_t'(L_t)L_t\{L_m(I_f)+L_t\}}{\{L_m(I_f)+L_t\}^2} < 0. \quad \text{(A.2.5)}$$

The denominator of equation (A.2.5) is a square term, hence positive. The numerator is negative. This is because, in the numerator, the per capita real income of the traditional farm sector ($y_t(L_t)$) is lower than the modern sector's per capita real income ($y_m(I_f)$), that is, $y_t(L_t) < y_m(I_f)$.

Also, the per capita real income of the workers in the *RNFS$_t$* (y_t) is negatively influenced by the volume of the workforce (L_t), that is, $y_t'(L_t) < 0$. Therefore, $\frac{\delta y_{na}}{\delta L_t} < 0$.

The slope of the per capita real income schedule of traditional agriculture is

$$\frac{\delta y_a}{\delta L_t} = -\frac{w_2 P_t'(L_t).P_a A}{\{w_1.P_m(I_f) + w_2.P_t(L_t)\}^2} > 0. \quad \text{(A.2.6)}$$

This slope is positive due to the fact that $P_t'(L_t) < 0$. In other words, the price of the *RNFS$_t$* output (P_t) bears a negative relationship with the volume of the workforce in that sector (L_t). As this volume of workforce expands, increased production and supply leads to increased pressure on the market, reducing the price of the *RNFS$_t$* output.

A.2.1.3 Shifts of the per capita real income schedules

The schedules can shift due to a change in the constant parameters of the model. The models have several parameters, such as A, P_a, w_1, w_2, and I_f. However, since we are concerned about the impact of FS growth, here we show how these schedules shift due to an expansion of FS investment. The effect of an expansion of FS investment on both these sectors can be obtained by partially differentiating equations y_{na} and y_a with respect to I_f.

The following results are obtained:

$$\frac{\delta y_{na}}{\delta I_f} = \frac{L_m'(I_f)L_t\{y_m(I_f) - y_t(L_t)\} + y_m'(I_f)L_m(I_f)\{L_m(I_f) + L_t\}}{\{L_m(I_f) + L_t\}^2} > 0. \quad \text{(A.2.7)}$$

Equation (A.2.7) is positive because employment and output in the modern sector is an increasing function of FS investment, that is, $L_m'(I_f) > 0$ and $y_m'(I_f) > 0$ and also $y_m(I_f) - y_t(L_t) > 0$.

$$\text{Similarly, } \frac{\delta y_a}{\delta I_f} = -\frac{w_1 P'_m(I_f).P_a A}{\{w_1.P_m(I_f)+w_2.P_t(L_t)\}^2} < 0. \tag{A.2.8}$$

Since all the individual components are positive in equation (A.2.8), due to the negative sign, $\frac{\delta y_a}{\delta I_f}$ is less than zero.

The result indicates that an ex pansion of FS investment shifts the y_{na} curve up and y_a curve down.

A.2.1.4 The impact of formal sector investment on employment in the traditional nonfarm sector

Our overall model is based on three equations. The first two equations represent the per capita real income schedule of traditional agriculture and the sector outside traditional agriculture. The third equation is the migration equilibrium condition, that is, $y_{na} = y_a$

These equations are presented below.

$$y_{na} = \frac{L_m(I_f)}{L_m(I_f)+L_t} y_m(I_f) + \frac{L_t}{L_m(I_f)+L_t} y_t(L_t)$$

$$y_a = \frac{P_a A}{w_1.P_m(I_f)+w_2.P_t(L_t)}$$

$$y_{na} = y_a.$$

Total differentiations of the three equations would capture the change of these variables with respect to the change of I_f and L_t. As stated above, we have assumed that $dP_a = dA = dw_1 = dw_2 = 0$. The total derivatives are provided below.

$$dy_{na} = \frac{L'_m(I_f)L_t\{y_m(I_f)-y_t(L_t)\}+y'_m(I_f)Lm(I_f)\{L_m(I_f)+L_t\}}{\{L_m(I_f)+L_t\}^2}dI_f + \frac{L_m\{y_t(L_t)-y_m(I_f)\}+y'_t(L_t)L_t\{L_m(I_f)+L_t\}}{\{L_m(I_f)+L_t\}^2}dL_t \tag{A.2.9}$$

$$dy_a = -\frac{w_1 p'_m(I_f).P_a A}{\{w_1.P_m(I_f)+w_2.P_t(L_t)\}^2} dI_f - \frac{w_2 p'_t(L_t).P_a A}{\{w_1.P_m(I_f)+w_2.P_t(L_t)\}^2} dL_t \tag{A.2.10}$$

$$dy_{na} - dy_a = 0. \tag{A.2.11}$$

Our objective is to find out the impact of an increase in FS investment (I_f) on employment in the traditional non-agricultural sector (L_t). Inserting dy_{na} obtained from equation (A.2.9) and dy_a obtained from equation (A.2.10), in equation (A.2.11) we get

$$\frac{L'_m(I_f)L_t\{y_m(I_f)-y_t(L_t)\}+y'_m(I_f)L_m(I_f)\{L_m(I_f)+L_t\}}{\{L_m(I_f)+L_t\}^2} dI_f + \frac{L_m\{y_t(L_t)-y_m(I_f)\}+y'_t(L_t)L_t\{L_m(I_f)+L_t\}}{\{L_m(I_f)+L_t\}^2} dL_t$$
$$= -\frac{w_1 P'_m(I_f).P_a A}{\{w_1.P_m(I_f)+w_2.P_t(L_t)\}^2} dI_f - \frac{w_2 P'_t(L_t).P_a A}{\{w_1.P_m(I_f)+w_2.P_t(L_t)\}^2} dL_t.$$

Rearranging, we get

$$-\frac{w_2 P'_t(L_t).P_a A}{\{w_1.P_m(I_f)+w_2.P_t(L_t)\}^2} dL_t - \frac{L_m\{y_t(L_t)-y_m(I_f)\}+y'_t(L_t)L_t\{L_m(I_f)+L_t\}}{\{L_m(I_f)+L_t\}^2} dL_t$$
$$= \frac{w_1 P'_m(I_f).P_a A}{\{w_1.P_m(I_f)+w_2.P_t(L_t)\}^2} dI_f + \frac{L'_m(I_f)L_t\{y_m(I_f)-y_t(L_t)\}+y'_m(I_f)L_m(I_f)\{L_m+L_t\}}{\{L_m(I_f)+L_t\}^2} dI_f$$

or

$$dL_t = \frac{\{w_1 P'_m(I_f)\}.P_a A\{L_m(I_f)+L_t\}^2 dI_f + [L'_m(I_f)L_t\{y_m(I_f)-y_t(L_t)\} + y'_m(I_f)Lm(I_f)\{L_m+L_t\}]\{w_1.P_m(I_f)+w_2.P_t(L_t)\}^2 dI_f}{-\{w_2 P'_t(L_t).P_a A\}\{L_m(I_f)+L_t\}^2 - [L_m\{y_t(L_t)-y_m(I_f)\} + y'_t(L_t)L_t\{L_m(I_f)+L_t\}]\{w_1.P_m(I_f)+w_2.P_t(L_t)\}^2}. \tag{A.2.12}$$

Based on the assumptions we have made on price, output, and employment of different sectors, both the numerator and the denominator of equation (A.2.1) are greater than zero.

This means $dLt/dI_f > 0$.

In other words, an expansion of FS investment increases employment in the $RNFS_t$.

A.2.1.5 The impact of formal sector investment on the incomes of agriculture and the nonfarm sector

This can be addressed using matrix algebra.*

Writing equations (A.2.9), (A.2.10), and (A.2.11) in matrix form, we get

$$\begin{bmatrix} \{L_m(L_t)+L_t\}^2 & 0 & [L_m\{y_t(L_t)-y_m(I_f)\}+y_t'(L_t)\{L_m(I_f)+L_t\}] \\ 0 & \{w_1.P_m(I_f)+w_2.P_t(L_t)\}^2 & w_2P_t'(L_t).P_aA \\ 1 & -1 & 0 \end{bmatrix}$$

$$\times \begin{bmatrix} dy_{na} \\ dy_a \\ dL_t \end{bmatrix} = \begin{bmatrix} [L_m'(I_f)L_t\{y_m(I_f)-y_t(L_t)\}+y_m'(I_f)L_m(I_f)\{L_m+L_t\}]dI_f \\ -w_1P_m'(I_f).P_aAdI_f \\ 0 \end{bmatrix}$$

Using Cramer's rule, one can solve dy_{na} or dy_a. We are considering here only dy_{na}.

$$dy_{na} = \frac{\begin{vmatrix} [L_m'(I_f)L_t\{y_m(I_f)-y_t(L_t)\}+y_m'(I_f)L_m(I_f)\{L_m+L_t\}]dI_f & 0 & [L_m\{y_t(L_t)-y_m(I_f)\}+y_t'(L_t)L_t\{L_m(I_f)+L_t\}] \\ -w_1P_m'(I_f).P_aAdI_f & \{w_1.P_m(I_f)+w_2.P_t(L_t)\}^2 & w_2P_t'(L_t).P_aA \\ 0 & -1 & 0 \end{vmatrix}}{\begin{vmatrix} \{L_m(I_f)+L_t\}^2 & 0 & [L_m\{y_t(L_t)-y_m(I_f)\}+y_t'(L_t)L_t\{L_m(I_f)+L_t\}] \\ 0 & \{w_1.P_m(I_f)+w_2.P_t(L_t)\}^2 & w_2P_t'(L_t).P_aA \\ 1 & -1 & 0 \end{vmatrix}}$$

$$dy_{na} = \frac{\begin{gathered}[L_m'(I_f)L_t\{y_m(I_f)-y_t(L_t)\}+y_m'(I_f)L_m(I_f)\{L_m+L_t\}]dI_f[w_2P_t'(L_t).P_aA] \\ +[L_m\{y_t(L_t)-y_m(I_f)\}+y_t'(L_t)L_t\{L_m(I_f)+L_t\}]w_1P_m'(I_f).P_aAdI_f\end{gathered}}{\begin{gathered}[\{L_m(I_f)+L_t\}^2][w_2P_t'(L_t).P_aA]-[L_m(I_f)\{y_t(L_t)-y_m(I_f)\} \\ +y_t'(L_t)L_t\{L_m(I_f)+L_t\}]\{w_1.P_m(I_f)+w_2.P_t(L_t)\}^2\end{gathered}}.$$

* Disclaimer: We acknowledge that the equations may be nonlinear and Cramer's rule applies only to linear systems. This exercise is illustrative and applicable only where linearity holds.

The numerator is negative because $w_2 P_t'(L_t) < 0$, $y_t(L_t) - y_m(I_f) < 0$ and $y_t'(L_t) < 0$. The value of the denominator can be positive or negative.

The denominator can be negative if the absolute value of $[\{L_m(I_f) + L_t\}^2][w_2 P_t'(L_t).P_a A]$ is greater than $[L_m(I_f)\{y_t(L_t) - y_m(I_f)\} + y_t'(L_t)L_t\{L_m(I_f) + L_t\}]\ dI_f\{w_1.P_m(I_f) + w_2.P_t(L_t)\}^2$.

Otherwise, it will assume a positive value. If the denominator is negative, the FS will have a positive positive on the average income of the sectors outside traditional agriculture. If the denominator is positive, the FS will have a negative impact.

Here we have shown the impact of I_f on y_{na}. The impact of formal sector investment on y_a can be obtained also in the similar way.

A.2.2 The share of own account enterprise in the gross value added of rural unincorporated non-agricultural enterprises and the value of the Crop Diversification Index across the major states of India

We assumed in our theoretical framework that the traditional nonfarm sector (such as the OAEs) is linked to traditional agriculture (such as basic cereals). On the other hand, the modern nonfarm sector is linked to modern agriculture and the FS.

Table A.2.2 provides support for the above assumptions. It can be seen that states (such as Assam, Bihar, and Odisha) that have a lower presence of the FS (i.e. low per capita net value added) accompanied by the lower land area under cereals production have a higher presence of OAEs. On the other hand, states that have a higher presence of the FS or produce more modern crops have a higher value of the Crop Diversification Index (CDI) and have a higher presence of modern firms (such as Establishment) in the informal sector. Examples of such states are Gujarat, Tamil Nadu, Maharashtra, and Karnataka.

Table A.2.2 The share of own account enterprise in the gross value added of rural unincorporated non-agricultural enterprises and the value of the Crop Diversification Index across the major states of India

Serial no.	State	Land area used for cereal production in gross cropped area of the state (%)	Per capita NVA of the formal sector in INR	Share of own account enterprise (OAE) in GVA of rural unincorporated non-agricultural enterprises	Crop Diversification Index (CDI)
1	Punjab	87.73	6399	66.05	0.63
2	Haryana	82.49	11776	48.32	0.71
3	Tamil Nadu	51.76	10667	48.67	0.84
4	West Bengal	68.14	2252	69.01	0.58
5	Andhra Pradesh	39.52	7928	58.2	0.86
6	Bihar	90.77	542	81.02	0.67
7	Uttar Pradesh	81.03	1859	68.08	0.71
8	Gujarat	25.47	14509	40.69	0.88
9	Assam	72.51	2098	70.31	0.48
10	Madhya Pradesh	47.29	2609	61.83	0.83
11	Rajasthan	38.90	5728	62.05	0.9
12	Karnataka	41.64	7563	59.72	0.94
13	Odisha	82.26	4337	67.44	0.37
14	Maharashtra	35.01	13950	59.46	0.9

Note: Higher share of OAE in GVA of rural unincorporated non-agricultural enterprises imply a lower share of Establishment and vice versa.

Sources: Computed using the following data sets: Agricultural Census 2015 (CDI data and share of cereals in the gross cropped area), NSSO (OAE data), and Annual Survey of Industries (for FS data).

3
The Changing Nature of the Global Rural Economy

Historically, the world has observed several phases of economic transformation. While human involvement in production and trade has been present since ancient times, significant and rapid advancements began in both domains with the advent of the Industrial Revolution. As the Industrial Revolution progressed, not only did the production of various items increase in quantity and variety, but also the places where they were manufactured became more and more distant from the people who would finally consume them. Initially, Great Britain assumed the forefront, and subsequently, other Western European countries began producing goods for the world market. The existence of colonies under Western hegemony also facilitated these productions and trade.

During this period, industries in the developing countries were predominantly village-based, unorganized, and traditional in nature. They were also considerably devastated by the colonial policies. The modern manufacturing industry, if it existed at all, was small in scale and had minimal influence on the economy. This course persisted until the time of decolonization, which happened around the 1950s.

Following decolonization, modern manufacturing capabilities steadily expanded to most sectors of the developing world, primarily owing to trade restriction and import substitution policies. This led to the growth of dualism in the erstwhile colonies, in which a sizeable modern sector began to coexist with an enduring traditional or informal sector.[29] Over

[29] It is important to emphasize that the difference in capabilities between the modern sectors of developing countries and industrialized ones is not very high or insurmountable. Rodrik (2013) asserts that modern manufacturing industries demonstrate unconditional convergence. In other words, despite geographical disadvantages, inferior institutions, or unfavourable policies, the modern industrial sector nonetheless reaches the global frontier. Favourable conditions only augment the speed in the process of convergence.

The Nonfarm Economy. Manojit Bhattacharjee, Saumya Chakrabarti, and Meenakshi Rajeev,
Oxford University Press.
DOI: 10.1093/9780198972013.003.0003

time, the modern sector largely assumed a greater share in the gross domestic product (GDP), while the traditional sector continued to assume a larger share in employment.

The advent of the internet and other communication technologies in the 1990s increased the complexity further by causing an unbundling in the production process itself, which continues to this day. In this contemporary globalized era, due to advancements in communications, goods are manufactured by sourcing inputs from many locations worldwide. The former colonizers, who previously participated in global production, now prioritize technology and knowledge generation and brand development. In contrast, the developing world primarily focuses on manufacturing, dedicating its efforts to a single part of a longer value chain.

This process of unbundling of production has opened up the opportunity for the erstwhile traditional/informal sector to integrate with the modern sector by supplying important inputs through subcontracting at cheaper rates. While this mode initially seemed quite resilient, the emergence of the COVID-19 pandemic, as well as geopolitical disputes and wars, presented challenges for this system. This is because the pandemic caused significant disruption in the worldwide supply chain.

As far as the impact of all these processes are concerned, it not only impacted the rural economy and agriculture but also brought about significant changes in the rural nonfarm sector. Our intention in this chapter is not to capture the processes and impacts of all these diverse global events on the local rural economies. Rather, we exclusively highlight the transformations that the global economy has experienced in the recent past (particularly during the past few decades) and study the meanings and implications of these changes with respect to the rural nonfarm sector (RNFS) of the developing world, along with agriculture. Specifically, the chapter explores the macro trends of whether the global phenomenon of capitalistic accumulation and growth, accompanied by production unbundling, has pulled the RNFS into the circuit of capital across the globe and transformed it by providing cheap access to capital, subcontracting deals, technology, or knowledge. In other words, we ask whether the developing world is witnessing the maturing of a comprehensive rural transformation in which a shift is happening from the traditional farm and nonfarm activities having low land or labour productivity to activities having higher levels of productivity and integration with the global value chains; or, whether the capitalistic transition of the rural economy of the developing world remains mostly elusive.

This chapter concentrates on developments at the macro level that occurred prior to the outbreak of the COVID-19 pandemic. The changes and challenges that were witnessed during and following the COVID-19 pandemic are discussed in Chapter 7.

In order to address the study objectives, we have segregated the world economy into different regions. When there is a lack of data at the regional level, we use country-level indicators.

Given the limited data, it is not possible to firmly establish the propositions based on the available information. However, this chapter offers some indications that support our theoretical conjectures presented in Chapter 2. Using data at the macro level, this chapter establishes that the creation and spread of dualism have occurred across the globe, along with accumulation. Chapter 4 uses existing literature from specific individual countries to provide a more detailed explanation of the factors that caused a spread of dualism. Chapter 5 provides more rigorous analysis in the context of India.

While the current chapter mainly offers some indications that support our main propositions, it delivers useful insights through a detailed review of worldwide data and certain approaches. This, in turn, has helped us formulate the policy recommendations detailed in the book's final chapter.

This chapter is subdivided into several sections. Section 3.1 highlights the expansion of the urban areas and the reduction in the size of the global rural economy overtime. Section 3.2 provides an account of the changes in the global employment structure that have been observed over the past two decades. Here, we have focused on sectoral employment across different rural regions of the world and showed that the decline in the size of the rural economy did not squeeze all the segments of the rural space. In fact, some rural sectors have experienced an expansion in employment. Section 3.3 then explores the reasons behind such changes using data from the farm and nonfarm sectors and highlight the proliferation of a dual structure in the rural economies of the globe (especially of the Global South). Finally, a concluding section is presented in section 3.4.

3.1 Rural to urban transition and the transformation of the global economy

Over the past few decades, the world as a whole has undergone a structural change. World Bank estimations show that with economic advancement, we have shifted from a predominantly rural to an urbanized world.[30] For instance, while in 1960, 66.38 per cent of the global population[31] resided in rural areas, in 2020, it was around 44.84 per cent. The decline in the share of the rural population in the total global population has happened mainly in the post-1980 era. One can understand this by comparing the average decadal decline in the share of the rural population before and after 1980. World Bank data shows that the share of the rural population declined on average by 2.86 percentage points per decade from 1960 to 1980 and by 4.2 per cent from 1980 to 2020. In this context, for the disaggregated trends, we introduce Table 3.1. This disaggregation, generates interesting insights that could be a step towards evaluating our fundamental analytical proposition of deepening rural dualism.

Table 3.1 displays that though the share of the population residing in rural areas in most regions of the globe has experienced a decline, the rate of decline was not uniform or linear across regions or countries. Based on the data, we can classify the regions into four categories. The regions classified as Europe and Central Asia and North America constitute the first category. In these regions, more than half of the population became urbanized way back in 1960. These regions are not the object of our analysis, since they are already developed. Nevertheless, countries in these regions can be used as a reference point in our analysis. Latin America and the Caribbean and North Africa can be considered as the second category. Though countries in these regions observed decline in rural population long ago, the regions are not yet developed. The third category

[30] The World Bank estimate on share of rural population in total population is calculated using data from the United Nations Population Division (UNPD) by subtracting the share of urban population from the total. One should note that there is no proper definition of the term 'rural areas'. National statistical department of each country has a definition of 'urban area'. Estimates on rural areas are obtained by netting out the corresponding urban values.

[31] Information on population and per capita GDP is provided in Table A.3.1 of the Appendix.

Table 3.1 Percentage of the population residing in the rural areas

Region name	1960	1980	2000	2020
East Asia and Pacific	77.40	72.27	58.58	39.30
Europe and Central Asia	44.44	35.02	31.26	27.39
Latin America and Caribbean	50.53	35.47	24.52	18.88
The Middle East and North Africa	65.08	50.39	41.40	34.03
North America	30.08	26.07	20.90	17.45
South Asia	83.26	77.67	72.62	65.12
Sub-Saharan Africa	85.31	77.66	68.65	58.75
World	66.38	60.65	53.31	43.85

Source: Database: World Development Indicators, World Bank.

consists of East Asian and Pacific countries. It is observed that the fall in the share of the rural population in this region have largely taken place over the past three decades. The last category constitutes South Asia and large parts of Africa. In most parts of Africa, and in densely populated South Asia, the share of the population residing in rural locations is still higher than 50 per cent (despite rural-to-urban migration and the tendency that more and more rural spaces are being renamed as urban, based on infrastructural changes).

The next question should obviously be what are the emerging patterns of the rural–urban employment that are taking place due to the change in the rural–urban population structure? Is it the case that the rural surplus labourers, mostly from agriculture, are transforming themselves into a productive urban workforce (whatever its extent across the globe), whereby the pool of labour in traditional activities of the rural regions keeps on contracting (as was envisaged by Lewis, 1954), and the process is faster in places where urbanization is happening fast (say, for instance, in East Asia)? Or is it a Harris–Todaro (1970)-type migration phenomenon, where rural-to-urban migration is giving rise to urban unemployment or underemployment, although the rural economy is getting some relief? Or is it that what is happening in the developing world's rural space is a much more complex process, contrary to the often-projected path of comprehensive market-orientated transition? With these questions, we proceed to section 3.2.

Table 3.2 Urban unemployment rate across different countries (%)

Urban unemployment	Northern Africa	South East Asia	South Asia	Sub-Saharan Africa	Latin America	East Asia
2019	13.17	3.26	7.07	3.47	8.71	4.86
2015	15.01	3.97	7.32	2.80	7.27	5.11
2010	12.84	4.94	7.24	3.02	7.58	5.30
2005	15.17	6.55	7.09	3.35	8.93	5.32

Source: International Labour Organization (ILO) estimates.

3.2 Global employment change: An account of the past two decades

In order to understand the emerging pattern of the rural–urban employment scenario, we first pay attention to the urban unemployment rates. In this context, Table 3.2 displays the urban unemployment rates in various regions of the world. Our data indicates that in all the examined regions, the urban unemployment rate either exhibits invariableness or a decline. For example, in South Asia and Latin America, between 2005 and 2019, the urban unemployment rate remained stable at about 7 or 8 per cent, but in East and Southeast Asia, it has decreased.

From Table 3.2, it appears that even though there has been migration from rural to urban areas or transformation of existing rural areas into urban spaces,[32] there has also been an associated expansion of employment. This suggests that rural to urban migration/transformation is not contributing to an increase in urban unemployment or a Harris–Todaro phenomenon.

However, this represents only one side of the overall change that has taken place. Table 3.3, which demonstrates the employment distribution across various sectors in rural and urban areas of the developing countries over two decades, indicates a more complex development pattern. It is observed that even though the share of rural employment in total employment has decreased in most areas, there have been two notable

[32] Transformation of rural spaces into urban should not be a dominant factor, since we are analysing data for just fifteen years.

Table 3.3 Distribution of employment over time in different sectors across rural and urban locations

Region	Year	Rural agricultural	Ruralnon-agricultural	Rural total	Urban total	Total
South Asia	2005	50.9	23.4	74.4	25.6	100
	2010	47.1	26.0	73.1	26.9	100
	2015	42.1	28.3	70.4	29.6	100
	2019	38.8	30	68.8	31.2	100
East Asia	2005	35.7	22.5	58.2	41.8	100
	2010	29.0	22.7	51.7	48.3	100
	2015	22.4	23.5	45.9	54.1	100
	2019	19.4	21.9	41.3	58.7	100
West Asia	2005	19.4	14.7	34.1	65.9	100
	2010	17.6	16.2	33.8	66.2	100
	2015	15.4	18.3	33.7	66.3	100
	2019	13.8	20.2	34.1	65.9	100
South East Asia	2005	40.0	22.1	62.1	37.9	100
	2010	36.5	25.2	61.7	38.3	100
	2015	30.0	24.4	54.3	45.7	100
	2019	26.0	30.0	56.0	44.0	100
Northern Africa	2005	27.7	23.5	51.2	48.8	100
	2010	24.8	26.9	51.7	48.3	100
	2015	22.9	28.6	51.4	48.6	100
	2019	20.0	31.1	51.1	48.9	100
Sub-Saharan Africa	2005	54.0	15.2	69.1	30.9	100
	2010	51.6	16.6	68.2	31.8	100
	2015	48.3	18.1	66.4	33.6	100
	2019	47.2	18	65.2	34.8	100
Latin America and the Caribbean	2005	13.5	10.1	23.6	76.4	100
	2010	11.4	10.8	22.2	77.8	100
	2015	10.1	11.3	21.4	78.6	100
	2019	9.9	11.4	21.4	78.6	100

Source: ILO estimates.

changes: a decrease in agricultural employment and an increase in employment within the RNFS. Stated otherwise, with an increase in the share of urban employment, we also have an increase in rural nonfarm employment. In regions such as South and West Asia and most of Africa, the growth rate of rural nonfarm employment is higher than that of the urban sector employment. This may be a result of availability of better jobs in the RNFS vis-à-vis agriculture, or it is possible that the urban economy is not able to create enough jobs to keep pace with the increased labour supply that is emerging from the outmigration of workers from the agricultural sector.

The world economy thus faces a unique situation. On the one hand, akin to the past experience of the developed world, the developing world, as well, is observing a decline in the share of agriculture with the growth of the economy. However, unlike in the developed world, the pattern of this growth is not characterized by a homogeneous transformation of the economy that causes a complete shift of employment from rural to urban locations. Rather, here we see that, with the growth of the urban economy, a section of the rural (nonfarm) economy is growing. It seems that a complementary relationship exists between the RNFS and the urban economy.

Two questions may arise in this context, as discussed in Chapters 1 and 2. First, what are the reasons behind the decline in agricultural employment? More precisely, one may ask whether the decline is a push effect out of agriculture, or a pull effect arising from the rural non-agricultural sector, or a combination of both.

According to the existing literature, in the absence of any barriers, surplus labour may migrate from the agricultural sector if the agricultural sector faces stagnation or there exist productivity or wage disparities between the non-agricultural economy and agriculture. Therefore, it is necessary to compare the value added per worker in the agriculture sector over time and compare it with that of the nonfarm sector. If the former is stagnant, and the gap between both the sectors is continuously increasing, we may reasonably hypothesize that a pull effect predominates over a push effect; conversely, if the latter is smaller or not gradually increasing, the opposite may be happening.

Information regarding value added per worker in the agricultural sector is available from the World Bank database. However, there is an absence of direct data regarding value added per worker in the RNFS. Consequently, we have compared the value added per worker in the agricultural sector with the overall value added per worker in the industrial and services sector (including rural and urban) in Table 3.4.

Table 3.4 Value added per worker (US dollars) in the agricultural and non-agricultural sectors (at 2015 constant prices)

	2005			2010			2015			2019		
Region	AGR	IND	SER	AGR	IND	SER	AGR	IND	SER	AGR	IND	SER
East Asia and Pacific	2,061	16,898	18,892	2,842	19,830	21,197	4,073	24,390	22,930	5,145	27,219	26,120
Europe and Central Asia	8,376	44,464	48,458	9,812	45,828	49,043	11,858	48,869	50,114	13,348	51,554	51,853
Latin America andCaribbean	4,350	21,780	16,716	5,238	22,498	17,915	6,129	23,214	18,598	6,509	21,949	18,048
Middle East and North Africa	6,185	32,652	19,651	6,885	33,460	21,974	8,410	35,234	24,439	10204	36,457	25,298
South Asia	1,307	4,100	4,381	1,414	4,489	5,829	1,718	4,894	6,944	2,105	5,478	7,644
Sub-Saharan Africa	1,064	10,342	6,502	1,270	10,966	6,997	1,408	10,217	7,077	1,480	9,749	6,693

Note: SER stands for services, IND is industrial sector.

Source: Computed using World Bank and ILO data.

Table 3.4 demonstrates that gross value added (GVA) per worker is higher in the industrial and services sectors across all areas in comparison to the agricultural sector. This observed disparity in GVA per worker may induce individuals to migrate from the agricultural sector to the industrial or services sectors.

However, it is also important to note that the agriculture sector is not stagnant enough to stimulate significant migration. In certain regions, the agricultural output per worker exhibits a greater growth rate, leading to a narrowing disparity between the agricultural sector and other sectors over time. The substantial expansion in the agriculture sector ought to have led to a slowing down in the migration rate. Furthermore, it is essential to acknowledge that the data shown in Table 3.4 pertains to the entire nonfarm economy, encompassing both formal and informal segments across rural and urban regions. Research has demonstrated the presence of significant productivity gaps and earnings variations between the formal and informal sectors (refer to Loayza and Rigolini, 2006; Oviedo, 2009) as well as between rural and urban regions (Table 3.5).

Thus, while it is possible to understand the motivations driving migration from rural to urban areas, particularly from agriculture to the formal sector (when feasible), explaining the factors that lead workers in rural regions to migrate from agriculture to the nonfarm sector, which is largely characterized by informal firms and lower productivity, is difficult.[33]

In other words, the flow of labour force towards the RNFS from agriculture cannot be explained fully by the difference in value added per worker between agriculture and the overall non-agriculture. Tentatively, it seems that the pull effect, as mentioned above, may not be that powerful and that the push effect may also be playing an important role, in this regard. Since we could not say conclusively whether the push or pull effect is dominating from the figures on value added per worker, for the processes of labour movement away from agriculture, we need to go deeper into the analysis.

Several studies can shed some light in this regard. In Africa, for instance, Mosley (2017) highlights the problem of abundance of natural

[33] In fact, there are countries that have observed a decline in average rural income over the years (see the figures for Bangladesh, Kenya, Ghana, and Jamaica from Table 3.5) accompanied by an increase in value added per worker in the agricultural sector. All these countries have experienced the shift of workers from agriculture to the rural nonfarm sector.

Table 3.5 Average monthly earnings of employees in rural and urban areas 2021 purchasing power parity (US dollars)

Country	Year	Rural	Urban	Monthly difference
Bangladesh	2013	399.496	500.217	100.721
	2017	356.57	487.07	130.5
Brazil	2013	466.474	814.022	251.207
	2019	546.401	1,010.926	544.452
Ecuador	2019	678.455	1,049.017	370.562
	2005	298.861	570.271	271.41
Ghana	2013	532.757	705.306	172.549
	2017	421.613	527.882	106.269
India	2005	376.174	545.946	169.772
	2019	615.386	942.331	326.945
Indonesia	2005	234.096	317.595	83.499
	2019	360.681	545.577	184.896
Jamaica	2008	502.388	708.404	206.016
	2014	401.216	638.539	237.323
Kenya	2005	244.639	597.087	352.448
	2019	208.203	431.191	222.988
Pakistan	2010	323.204	446.297	123.093
	2019	490.673	674.701	184.028
Sri Lanka	2010	316.035	424.887	108.852
	2019	621.859	866.631	244.772
Thailand	2007	579.524	1,014.82	435.296
	2019	1,001.68	1,436.073	434.397
Vietnam	2010	333.363	445.265	111.902
	2019	768.399	1,022.11	253.711

Source: ILO estimates.

resource (which he terms as a 'natural resource curse') as the principal problem for individuals engaged in the non-mining sector (which also includes agriculture). In many parts of Africa, the abundance of natural resources has adversely affected the non-mining sectors of the economy. This is because natural, resource-dependent growth leads to export surpluses generated by natural resources or the mining sector. This, in turn, can appreciate a country's exchange rate and thus damage the non-mining sectors by making its output less competitive in the world market. Presence of the 'natural resource curse' can accentuate an out-migration of workers to sectors that are linked to mining activity. This 'natural resource curse' problem is present not only in African countries but also in countries like Venezuela, Russia, and many others.

However, expansion that is driven by natural resources may not always have a negative impact. Governments of a number of developing economies, including East Asian countries such as China and Southeast Asian nations like Indonesia, along with Latin American countries like Brazil, have actively devalued their exchange rates to safeguard their vibrant traded-goods sectors (World Bank, 2003; Rosser, 2004; Sala-i-Martin and Subramaniam, 2013).

This difference in policy measures across nations to protect the non-mining sectors from currency appreciation exists due to the presence/absence of strong mining sector lobby in some countries. The mining industry is often influenced by special interest groups that can hinder economic growth in various resource-dependent economies. The government is typically urged to avoid devaluation, as this would raise the cost of capital goods predominantly utilized in the mining sector.

Apart from the natural resource curse, several other factors may compel or induce individuals to leave the agricultural (and allied activity) sector and shift to the rural non-agricultural sector. For instance, a few African studies argue that due to the presence of land scarcity, households may respond by shifting labour to rural nonfarm activities rather than migrating to other places (Jayne et al., 2014a, 2014b). Agrarian land (including common land) scarcity may arise in developing countries because of an increase in population density, government policy inducements towards land use for a variety of economic activities (other than traditional agriculture and long-established commons-based livelihood generation activities), and/or increased demand for agricultural land (including commons) by the domestic and foreign capitalistic companies for commercial use in addition to mining (Harvey, 2003, Jayne et al., 2014a, 2014b; Dell'Angelo et al., 2017).

Though it is difficult to provide sufficient data on all the above-mentioned aspects, increasing population density and fragmentation of landholdings are observed in most developing countries (Lowder et al., 2014, 2016). Table 3.6 shows the trends in the average size of agricultural

Table 3.6 Trends in the average size of agricultural landholdings (ha) across different countries over time

Year	1960	1970	1980	1990	2000
Argentina	371.3	–	–	469.0	582.5
Bangladesh	1.4	–	1.3	–	0.3
Brazil	74.9	60.0	70.7	64.5	72.8
Egypt	1.6	–	1.0	0.9	0.8
India	2.7	2.3	2.0	1.6	1.3
Indonesia	1.2	1.1	1.1	0.9	0.8
Jamaica	4.4	3.1	2.9	–	2.2
Jordan	–	7.0	5.9	–	3.3
Madagascar	1.0	–	1.3	–	0.9
Malawi	–	−1.5	−1.2	−0.7	–
Mexico	123.9	137.1	–	41.4	–
Nepal	–	1.0	1.1	0.9	0.8
Pakistan	3.5	5.3	4.7	3.8	3.1
Panama	19.0	18.2	14.7	13.8	11.7
Paraguay	108.7	–	88.1	77.5	–
Peru	20.4	16.9	–	20.1	–
Philippines	3.6	3.6	2.9	2.2	2.0
Thailand	3.5	–	3.7	3.4	3.2

Source: Computed from Lowder et al. (2014).

landholdings across different developing countries. One finds that in most of the countries, the average size of land holdings has reduced substantially. In some instances, this might have caused an increase in the number of unviable land holdings, leading to an increasing cost of cultivation. For example, in the year 2000, in Bangladesh, India, and Nepal, the average sizes of land holdings were 0.3, 1.3, and 0.8 acres, respectively. In the recent period, this might have reduced further. This should have a significant impact on the size of the RNFS with a pushed migration or employment diversification towards this sector.

Now, we consider the next driver of agrarian land scarcity, as mentioned above, that is, government and private inducements for commercial use of private land and commons (away from traditional livelihood generation activities). We know that government and/or private policy/

interest-determined urbanization, large-scale rural industrialization, and infrastructure development unquestionably affect agrarian land supply and thereby could engender a push-driven movement of labour away from traditional farming and allied activities (Ghatak and Mookherjee, 2014; Pandey and Seto, 2015; Bren d'Amour et al., 2017).

However, much less discussed is the widespread, ongoing phenomenon of large-scale cropping pattern change (away from traditional, small-scale, basic food crop farming) across the globe and especially its impact on the RNFS. We now take up this often-neglected issue of the impact on the rural nonfarm economy due to large-scale crop diversification. A reading of the recent literature would be helpful in understanding this effect on the nonfarm sector (Chakrabarti and Kundu, 2009a; Kundu and Chakrabarti, 2010; Chakrabarti, 2014a; Datta and Chakrabarti, 2024).

The arguments in favour of large-scale crop diversification towards high-value crop (HVC) (like fruits, flowers, vegetables, agro-fuel, and feedstock), as proposed by The World Bank (2007) in its World Development Report (WDR), are as follows:

1. Traditional agriculture is non sustainable (as it is water-intensive) and non-profitable.
2. HVC has a large domestic urban market.
3. There is a high-value export market for HVC.
4. There is the availability of the modern supply chain, which is helpful for large-scale HVC cultivation. Thus, technological feasibility makes the large-scale HVC economy a real possibility.

However, it is also argued in the WDR 2008 (World Bank, 2007) that large-scale diversified agriculture (the so-called evergreen revolution) is possible only 'with the entry and rapid growth of supermarket chains and the (large scale) food processing and foodservice industries' (World Bank, 2007, p. 124). This is because the much-talked-about green revolution (involving large-scale HVC cultivation) requires a highly sophisticated, capital-intensive, and integrated cultivation, harvesting, handling, storing, processing, packaging, transporting, and selling system, that is, a highly sophisticated supply chain. This gives corporate capital a huge scope to enter into agriculture, which is not possible with traditional farming; indeed, the large-scale crop diversification experiences of the Global South also show that.[34]

This entry of corporate capital into the fields of agricultural and allied activities (including commons), in its turn, has been found to engender a variety of exclusionary processes. The World Bank (2007), in this regard, has noted the following instances of exclusion:

1. Exclusion of asset-poor farmers from corporate-led (contract-based) large-scale crop diversification processes, as the HVC economy is highly capital and technology-intensive, and the asset-poor farmers are incapable of finding a place in the sophisticated, vertically integrated supply chain;
2. exclusion of small processing, packaging, transportation firms from the corporate supply chain due to asset poverty and transaction cost. As these small firms are asset-poor, they are unable to participate in the modern supply chain. Further, for corporate capital, it is always better to either vertically integrate the collection, processing, packaging, storing, and transportation processes or contract with only larger firms to reduce transaction costs;
3. eviction of small retailers with the growth of supermarkets through cut-throat competition.

Thus, the large-scale commercialization of agriculture and allied activities (including that of commons) is a major process of exclusion of the traditionally employed mass of the population (engaged in

[34] The ProSAVANA project was decried as the largest land conversion for the so-called evergreen revolution in Africa. This ambitious Brazil–Japan–Mozambique development project was slated for turning 35 million hectares (over 85 million acres) of Mozambique's supposedly unoccupied savannah lands into industrial-scale soybean farms modelled on—and with capital from—Brazil's savannah lands in its own southern Cerredo region (Wise, 2015).

Millions of hectares of farmland in Latin America have been taken over by foreign investors over the past few years for the production of food crops and agrofuels for export. Much of the money comes from United States and European pension funds, banks, private equity groups, and wealthy individuals like George Soros, and it is being channelled through special farmland investment vehicles set up by both foreign and local companies (GRAIN 2010).

According to China's Ministry of Agriculture, over 1,300 Chinese enterprises had overseas investments in modern agriculture, forestry, and fisheries valued at $26 billion in 2016. The investments include sophisticated crop and livestock farming, fishing, processing, farm machinery, inputs, seeds, and logistics in over 100 countries. China's National Bureau of Statistics reports that foreign investment in such high-value farming, forestry, and fishing grew five-fold between 2010 and 2016 (Gale and Gooch, 2018).

traditional farming and allied activities and even traditional age-old nonfarm). This vast excluded mass is pushed out of the traditional activities and fuels the (relatively new non-conventional) RNFS sector to grow (along with the urban economy). The following crucial observation derived from a large number of studies is a clear recognition of this push-driven expansion of the RNFS across the Global South:

'Small scale farming remains the main means of food production globally, and the world's rural populations depend heavily on local land and natural resources and self- subsistence. [. . .] However, since about 2008, an emerging phenomenon of global large- scale land acquisitions (LSLAs) [. . .] might be altering this picture' (Dell Angelo et al., 2017, p. 1, emphasis added) . . . . 'The ongoing LSLAs are associated with a change in production system, from subsistence and small holding to commercial farming, that entails fundamental social transformations. [. . .] Critics have pointed out that this is correlated with a process of dispossession, a transformation of social networks, an increase in conflict, and loss of livelihood strategies, assets, traditional knowledge, environmental stewardship, food security, and productive opportunities' (ibid., p. 8, emphasis added; also see Chakrabarti (2016) in this regard).

Consequently, we could infer from the preceding discussion that if it is found that, across the Global South, there is substantial crop diversification, we could tentatively say that there could be a push-driven migration and/or employment diversification away from the traditional farming and allied activities to the relatively new nonfarm sector, ballooning its size.

Table 3.7, in this context, provides information on the cropping pattern across different regions of the globe over a decade. It can be seen that, for most regions, the area under production of cereals has declined. On the other hand, the area used for non-cereal crops has increased. It is possible that such changes might have altered the requirements of labour and/or land in the agricultural sector (and in allied and traditional agriculture-linked nonfarm sectors, too), and thus, there is an outflow of labour to other (relatively new) rural activities and to cities.

Table 3.7 Area under different types of crops (%)

Region	Year	Cereals	Pulses	Oil crops	Others	Total
South Asia	2005	58.2	10.5	18.3	13.1	100
	2010	56.4	11.7	17.5	14.5	100
	2015	55.0	11.6	17.7	15.7	100
East Asia	2005	50.8	2.2	17.9	29.1	100
	2010	53.0	1.8	15.9	29.3	100
	2015	56.3	1.5	12.9	29.3	100
West Asia	2005	68.1	4.8	9.2	18.0	100
	2010	65.6	4.0	10.6	19.8	100
	2015	64.0	3.7	11.4	20.9	100
South East Asia	2005	51.5	4.0	19.4	25.2	100
	2010	49.0	4.1	22.9	24.0	100
	2015	45.4	4.3	23.8	26.5	100
North Africa	2005	68.5	2.5	16.6	12.4	100
	2010	61.8	3.4	19.1	15.7	100
	2015	59.0	3.1	21.8	16.0	100
Sub-Saharan Africa	2005	46.6	11.1	14.1	28.2	100
	2010	46.7	11.6	13.9	27.9	100
	2015	42.1	10.9	15.3	31.7	100
Latin America and the Caribbean	2005	38.4	5.6	31.8	24.1	100
	2010	36.2	5.7	33.1	25.0	100
	2015	35.6	4.9	36.6	22.9	100

Source: Food and Agriculture Organization (FAO) estimates.

3.3 The nature of nonfarm sector employment: Symptoms of development or dispossession?

In the preceding sections, we have seen that the RNFS is growing in most regions of the globe; however, we could not shed much light on the nature of employment generated in this sector and, more importantly, on the causes of this expansion of the RNFS (in support of the propositions of our previous theoretical perspective). We have understood, through our analysis above, that there is an exodus of the labouring population from agriculture across the Global South, and a part of this migrant/

diversifying mass is thronging the RNFS. However, we could not say conclusively whether this shift is due to the push factors working within agriculture or to a variety of pulls from the rural–urban modern sectors. Now, we wish to explore this crucial question further.

One can expect a deterioration in the quality of employment if push factors operating within agriculture are causing an increase in employment in the nonfarm sector. Stated otherwise, a deterioration in the quality of employment (with increasing quantity) could be a mark of push from agriculture; this is because, it could be conjectured, being pushed out of agriculture, a section of the migrating/diversifying mass is compelled to engage in under-remunerative activities (supplementary/substantive). The push factors are responsible for this unfavourable shift and/or even diversification. On the other hand, there can be a qualitative improvement if the nonfarm sector gets linked to the capitalistic rural or urban modern sector, and the latter exerts a pull on the former. Thus, an improvement in the quality of nonfarm employment (along with expanding quantity) should be a mark of pull-driven expansion.

Given these conjectures, it is important to note that most jobs that are created in the non-agricultural economy in most parts of the Global South are of an informal nature. Table 3.8 shows the informal employment rate in the non-agricultural sector of selected countries. It is seen that in most parts of South Asia and Africa, informal employment is very high and has increased even further in some cases. The International Labour Organization, in its report *Women and men in the informal economy: A statistical picture* (ILO, 2018) shows that, excluding agriculture, half of the employed individuals are engaged in informal activities. This proliferation of informal activities could be a mark of push-driven migration/diversification away from agriculture because we know that informal activities, in general, are under-remunerative.

Apart from the proliferation of informal jobs, changes are happening in other dimensions as well. For instance, Table 3.9 provides information on the changes in the nature of occupation between 2005 and 2015. The table shows that the share of employees in total employment is increasing in rural areas and that of self-employment is declining, although self-employment still constitutes a sizeable and larger fraction.

An increase in the share of employees in total employment may have several interpretations; either it may mean an increase in the share of

Table 3.8 Informal employment rate in the non-agricultural sector (%)

Country	2009	2010	2011	2012	2013	2014	2015	2016	2017	2018	2019	2020
Argentina	49.4	48.2	47.6	47.7	47.3	46.8	–	–	47.9	48.1	49.4	46.4
Bangladesh	–	82.2	–	–	82.4	–	–	–	91.3	–	–	–
Brazil	42.0	–	38.5	38.2	37.1	37.8	38.3	42.5	44	44.7	44.9	44
Egypt	39.4	43.1	43.8	41.6	42.9	–	47.2	50.5	52.9	54.2	56.3	–
Ghana	–	–	–	–	–	–	–	52.1	51.9	52	51.7	51.1
India	–	75.3	–	74.8	–	–	–	–	–	80.3	79.8	80.1
Indonesia	–	–	–	–	–	–	–	78.5	78.5	76.5	74.7	–
Jamaica	–	–	–	–	–	–	–	52.1	51.9	52.0	51.7	51.1
Mexico	54.6	54.9	54.9	54.9	54.2	53.1	53.4	52.9	52.6	52.5	52.7	50.4
Pakistan	67.3	67.7	69.5	–	69.2	72.0	71.2	–	–	71.6	–	–
Rwanda	–	–	–	–	–	–	–	–	68.2	68.7	68.9	–
South Africa	33.4	33.9	32.5	31.4	32.0	32.0	34.2	33.8	34.2	34.7	34.6	31.3
Thailand	–	–	–	–	–	63.4	62.4	63.4	53.7	51.9	–	–
Uganda	–	–	–	83.2	–	–	–	–	85.0	–	–	–
Viet Nam	65.9	–	–	–	62.2	57.6	57.1	56.3	56.1	54.9	54.2	54.9
Zimbabwe	–	–	62.5	–	–	66.0	–	–	–	–	74.1	–

Source: ILO estimates.

Table 3.9 Distribution of employment by type of occupation (%)

Region	Year	Rural			Urban		
		Employees	Self-employment	Total	employees	Self-employment	Total
South Asia	2005	12.87	87.13	100	45.35	54.65	100
	2015	16.81	83.19	100	49.64	50.36	100
East Asia	2005	28.69	71.31	100	69.81	30.19	100
	2015	32.17	67.83	100	72.27	27.73	100
West Asia	2005	41.76	58.25	100	63.35	36.66	100
	2015	52.22	47.78	100	69.62	30.38	100
South East Asia	2005	28.3	71.7	100	56.43	43.57	100
	2015	37.04	62.96	100	62.45	37.55	100
Northern Africa	2005	43.28	56.73	100	68.51	31.49	100
	2015	49.23	50.77	100	70.86	29.14	100
Sub-Saharan Africa	2005	11.74	88.26	100	37.36	62.64	100
	2015	14.24	85.76	100	40.55	59.45	100
Latin America and	2005	40.7	59.3	100	66.83	33.17	100
the Caribbean	2015	45.61	54.39	100	68.46	31.55	100

Source: Computed using ILO data.

Table 3.10 Distribution of informal employment according to skill type in rural areas (%)

Country	Year	High	Medium	Low	Not classified	Total
Brazil	2019	1.9	67.4	28.4	2.3	100
	2016	1.8	64.8	27.3	6.1	100
Ecuador	2019	0.46	60.42	39.11	0	100
	2007	1.42	48.53	50.03	0	100
Egypt	2019	18.0	76.07	6.96	0.06	100
	2007	2.82	92.3	4.83	0.46	100
Ghana	2015	2.7	89.9	7.4	0	100
	2013	1.5	94.5	3.7	0.3	100
Indonesia	2019	5.2	74.7	20.1	0	100
	2016	5.6	76.5	17.6	0.3	100
Thailand	2018	6.3	82.2	11.5	0	100
	2014	6.1	83.9	9.9	0.1	100
Pakistan	2019	3.2	79.9	16.9	0	100
	2006	9.9	76.0	14.1	0	100
Uganda	2019	3.3	84.7	11.8	0.2	100
	2010	2.2	88.6	8.1	1.1	100
Zimbabwe	2019	1.13	86.07	12.8	0.15	100
	2014	0.76	91.93	7.3	0	100

Source: Computed using ILO estimations based on different national surveys.

casual workers or it may mean an increase in quality jobs. Table 3.10, in this context, shows the distribution of employment by type of skills in informal jobs in rural areas. The time periods used here are not uniform across countries due to the unavailability of data. We have considered the first and the latest time periods for which data is available for each country from the ILO data set. It can be seen that, in the past two decades, in the countries for which the data are presented, in most countries there has been a simultaneous expansion of low- as well as medium- and high-skilled jobs.[35] This, to some extent, indicates that the change that is

[35] High-skilled workers consist of managers, professionals, technicians, and associate professionals. Medium-skilled workers consist of clerical support workers; service and sales workers; skilled agricultural, forestry, and fisheries workers; craft and related trade workers; plant and machine operators; and assemblers. People engaged in elementary occupations have been categorized as low-skilled workers.

happening in the economy is creating a dualism. On the one hand, it may generate better and more inclusive employment. On the other hand, it might be generating or sustaining petty, low-skilled work. Thus, it is important to note that there is no compatibility or one-to-one correspondence between an increase in nonfarm jobs and the generation of better employment. There is not only an ongoing trend of the proliferation of the farm–nonfarm divide but also an emerging phenomenon of intra-nonfarm dualism.

Table 3.11 shows the distribution of employment in terms of size of the firms. While the number of firms that have not stated the firm size is large for most countries, from the table it is seen that in countries in which most respondents have reported their size of firms, (such as Ecuador, Ghana, and Uganda), have seen an expansion of the smaller-sized firms.

Table 3.11 Distribution of informal employment in terms of size of the firms in rural areas (%)

Country	Year	1–4	5–49	50 and above	Not stated	Total
Bangladesh	2017	73.6	10.4	4.1	11.9	100.0
	2010	93.6	3.0	2.9	0.4	100.0
Brazil	2019	83.8	6.6	1.1	8.5	100.0
	2016	41.3	3.0	0.5	55.1	100.0
Ecuador	2019	77.7	21.1	1.2	0.0	100.0
	2001	63.9	28.2	7.9	0.0	100.0
Egypt	2019	3.4	0.9	0.4	95.3	100.0
	2008	5.8	4.0	1.3	88.9	100.0
Ghana	2015	82.8	6.2	0.5	10.5	100.0
	2013	68.4	25.3	0.5	5.8	100.0
Jamaica	2019	83.7	10.5	1.0	4.8	100.0
	2016	84.1	9.2	0.9	5.8	100.0
Thailand	2019	11.6	10.8	1.2	76.5	100.0
	2014	9.4	10.1	2.1	78.4	100.0
Uganda	2017	80.8	18.1	0.9	0.2	100.0
	2012	67.5	24.6	1.5	6.4	100.0
Zimbabwe	2019	25.6	5.0	1.8	67.6	100.0
	2011	5.2	2.4	2.4	90.0	100.0

Source: Computed using ILO estimations based on different national surveys.

In order to provide a glimpse of the extent of the income difference between high-skilled work, on the one hand, and people engaged in low-skilled work or elementary occupations, on the other, we have computed the average monthly earnings of employees at different skill levels in occupations in US dollars for different countries. It is to be noted that the figures in Table 3.12 are national-level average figures, which include both rural and urban areas. The table reveals that a huge gap exists between high- and low-profile works in all the countries for each year under consideration. Table 3.12 also reveals that the mean income gap between high- and low-profile work has either widened or is invariable over time. Finally, we have Table 3.13, which focuses only on rural areas to elaborate on this issue further.

Table 3.13 shows the annual per capita consumption expenditure (PCE) for different countries in local currency units across different economic classes in rural areas. From the data set, we could get only four countries for which rural data was available for at least two time periods, namely, China, India, Indonesia, and Mongolia. The countries here are subdivided into differently ordered income fractiles. The poorest income fractile takes the value of 1, while the higher fractile takes a higher value. We dropped China, since there were no two time periods having the number of fractiles for the country.

From the table, it is observed that the gaps in PCE between the lower fractiles and the higher ones have increased over time for most countries. In order to understand this augmentation of inequality over the years among the different economic classes, one needs to compare the growth in PCE of the poorest class and the richest class between the two time periods provided. From the table, one can see that in the case of Indonesia and India, the gap has expanded, while for Mongolia, it has remained the same. For instance, in Indonesia, while PCE increased by 1.07 times for the poorest class, for the richest class, it grew by a factor of 1.45.

Thus, once again, we find support for our hypothesis of the proliferation of a dual structure in the rural economies of the globe.

3.4 Conclusion

This chapter highlighted the changes that the rural economy has experienced globally over the past few decades. Our special focus was on the

Table 3.12 Average monthly earnings of employees at different skill levels in occupations in US dollars (rural and urban)

Country	Year	High skill	Medium skill	Low skill	Difference between high skilled and low skilled	Difference in differences
Argentina	2019	748.855	504.496	266.208	482.647	–
	2013	1,241.494	904.867	467.577	773.917	291.27
Bangladesh	2017	272.095	134.446	93.59	178.505	–
	2013	211.109	144.947	101.036	110.073	68.432
Brazil	2016	962.355	437.954	272.101	690.254	–
	2009	952.71	402.093	265.285	687.425	2.829
	2001	503.571	160.457	128.522	375.049	–
Ecuador	2019	903.815	425.237	331.692	572.123	–
	2009	594.766	283.43	195.111	399.655	172.468
Egypt	2015	272.689	212.079	174.84	97.849	–
	2010	137.582	140.733	97.288	40.294	57.555
Ghana	2017	273.991	168.276	107.735	166.256	–
	2013	477.849	257.522	206.193	271.656	–105.4
Indonesia	2019	290.51	176.138	119.016	171.494	–
	2007	193.225	104.918	73.998	119.227	52.267
Jamaica	2014	662.59	250.897	161.285	501.305	–
	2008	819.19	354.164	212.042	607.148	–105.843
Kenya	2019	343.013	113.806	47.149	295.864	–
	2005	255.556	78.105	45.169	210.387	85.477
South Africa	2020	753.17	332.30	166.48	586.69	–
	2007	1,221.093	423.163	234.996	986.097	–

Table 3.13 Annual per capita consumption expenditures in local currency units across different economic classes (income fractiles) in rural areas

Economic class	Indonesia		India		Mongolia	
	1993	2005	2002	2005	1993	1998
1	747,125	801,003	2,456	2,383.37	5,877.95	39,729.2
2	914,899	1,082,321	3,089	2,991.12	12,849.5	86,723.2
3	1,015,884	1,227,896	3,418	3,329.72	21,043.9	141,890
4	1,102,888	1,342,222	3,710	3,615.19	28,199.7	190,246
5	1,179,121	1,447,090	3,968	3,869.3	34,614.8	233,381
6	1,250,172	1,547,434	4,211	4,100.12	43,081.3	290,591
7	1,320,074	1,648,276	4,446	4,347.32	48,518.8	327,142
8	1,390,622	1,751,811	4,684	4,604.43	53,726.4	362,331
9	1,462,814	1,860,955	4,943	4,851.38	77,284.2	521,247
10	1,540,501	,1969,835	5,207	5,123.63	–	–
11	1,623,351	2,086,631	5,484	5,407.78		
12	1,713,348	2,218,265	5,777	5,712.87		
13	1,811,280	2,357,439	6,090	6,054.72		
14	1,920,924	2,517,064	6,457	6,437.74		
15	2,046,298	2,716,600	6,903	6,892.3		
16	2,207,322	2,958,578	7,427	7,462.53		
17	2,416,864	3,263,637	8,122	8,229.76		
18	2,706,051	3,711,829	9,056	9,298.5		
19	3,197,982	4,498,972	10,479	11,196.8		
20	5,128,293	7,443,335	14,422	21,212.2		

Source: Milanovic (2013).

RNFS. We found that over the past few decades, the agricultural sector has squeezed in terms of employment share in most rural regions of the globe, and this decline has caused two simultaneous developments. On the one hand, there is an expansion of urban employment, and on the other hand, there is also an increase in employment in the RNFS. As far as employment in the RNFS is concerned, we found that there is a simultaneous expansion of modern/formal and elementary/informal jobs. This indicates the creation of a new form of dualism that is associated with the present development process, over and above the traditional farm–nonfarm dichotomy.

Mainstream development discourse opines that with the overall growth and some institutional changes in the economy, there would be a comprehensive structural transformation; non-capitalist agriculture would squeeze and its resources and surplus labour would be absorbed into the circuits of the growing capitalist sector, and thereby, an overall transition would be initiated. However, our above analysis of the trends of the Global South has shown that not only is the traditional divide between the farm and nonfarm proliferating, but also there are the emerging phenomena of intra-farm and especially intra-nonfarm dualities. While there is the modernization of a part of the agricultural sector, a much larger part remains trapped in perpetual low-level equilibrium; on the other hand, more glaringly, not only is there the expansion of the pool of modern nonfarm jobs but also a persistence (and even deepening) of misery due to the proliferation of the large low-value-adding traditional segment of the nonfarm sector. In the rural economy, this spread of fissure within the nonfarm sector is even more distinct.

The next issue discussed in this chapter was the cause of this phenomenon of deepening dualism. It has been shown, albeit tentatively, that a section of the agricultural labour force is migrating/diversifying towards the RNFS (over and above rural–urban migration) due to two sets of forces—pull and push. The rural–urban modern sector growth is pulling a relatively advanced section of the surplus labour force from agriculture, and this migrant/diversifying population is getting absorbed in the relatively modern rural–urban nonfarm activities. On the other hand, the ongoing agrarian crisis is pushing out a relatively backward section of the agrarian labour force that is compelled to get engaged in low-value-adding nonfarm activities (mostly rural), thereby spreading/multiplying this segment of the nonfarm sector. Thus, the pull and push factors conjointly spread the RNFS and spread and deepen its fissures too.

In our above exploratory data analysis, there are certain limitations as well. In this chapter, due to the unavailability of data, we could only indicate certain changes. A more disaggregated analysis is required to pinpoint the factors that are influencing these changes. This issue is taken up in Chapters 4–6. In Chapter 4, we present selected country-specific evidence that shows the generation of dualism. This is followed by chapters that have done a more disaggregated analysis based on secondary data from India.

The reasons for taking up India as our focus of analysis are that India is a large country case with a consistently high growth rate, having a very large and diverse rural sector showing simultaneously glaring signs of prosperity and poverty, where traditional agriculture has been suffering for a long time, and the RNFS is spreading pretty fast. Given such a setting, we could analyse the questions set earlier in the book. What is the pattern of expansion of the RNFS, and what is its emerging structure? Which are the forces behind this expansion? Why is there an agrarian crisis despite consistent economic growth? And finally, how is this crisis feeding the process of expansion of the RNFS?

A.3 Appendix

Table A.3.1 Population and gross domestic product per capita across various regions of the globe

Region name	2015	
	Population	GDP per capita current USD
Africa Eastern and Southern	593,871,847	1,549.03794
Africa Western and Central	401,586,651	1,894.310195
East Asia and the Pacific	2,291,503,725	9,579.474371
Europe and Central Asia	906,669,764	22,619.69884
Latin America and the Caribbean	622,301,041	8,630.85569
The Middle East and North Africa	425,821,771	7,269.495916
North America	356,507,139	55,542.96607
Pacific Island small states	2,353,578	3,832.184552
South Asia	1,749,417,067	1,543.048131
Sub-Saharan Africa	995,458,498	1,688.327251
World	7,347,679,005	10,222.60827

Source: World Bank.

4

Rural Economies of the Developing World

Micro Perspectives

Chapter 3 used region- and country-level data to show certain macroeconomic trends relating to the rural economy and the changes taking place in those economies. These trends are captured using indicators such as rural–urban employment and unemployment patterns, changes happening within agriculture, and the nature of rural nonfarm employment. The analysis presented reveals certain intriguing trends, including a decreasing trend in urban unemployment, despite rural-to-urban migration, and an increasing level of rural nonfarm employment.

The discussion concludes that dualism has been observed in these economies, especially the nonfarm sector, and we argue that such dualism is deepening over time, especially in certain developing nations. It is argued that a segment of the agricultural labour force is migrating or diversifying into the rural nonfarm sector (beyond rural–urban migration) due to both pull and push factors. On one hand, the growth of the rural–urban modern sector is attracting a more advanced segment of the surplus labour force from agriculture, which is then absorbed into relatively modern rural–urban nonfarm activities. On the other hand, the ongoing agrarian crisis and formal sector expansion are pushing out a more disadvantaged section of the agricultural labour force, forcing them to engage in low-value, predominantly rural, nonfarm activities. This dynamic contributes to the expansion of the rural nonfarm sector while also deepening its internal disparities.

While this analysis at a macro level, using quantitative data, has been revealing, to arrive at certain conclusions about the rural economy, we

The Nonfarm Economy. Manojit Bhattacharjee, Saumya Chakrabarti, and Meenakshi Rajeev,
Oxford University Press.
DOI: 10.1093/9780198972013.003.0004

present selected country-specific evidence in the present chapter. The attempt, thus, is to present a micro perspective that brings to light certain nuances that macro analysis may hide. While presenting these micro perspectives, we also incorporate in our analysis other factors (such as state policies, climate change, etc.), which also have implications for income generation and employment formation.

This study focuses on Asian and African countries, where a significant portion of the population continues to reside in rural areas. The analysis concentrates on three developing nations in Africa—Rwanda, Ethiopia, and Ghana—and four in Asia—Indonesia, Vietnam, Sri Lanka, and Pakistan. This study relies predominantly on secondary information sources and a literature review specific to the country in question.

It is important to recognize that these countries are at different levels of development (as classified by the World Bank) and have different sizes of the formal economy. Therefore, not necessarily all these economies will portray exactly the same development problem as presented in the theoretical framework. However, from these micro-level perspectives, it will be evident that the dualism problem is universal, and the existing fissures can intensify with capital accumulation.

Section 4.1 presents the insights we obtained from the three African countries. This is followed in section 4.2 by our insights from Asia. A concluding section is presented in section 4.3.

4.1 Some insights from Africa

We consider two of the low-income nations (as per the World Bank classification) of the African continent (viz., Ethiopia and Rwanda) and the lower-middle-income nation of Ghana.[36] The objective is to understand their development experiences in terms of employment formation and income generation in the rural agricultural and nonfarm sectors. These experiences may help us understand the basis of duality formation in the presence of limited formal sector accumulation.

[36] These countries differ in terms of the size of the modern sector. According to International Labour Organization (ILO) estimates, the proportion of formal employment was around 22 per cent in Ghana in 2015. This figure was much lower for Ethiopia (around 16.5 per cent in 2021) and Rwanda (15.7 per cent in 2017).

4.1.1 Ethiopia

Ethiopia continues to rely heavily on agriculture as the backbone of its economy. Based on data from two large-scale surveys—price data from the Central Statistical Agency of Ethiopia, and the Agricultural Growth Programme of Ethiopia—it was seen that nonfarm income constitutes only 18 per cent of total income (Bachewe et al., 2016). In comparison, crop income dominates, with a share of 71 per cent, while livestock income contributes 11 per cent. However, the agricultural sector is facing numerous challenges that have made livelihood sustainability a challenge for people who depend solely on this sector. Therefore, the demand for nonfarm employment is rising.

First, it is essential to recognize that, in Ethiopia, the state owns all the land. The Ethiopian law entitles the rural residents to acquire lands at no cost. Nonetheless, due to population expansion, it has become increasingly challenging to realize this right (Bezu and Holden, 2014). As a result, landlessness, accompanied by unviable-sized landholding, is emerging, forcing many people, especially young people, to look for other ways to make money instead of farming.

The second reason for the growth of nonfarm employment is the decline in agricultural productivity. Multiple factors are contributing to this problem. Neglo et al. (2021) observed that just 34 per cent of agricultural families used fertilizers for their crops, while only 5 per cent had irrigation systems. Furthermore, 38 per cent owned land holdings less than 0.5 hectares. All these factors lead to a decrease in agricultural productivity and subsequently increased demand for engaging in nonfarm activity, particularly for low-income households. In fact, 34 per cent of the national population works in nonfarm activities (Neglo et al., 2021).

Engaging in nonfarm activities has generally allowed rural households in Ethiopia to earn significantly more than those dependent solely on agriculture. Additionally, participation in these activities enables households to hire farm labour, ultimately enhancing agricultural productivity. Thus, as shown in Chapter 3 with data, the increasing prevalence of the nonfarm sector is observed (through various existing studies) in some of the poorest agrarian countries, like Ethiopia, as well.

The main nonfarm income activities carried out in the country are home-based businesses or services (10 per cent), selling processed food and drinks (6 per cent), and trading goods in the marketplace or as roadside vendors (4 per cent) (CSA, 2017). For instance, lower-income households were mainly involved in activities such as selling local liquor and homemade food, which did not require large-scale investment. On the other hand, wealthier households were more involved in trading cattle and food grains, which had the potential for greater profits due to linkage with the urban modern economy. However, these nonfarm opportunities are not equally available to all households due to the presence of several constraints (Barrett et al., 2001) and also owing to the small size of the modern economy. Thus, evidence of dualism mentioned in the previous chapters exists in Ethiopia.

Empirical analysis has evidenced that distress-push factors, such as small or infertile land and high poverty, as well as demand-pull factors, such as proximity to urban centres, influence the prevalence of nonfarm activities. Based on how these push and pull factors interact, nonfarm activities can be split into two groups: those that poor people need to do to survive and those that wealthy families can use to make money (Atamanov, 2012).

In Ethiopia, certain other factors also cause dualism. For instance, it has been observed that the female-headed households earn less from nonfarm activities than their male-headed counterparts, underscoring gender disparities in economic opportunities. The female-headed households face limitations due to restricted access to resources and credit. Limited access to credit is itself a major constraint for households attempting to enter high-return nonfarm businesses. Membership in cooperatives and access to agricultural extension services positively impact participation as well. This is because they provide resources and information that enable rural households to diversify their income sources. Kowalski et al. (2016) noted that the establishment and operation of nonfarm enterprises primarily occurred during harvest periods. This was due to an increase in both capital/finance and local demand generated by agricultural income and seasonal purchasing power in the community.

Various other demographic, economic, and institutional factors also significantly impact the likelihood of households engaging in non-agricultural income-generating activities (Kowalski et al., 2016; Asfaw et al., 2017). Younger individuals, for example, are more inclined to seek employment outside agriculture, whereas older individuals tend to rely on subsistence farming. Additionally, larger households are more likely to engage in nonfarm activities to supplement agricultural earnings (Neglo et al., 2021; Yaried et al., 2024).

Education and health are an important source of generating inequality. Households with higher education levels are more engaged in nonfarm enterprises, as education provides skilled employment opportunities with higher pay (Neglo et al., 2021; Yaried et al., 2024). Poor health status negatively impacts participation, as nonfarm work often requires physical labour (Neglo et al., 2021). Furthermore, households with higher livestock ownership are less likely to engage in nonfarm activities, as livestock is an alternative income source. On the other hand, crop failures and food insecurity push vulnerable households to seek nonfarm employment as a coping mechanism (Neglo et al. 2021). Thus, this country-specific case study has brought out several diversified factors that led to this dualism.

However, compared to other regions in the world, nonfarm and off-farm income in Ethiopia remains low. Rijkers et al. (2008) observed that only 2 per cent of all rural households in Ethiopia solely relied on nonfarm income, while 25 per cent of households had an income source from nonfarm activities. Key constraints reported were mainly a lack of access to credit, a lack of marketing promoting homemade goods, and poor infrastructure (Zerai and Gebreegziabher, 2011). Studies from Africa, Asia, and Latin America indicate that off-farm income constitutes 36 per cent, 50 per cent, and 43 per cent of total rural income, respectively. Ethiopia's share of 18 per cent lags behind this average, reflecting its largely agrarian economy (Reardon et al., 2006).

Nevertheless, even with a large agrarian base, it is seen that the nonfarm sector is expanding over time, and within it, dualism is spreading due to differences in resources or skills and the presence of a small-sized formal sector/urban area; that is, it is creating a pull effect.

Next, we discuss the case of Rwanda, which is another economy within Africa with a low degree of development and very low per capita income.

4.1.2 Rwanda

As in the case of Ethiopia, Rwanda also has a large percentage of the population—as high as 72 per cent of the working population—dependent on agriculture as their main source of livelihood (Tuyishime et al., 2020). The high population density, land distribution issues, inefficient or outdated farming techniques, and soil erosion make it difficult for rural households to solely depend on cultivation. Most rural landholders, therefore, have shifted towards agricultural wage labour to supplement their income. The primary reason for this was the lack of assets, minimal land holdings and livestock, and access to capital, which is required to invest in a nonfarm enterprise (Schmidt et al., 2024). These barriers led to reliance on unskilled casual labour opportunities for survival rather than the development of the nonfarm sector (Howe and McKay, 2007).

This was confirmed by a study by Schmidt et al. (2024) using a Rwanda household survey conducted in 2022 by the International Food Policy Research Institute (IFPRI) to assess employment profiles in rural Rwanda. In particular, 2020 households from 202 different areas were considered through the survey. The results of their survey showed that 99.3 per cent of the households were involved in agriculture and 73.5 per cent in raising livestock, thereby showing signs of pluri-activities. For other income sources, 62.3 per cent of households engage in wage labour, of which 60.2 per cent undertake only agricultural wage labour. Nonfarm business ownership represents a smaller share, with only 10.7 per cent owning a business.

Rural households generate approximately 41 per cent of their total earnings from agricultural production, while the share of livestock production is 11 per cent. Although agricultural wage labour is the lowest-paying off-farm activity, it remains one of the most common income diversification strategies, contributing 14 per cent to overall rural household earnings. In contrast, non-agricultural wage activities offer higher income potential, making up 21 per cent of rural household income, despite involving fewer participants (Schmidt et al., 2024). Dabalen et al. (2004) observed that participants who were self-employed in the nonfarm sector in rural areas had significantly higher incomes than agriculture workers and wage employees. Those households who diversified their income were one quintile higher (fourth quintile in comparison to third quintile in consumption distribution) than the average non-diversified household. Thus, nonfarm activities help them to supplement their income.

Only 11 per cent of smallholder households engage in nonfarm businesses, which collectively contribute about 5 per cent of rural income in Rwanda. More than three-quarters of these households operate businesses focused on the wholesale or retail trade of agricultural products. Most of these micro enterprises are informal in nature and operate without hired employees (Abbott et al., 2012). Thus, once again through the case of Rwanda, we observe what we concluded in Chapter 3 that subsistence nonfarm activities dominate the rural areas of the poorer countries.

Participation in Rwanda's nonfarm sector is influenced by a variety of economic, social, and institutional factors. A household's decision to participate in this sector is influenced both by their productive assets (such as skill, education, financial status, etc.) and the opportunities available (Dabalen et al., 2004). Attainment of secondary-level education has been positively associated with nonfarm earnings (Nilsson, 2019). Education is linked to a higher likelihood of self-employment for men, while for women, only post-primary education has a significant impact as seen by the econometric exercises carried out by some scholars (Nilsson, 2019; Dabalen et al., 2004). Additionally, education has an even stronger correlation with wage employment for both genders, with the effect increasing at higher education levels—especially for those with secondary or tertiary education. Education is more strongly associated with self-employment in enterprises that have assets. This aligns with the idea that such businesses require more complex skills (Dabalen et al., 2004).

Industrial diversity has also had a positive effect on the nonfarm participation rates in the country (Nilsson, 2019). This indicates that areas with a greater breadth of industrial activities tend to have higher per capita nonfarm income, perhaps through the linkage effects. Rural households located in more economically diverse regions are better positioned to generate nonfarm income compared to those in less diverse areas. This aligns with the idea that diverse economic environments foster opportunities for learning and adaptation, ultimately increasing participation in nonfarm income-generating activities (Conley and Udry, 2001). Additionally, clustering in services also has a significant impact, highlighting the presence of notable spill-over effects. This supports the notion that a strong local concentration of service activities acts as a pull factor, enhancing rural households' ability to diversify their income sources and benefit from economies of scope in production (Davis et al., 2014). Thus, it is observed that certain regions and more privileged sections of society, such as those with both financial and human capital, are able to take up more remunerative nonfarm activities, while the less privileged ones remain in the low-paying nonfarm sector, or traditional agriculture, or engaged as casual labour.

The country-specific case studies of Rwanda and Ethiopia show that, at lower levels of economic development, there are forces that sustains duality. Though the formal sector in these economies is not large enough to induce a push effect through land conversion or price movements (though inflation may exist), however, the pull effect may generate a duality. The predominance of lack of skills among the workers and differences in skill and resource accessibility implies that this dualism may become augmented as the economy experiences higher levels and rates of capital accumulation.

4.1.3 Ghana

Ghana is a lower-middle-income country as per the World Bank classification. The size of the formal sector in this country is larger in terms of output and employment as compared to Ethiopia and Rwanda. Ghana is also endowed with certain valuable natural resources, such as gold and crude oil (Asumadu et al., 2021). All these factors have implications on its growth and employment formation.

Even though Ghana is a middle-income country, poverty remains a significant concern, particularly in rural areas, where 37.9 per cent of households live in poverty, compared to only 10.6 per cent in urban areas. Notably, 78 per cent of the nation's poverty is concentrated in rural regions, revealing rural–urban dualism. Most rural households rely on agriculture for their livelihood (Nkegbe et al., 2019). However, the prolonged dry season, especially in northern Ghana, leaves farmlands unused for approximately seven months each year, and we see the impacts of environmental factors on rural livelihood.

Economic and institutional policies implemented in the 1990s further exacerbated the situation by increasing foreign imports of products like rice and poultry, which reduced demand for locally produced goods

(Marchetta, 2013). Compounding these issues, the agricultural sector has suffered from limited government investment and slow technological adoption. Many public investment projects initiated in the 1970s were discontinued due to a lack of financial resources, further hindering the sector's development. As a result of some of these government policies, the agricultural sector has struggled to sustain rural livelihoods. This has led many farm households to diversify their income sources by engaging in nonfarm economic activities. Part-time and seasonal work in nonfarm sectors is especially common in areas with a single agricultural season and relatively low productivity. Such employment plays a vital role in diversifying income and providing access to cash during critical periods. This is essential in a country like Ghana, where agricultural production is low, rural savings are non-existent, and credit and insurance are difficult to access (Reardon, 1997).

Recent research works argue that there is also the presence of the 'natural resource curse' ('Dutch disease') on the Ghanaian economy, particularly in the agricultural sector, after extraction of oil started commercially in 2010, which has resulted in currency appreciation (Acheampong and Baah-Kumi, 2011; Asumadu et al., 2021). The impact of Dutch disease can be observed from the dwindling performance of the agricultural sector. The share of the agricultural sector in gross domestic product (GDP) in 2010 was 29.8 per cent, and it declined to 18.24 per cent in 2020 (Asumadu et al., 2021).

Further, some areas within Ghana have experienced an expansion of urban areas. Osumanu and Ayamdoo (2022), have reported, in their study, that owing to the expansion of unregulated commercial and residential projects in several urban areas, agricultural activities (particularly areas under cultivation) in the surrounding regions have declined. All these factors have resulted in outflow of workforce to the nonfarm sector.

The Ghana Living Standards Survey (GLSS) conducted in 2016–2017 reported that 50.5 per cent of households in urban areas operate a nonfarm enterprise, while 34.6 per cent in rural settings engage in nonfarm enterprises. A total of 6.6 million people is working in 3.8 million nonfarm enterprises, highlighting the importance of nonfarm enterprises in Ghana (Ayambila, 2023).

Most nonfarm activities in Ghana can be classified into extractive, manufacturing/processing, constructive, commercial, and direct services (Dary and Kuunibe, 2012). Women dominate commercial services in jobs such as food vending, extractive industry (pito brewing and shea butter making), and manufacturing/processing activities (fuel wood production), while men dominate construction and direct service activities such as woodwork, masonry, carpentry, butchery, etc. (Dary and Kuunibe, 2012).

The government of Ghana has also launched several initiatives to promote nonfarm employment as a strategy to diversify rural livelihoods, reduce poverty, and stimulate economic growth. Recognizing the limitations of the agricultural sector in sustaining rural incomes, these initiatives aim to create alternative income-generating opportunities, particularly in rural areas. The National Entrepreneurship and Innovation Plan (NEIP) launched in 2017, provides training, funding, and business support services to entrepreneurs, particularly young people, to encourage the development of small and medium-sized enterprises (SMEs) in nonfarm sectors such as manufacturing, services, and technology.

Similarly, the One District One Factory (1D1F) Initiative is a flagship industrialization programme aiming to establish at least one factory in each of Ghana's districts, focusing on agro-processing, manufacturing, and other nonfarm industries. The initiative seeks to create jobs, boost local economies, and reduce reliance on agriculture. The Medium-Term Agriculture Sector Investment Plan (METASIP II) (2014–2017) and METASIP III (2018–2021) also have objectives that promote livelihood diversification.

However, various studies have found that multiple factors drive participation in remunerative nonfarm activities and migration (Dary and Kuunibe, 2012; Senadza, 2012). Education is a key determinant of off-farm diversification, since higher education ensures participation in high-skilled and therefore high-paying nonfarm activities. On the other hand, a lack of education leads to lower-paying casual wage labour (Abdulai and Delgado, 1999; Anang, 2017). Additionally, proximity to markets and infrastructure also encourages participation in nonfarm activities. Coastal and forest households in Ghana participated more in nonfarm activities than in the savannah belt. This regional difference was attributed more to the developed nature of the coastal and forest belts, which exerted a significant influence on the adopted diversification strategies (Senadza, 2012).

Despite an increase in the number of people participating in nonfarm activities, Ayambila et al. (2017) identified several barriers to entry in better nonfarm jobs. Limited access to credit was a major hindrance towards establishing rural enterprises. Additionally, households without electricity or those experiencing frequent blackouts were less likely to operate nonfarm enterprises. Access to electricity enabled self-employed individuals to work more days and extend their working hours into the evening. Furthermore, mobile phone ownership was associated with an increase in working days, with individuals who owned mobile phones working 39.87 days more than those without.

Thus, we observe that a more developed and relatively higher-income country such as Ghana has more people engaged in nonfarm activities, and state policies play a role in developing this sector. However, within the nonfarm sector, there is dualism, with some segments engaged in higher-end nonfarm and some segments of people in the low-subsistence nonfarm sector. Further, unlike Ethiopia and Rwanda, it is observed that expansion of nonfarm activities is also happening due to expansion of urban areas and mining activities. In other words, the formal sector is also having a push effect.

We next move on to a few Asian cases.

4.2 Insights from Asian Nations

4.2.1 Pakistan

Pakistan is considered a lower-middle-income country according to the World Bank classification. In rural Pakistan, the nonfarm sector has become increasingly important as an alternative income source for agricultural households, which corroborates what the data shows in Chapter 3. According to the Labour Force Survey (LFS), more than half of the rural labour force is employed in nonfarm activities. This shift from farm to nonfarm employment is driven by several (pull and push) factors, including overseas migration, unequal land distribution, and stagnant agricultural productivity (Farooq and Younais, 2022). Multiple studies (Iqbal et al., 2021; Jabbar et al., 2023) have acknowledged the impact of nonfarm activities on income diversification and livelihood sustainability. A survey of 290 farm households in Punjab, Pakistan by Iqbal et al. (2021) showed that 79 per cent of the farmers surveyed were involved in nonfarm activities, with such income contributing approximately 15 per cent of their total household earnings. In another study by Jabbar et al. (2023) of 441 farmers in Rawalpindi, Chakwal, and Jhelum of the Punjab district, 42 per cent of the farmers were involved in nonfarm activities, while in Sindh province, out of 400 farm households, 69 per cent were involved in nonfarm activities (Nazir et al., 2018). The Household Integrated Economic Survey (HIES) 2013–2014 reports that Pakistan has over 5 million rural nonfarm enterprises, with 19 per cent of rural households owning such businesses. These enterprises are primarily micro-scale and often operate informally, facing challenges such as limited marketing, accounting, and IT services (Farooq and Younais, 2022).

Regional differences were also seen in the type of nonfarm activities. Rural districts were primarily dependent on labour activities in construction, transportation, etc. (Iqbal et al., 2021). In addition to regional differences, studies have identified several socio-economic and geographic variables that influence participation in nonfarm activities. Higher education levels and access to roads and urban markets was seen to significantly increase the likelihood of engaging in service-orientated and self-employment jobs. Conversely, farmers with more years of farming experience were more likely to engage in off-farm labour to supplement their agricultural earnings (Kanwal et al., 2016).

The nonfarm sector has significantly benefited the 68 per cent of Pakistan's population residing in rural areas (Kazmi et al., 2023), either directly or indirectly. According to the HIES (2013–2014), 57 per cent of the poorest households rely on non-agriculture-based activities, particularly non-agricultural wages, highlighting the sector's role in providing livelihoods for vulnerable populations. In contrast, wealthier households are more likely to own nonfarm enterprises, with 31.8 per cent of the richest households owning such businesses compared to just 12.2 per cent of the poorest households (Farooq and Younais, 2022). The sector also plays a crucial role in reducing multidimensional poverty (MP).

Households engaged in nonfarm activities experience lower poverty levels and higher per capita consumption than those dependent solely on agriculture. For example, the headcount poverty rate is 19.4 per cent among households with nonfarm enterprises, compared to 22.6 per cent for those without. Similarly, the Multidimensional Poverty Index (MPI) is lower for households with nonfarm enterprises (17.3 per cent) than for those without (26.8 per cent) (Farooq and Younais, 2022). Thus, as our data from Chapter 3 shows, the nonfarm sector is increasingly becoming prominent in the rural economy, but certain endowed sections have benefited much more from the development of the sector.

Despite its contributions, the nonfarm sector in Pakistan faces significant challenges. The informal nature of most enterprises restricts the growth of this sector due to limited access to financial services, internet and mobile technology, and access to markets. This is reflected in the high closure rate of nonfarm enterprises, with a fall in the number of operating enterprises by 15.4 per cent from 2001 to 2010 (Farooq and Younais, 2022).

Some studies have identified the presence of a complementary relationship between informal employment and growth of the formal sector in Pakistan (Kemal, 2007; Mughal and Schneider, 2020). This is because, in Pakistan, a formal business is liable to pay tax for hiring permanent employees. However, in employing informal or contractual employees, no such liability exists. This is cited as one of the reasons why many small-level firms generate informal employment as they observe growth in their business (Kemal, 2007; Mughal and Schneider, 2020). It is important to note that although such practices may generate employment, they would also accentuate the difference in earnings between contractual and permanent workers or employers.

4.2.2 Sri Lanka

The Sri Lankan economy has seen a structural transformation in the past few years, moving from agricultural to industrial and service sectors. However, despite this diversification, a large percentage of the population in Sri Lanka is based in rural areas (Deininger et al., 2007). In 2023, of 6.4 million rural workers, approximately 73 per cent were engaged in nonfarm activities (World Bank Group, 2021). This reflects a marked shift from agricultural employment to services and industry. This World Bank Group (2021) study, covering the period from 2006 to 2016, showed that employment growth during this period was dominated by the services sector, which added nearly 430,000 jobs. By contrast, the agricultural sector witnessed a net loss of 35,000 jobs, predominantly in wage employment. Among nonfarm employment, about 3.3 million rural workers were involved in wage employment, while 1.3 million were self-employed (World Bank Group, 2021).

The nonfarm sector is diverse. Within the nonfarm sector, around 17.5 per cent of the rural nonfarm workers were employed in trade, followed by 11.4 per cent in construction, 9.9 per cent in textiles, apparel, and public administration, and 8 per cent in transportation. There is a noticeable gender-based variation in employment sectors. For instance, rural women are heavily involved in textiles (21.2 per cent), education (12 per cent), and public administration (11.3 per cent), while men dominate sectors like transportation and construction (World Bank Group, 2021). However, it is often seen that rural nonfarm enterprises are typically small, with an average workforce of 2.4 individuals, including household members. The majority (81 per cent) operate with fewer than three workers, while only 5 per cent of firms employ more than five workers (Deininger et al., 2007).

Nonfarm income sources can be broadly categorized into government jobs, private-sector employment, and self-employment. Over the past decade, the nonfarm sector, particularly services, has seen significant growth, adding approximately 430,000 jobs between 2006 and 2016. This expansion has drawn rural workers to nonfarm jobs, especially those offering higher wages and greater stability. Nonfarm self-employment and public-sector jobs tend to provide higher incomes compared to unskilled nonfarm work, with average monthly earnings ranging from 33,002 Sri Lankan rupees for self-employed workers to. 38,609 Sri Lankan rupees for public-sector employees (World Bank Group, 2021).

Therefore, one of the primary drivers of the migration from the farm to the nonfarm sector in Sri Lanka is the diverse income opportunities offered by the nonfarm sector, which are crucial for improving household welfare, particularly for those engaged in subsistence farming (De Silva and Kodithuwakku, 2005). Given the limited productivity of the agricultural sector, nonfarm employment has emerged as a viable pathway to higher incomes and poverty reduction. For example, a study by Weerahewa et al. (2021) in the Thirappane Village Tank Cascade System (VTCS) highlights that farm wages are very low due to small landholdings and the volatile market conditions people face in the area, making off-farm employment in activities such as brick manufacturing, pottery, and cadjan weaving (Navaratne, 2000) an attractive alternative for many households. The initial shift into nonfarm activities was driven by necessity, as limited prospects for full-time work, uncertainty, and income instability compelled households to engage in multiple income-generating activities. The decision to adopt pluri-activity was initially motivated by 'push' factors for both poor and wealthier households. However, wealthier households were eventually able to establish their own off-farm businesses, while poorer households were engaged in selling wage labour (De Silva and Kodithuwakku, 2010).

Education has also played a pivotal role in increasing participation in nonfarm activities. However, a notable skills barrier exists, as education significantly influences access to skilled nonfarm jobs, which generally offer better pay than unskilled farm work. Higher levels of education enhance the likelihood of securing nonfarm employment, as individuals with more education have better access to information, skills, and networks that facilitate entry into non-agricultural sectors. The study in Thirappane reveals that individuals with formal education are more inclined to pursue nonfarm employment due to its better wages and working conditions compared to traditional farming (Weerahewa et al., 2021). For instance, 23 per cent of public-sector employees hold a bachelor's degree or higher, whereas only a negligible percentage of farmers have similar qualifications (World Bank Group, 2021). Improved access to infrastructure, such as roads, markets, and technology, has further facilitated the shift towards nonfarm employment. Households with better access to these resources are more likely to diversify into nonfarm activities, underscoring the importance of infrastructure development in supporting this transition.

Despite its growth, the nonfarm sector faces challenges, such as limited access to credit, inadequate infrastructure, and skill mismatches. Notably, electricity is the most significant constraint, cited by approximately one-quarter of enterprises. This is followed by the cost of credit (12 per cent), lack of market demand (11 per cent), road access (8 per cent), water supply (7 per cent), access to market information (6 per cent), and road quality (5 per cent) (Deininger et al., 2007).

Studies have also cited the dominance of informal firms and informal employment with poorer working conditions and low remunerations within the nonfarm sector (Ruppert Bulmer, 2020; World Bank 2020a).

According to the World Bank (2020a), complexity of labour regulations is one of the primary factors that encourage informality. However, it has also pointed out that since formalization does not ease other constraints as cited above, there exist fewer incentives to formalize. De Mel et al. (2012) carried out an experiment in which they induced several informal firms to register for tax purposes by providing information and reimbursing the registration cost. In their experiment, they found that even after incentivizing, a substantial number of firms did not formalize, since the land in which they were doing their business was public land owned either by the government or a temple. Therefore, initial endowments also affect transformation. Further, akin to Pakistan, they found that demand for formalization is less among smaller firms, possibly because the benefits for them are less than the cost (such as tax).

The above studies show the reasons why, with growth of an economy, some firms may prefer to remain outside the larger capitalist or formal segment.

4.2.3 Vietnam

The reform policy or 'Doi Moi' introduced in Vietnam in 1986 led to a significant transformation of the country from a command economy towards a market-oriented economy. There was a notable reduction in the contribution of agriculture to GDP and employment, and household businesses became the primary source of job creation in the economy (Nguyen et al., 2021). The share of the labour force engaged in agriculture declined from 79.6 per cent in 2001 to 33.61 per cent in 2022, while the share of industry and services increased proportionally. At the household level, diversification into nonfarm activities has become a prominent livelihood strategy. Between 2008 and 2012, the proportion of households solely engaged in agriculture dropped from 56.0 per cent to 21.3 per cent, while those combining farming with waged labour increased from 12.2 per cent to 44.3 per cent. By 2016, the income from nonfarm activities had also risen to 73 per cent from 48 per cent in 1993 (Pham et al., 2024). Many households have used the increased income from nonfarm activities to reinvest in farm activities, such as buying new equipment or crop diversification, thereby ensuring increased farm income too (Mulia et al., 2021). Looking at regional variations, the nonfarm earnings of rural households were the highest in the Red River Delta (67.06 million VND (Vietnam Dongs)) and the South Eastern Area (76.40 million VND), mainly due to their proximity to developed cities such as Hanoi and Ho Chi Minh City, showing again urban linkages benefiting the rural nonfarm. Regions located at a distance from developed cities, such as the Central Highland, Midland, and Northern mountainous areas, have lower earnings from nonfarm employment (28.29 million VND and 31.68 million VND, respectively) (Nguyen et al., 2021).

Employment diversification in rural Vietnam takes three primary forms: agriculture combined with wage nonfarm employment, agriculture combined with household enterprise, and engagement in all three activities. Households engaged in both wage employment and enterprise activities experienced the highest welfare gains, with consumption levels 23 per cent higher than those specializing in agriculture (Bui and Hoang, 2021). Among nonfarm activities, industrial jobs such as food processing, woodwork, mining, and manufacturing of textiles are undertaken by only 0.5–2 per cent of the labour force (Brünjes and Diez, 2016). These jobs are primarily taken up by young male members with lower levels of education and are usually low-paying. Only a small proportion of these industrial jobs provide non-monetary benefits such as accommodation and food. A larger percentage of people work in the construction sector, where wages are higher. However, these jobs are temporary, and the average annual wage is much lower despite high daily wages. Typically, it is the household head who engages in construction work during the off-season when farming activities are not required. Thus, construction serves as a supplementary income source but is not a viable year-round occupation (Brünjes and Diez, 2016). Service-sector jobs such as drivers, woodworkers, hawkers, watchmen, house helps, etc. were taken up by young males with medium levels of education and more frequently found in urban areas. Most of these jobs paid well and were permanent, resulting in yearly incomes comparable to those in the industrial sector. In the rural areas, service jobs were mainly public-sector roles such as government employees, teachers, police personnel, and nurses. These were held by older males with higher levels of education. These positions were high-paying and included non-monetary employment benefits such as health insurance (Brünjes and Diez, 2016).

The transition of households towards nonfarm employment is driven by various socio-economic factors along with other strategic considerations. While economic incentives draw some rural residents to nonfarm activities with the prospect of higher income, others are pushed into diversification by the need to manage risks and overcome challenging circumstances in traditional agricultural work.

Interestingly, the literature talks about one of the most significant determinants of nonfarm employment in rural Vietnam as being social capital. Brünjes and Diez (2016) and Chuong (2023) observed that individuals are more likely to secure employment in a given sector if a family member is already employed in that sector. This suggests that family networks play a crucial role in job access, as household members often assist one another in finding work opportunities. Such reliance on social capital is particularly pronounced in informal and semi-skilled labour markets, where personal connections often matter more than formal credentials. However, this also means that those lacking strong social networks may face difficulties entering certain job markets, reinforcing existing social inequalities.

Education is another key factor influencing employment opportunities, though its impact varies by sector (Van Vu, 2020). Higher education levels are positively associated with participation in private and public service jobs, where formal qualifications and vocational training are often prerequisites. Public-sector jobs, in particular, demand higher levels of education, including university degrees and vocational certificates, making them among the most secure and desirable forms of employment. In contrast, education does not significantly affect participation in industrial or construction jobs. This suggests that lower-skilled labour markets rely less on formal education and more on physical ability and experience. Gender and experience further influence job access, particularly in the construction and private sectors. Jobs in construction tend to be male-dominated due to the physically demanding nature of the work.

In contrast, private service jobs, such as house help or shop workers, may be more accessible to women.

Geographical factors and better access to infrastructure facilities also shape employment opportunities, particularly for industrial and private service jobs, which are more concentrated near urban centres. The study finds that individuals living closer to provincial capitals have greater access to nonfarm wage employment, while those in more remote areas are often stuck with agricultural work. Additionally, improvements in IT facilities also play an important role in encouraging rural households to engage in nonfarm work (Bui and Hoang, 2021; Do et al., 2022).

Ethnicity plays a significant role in determining access to nonfarm employment in rural Vietnam, with ethnic minorities facing considerable challenges in securing jobs in certain sectors. Ethnic minorities are less likely to participate in industrial, construction, and private service jobs compared to the Kinh majority. One of the major factors limiting ethnic minorities' participation in private nonfarm sectors is their lower level of education and vocational training. They are, however, not significantly disadvantaged in public-sector employment. This is likely due to government initiatives aimed at supporting minority communities, such as Program 135, which seeks to improve economic opportunities for disadvantaged groups. The absence of significant discrimination in public employment suggests that affirmative action policies may have played a role in ensuring greater access to government jobs for ethnic minorities. However, since public-sector jobs are limited in number and require higher education, they do not provide a widespread solution to employment challenges faced by ethnic minorities in rural Vietnam.

Geographical factors also play a role in restricting nonfarm employment opportunities for ethnic minorities. Many minority communities live in remote or mountainous regions, far from urban centres, where most industrial and service jobs are concentrated. Limited transportation infrastructure and higher commuting costs make it difficult for minority workers to access nonfarm employment, reinforcing their dependence on agriculture.

Overall, the entry requirements for nonfarm wage employment in rural Vietnam highlight the interplay of education, social capital, health, gender, and geography. While formal education and vocational training are crucial for securing stable, high-paying jobs in the public and private service sectors, social networks and physical ability remain critical determinants of access to industrial and construction jobs. These findings suggest that policies aimed at expanding employment opportunities in rural areas should consider both skill development and social inclusion measures to ensure that disadvantaged groups, including ethnic minorities and those without strong family networks, are not excluded from nonfarm labour markets.

4.2.4 Indonesia

According to the World Bank classification, Indonesia is categorized as an upper-middle-income nation. The economy of Indonesia has always observed an impressive growth rate, and the state has always initiated reforms to sustain it.

Historically, Indonesia has been predominantly an agrarian economy. In 1997, as much as 60 per cent of the labour force was engaged in agricultural activities. The figures were much higher for rural areas (Rigg, 1997).

However, over time, the situation has changed. The Indonesian economy grew between 2001 and 2018 at about 5.3 per cent (Adi et al, 2022; World Bank, 2024). Simultaneously, one also observes a decline in the share of agriculture output in overall GDP and agricultural employment in total employment (Sudaryanto, 2020; Abduh, 2023). In other words, with the growth of the economy, the nonfarm sector grew rapidly. Initially, the villages situated on the fringes of urban areas got transformed. Over time, the nonfarm sector also grew in places that were located in faraway areas (Leinbach, 2003).

This sustained growth, and the associated transformation of the Indonesian economy had several implications for the economy. These are delineated below.

First, it led to the development of the economy in several social indicators. For instance, the poverty head count ratio fell from 20 per cent to 13 per cent between 2007 and 2018 (Ralston et al., 2020).

Second, even though the country experienced improvement in several social indicators, studies also report increase in inequality (Dartanto and Sofiyandi, 2017; Ralston et al., 2020; Sen, 2024). According to the ILO (2015), though Indonesia observed a fast increase in wage employment, one in three regular employees (33.6 per cent) in Indonesia received a low wage.

Existing studies have attributed this rising inequality to several factors. For instance, according to Ralston et al. (2020), people living closer to urban agglomeration in the Java–Bali region, or near to the cities in Sulawesi and Sumatra, have been able to get better off-farm jobs. On the contrary, people in Eastern Indonesia did not get such benefits. There are also differences in skills across population that have contributed to rising inequality (Mulyaningsih et al., 2021). According to Lee and Wie (2015), owing to the diffusion of foreign technologies and foreign direct investment, there has been an increase in demand for skilled labour in the industrial sector, and this has increased wage inequality. Differences in the size of land holdings among farm households have also contributed to rising inequality (refer to Yamauchi, 2016). Apart from this, non-compliance of minimum wage legislation, particularly in the informal sector, is another factor that augments inequality (Hohberg and Lay, 2015; Azzahra et al., 2024).

Third, owing to the growth rate of the economy, one also observes an increase in real wage rate in both the farm and the nonfarm workers (Otsuka et al., 2016; Yamauchi, 2016). Consequently, it has created problems for the smaller farmers (who are the majority in numbers) in the farm sector due to the increased cost of production, for having smaller-sized land holdings, and due to the absence of resources, they could not substitute labour by machines (Yamauchi, 2016). On the contrary, relatively large farmers have expanded agricultural production by renting in land (reverse tenancy) and have also gained by substituting labour by machines (Yamauchi, 2016). Stated differently, as far as the agricultural sector is concerned, the rising growth rate owing to faster capital accumulation has caused a push effect for the smaller farmer and a pull effect for the larger ones. In this context, one should note that the majority of these small farmers are poor and possess lower average years of schooling compared to the national standard (Sudaryanto, 2020). Thus, this pushed workforce is expected to join the unskilled workforce and expand the rising inequality.

The Indonesian economy thus portrays a classic example of how formal sector capital accumulation can create both push and pull effects in the traditional agricultural sector (dominated by small farmers) and thus generate nonfarm employment characterized by inequality and dualism owing to skill differences.

4.3 Conclusion

In this chapter, we have presented the development experiences of seven individual countries (which we call 'micro perspectives') to understand certain nuances of development that can get hidden while analysing data at the (supranational) regional level. We have considered both poorer and relatively richer nations from the developing world of Africa and Asia. We have observed certain uniformity in the experiences of the countries as well as certain features that differ across the low-income countries from the middle-income ones.

The uniform trends we observed are as follows. Across both poorer and relatively richer countries, it has been observed that rural agriculture has been declining over the years, and the nonfarm sector is increasing both in output and employment. Further, duality exists in both farm and nonfarm economies. Human capital, financial capital, social capital and geography are seen as contributing to the success of the households taking up better income-generating activities in the nonfarm sector.

We also observed certain differences across the relatively richer nations and the poorer ones. While in poorer nations, the formal sector generates only a pull effect for agriculture and the nonfarm sector (e.g. in Ethiopia and Rwanda), which in turn creates duality, in the relatively richer nations, formal sector accumulation generates both push and pull effects (say, for instance, in Indonesia or Ghana) for the farm and nonfarm sectors, as theorized in Chapter 2. In low-income countries, the decline in agricultural population is largely due to the push effect arising from higher population growth, state policies, and climatic factors.

In some countries (for instance, in Sri Lanka and Pakistan), we observed that certain institutional factors create impediments in the transformation of the economy. The informal sector, particularly smaller firms, generally enjoys certain benefits (say, for instance, production on public land or tax exclusion, etc). Since small firms don't have the economies of scale, leaving these benefits may reduce their income. This, in turn, augments informality.

5

The Rural Nonfarm Sector in India

Imprints of Deepening Dualism

In Chapters 3 and 4, we highlighted the changes that the rural economies of the Global South have experienced over the past few decades. Chapter 3 highlighted the broad trends, and Chapter 4 provided micro perspectives from some selected countries of the Global South. Our emphasis was on the rural nonfarm sector (RNFS); nevertheless, we also noted the emergence of heterogeneities within the agricultural sector and its implications for the rural nonfarm economy. The chapters helped us to put forward certain observations in support of some of the theoretical propositions presented in Chapter 2. Specifically, we could establish that agricultural employment has declined over time in the Global South, and this has caused not only the growth of urban employment but also an expansion of jobs in the RNFS. We have also shown the simultaneous expansions of skilled jobs and unskilled elementary occupations in rural areas over time. The micro perspectives have helped us in relating the changes that some countries of the Global South have experienced with formal sector accumulation.

However, the questions raised in the introductory theoretical chapters (such as how the traditional and modern segments of the rural farm–nonfarm economy have contracted/expanded owing to the growth of the formal sector) could not be established firmly. We now focus more with an in-depth analysis using data available from India.[37]

[37] India is taken up for our study for several reasons. First of all, Chapter 3 showed that more than 50 per cent of the South Asian population resides in rural areas. Second, among the South Asian countries, India is the largest country and has experienced rapid growth in recent years, and one also finds large variation across different sub-national states. Third, there is a large presence of informal sector in the country. Finally, the country has rich data pertaining to rural areas and informal economy. All these factors helped us to study rural India in a more granular way by undertaking a state-level analysis.

The Nonfarm Economy. Manojit Bhattacharjee, Saumya Chakrabarti, and Meenakshi Rajeev,
Oxford University Press.
DOI: 10.1093/9780198972013.003.0005

Before we start, let us reiterate our main theoretical conjectures.

As stated in the previous chapters, several conjectures exist in the literature about the changes in the rural farm–nonfarm economy that are happening globally. While one set of studies presumes a decline of the traditional (farm–nonfarm) sectors and growth of the modern (farm–nonfarm) segments over time (Ranis and Stewart, 1993; Marjit, 2003), there are also studies which have argued that growth of the (rural–urban) formal economy will cause dispossession and thereby an expansion of the traditional/subsistence/need-orientated nonfarm activities (Harvey, 2003; Sanyal, 2007; Bhaduri, 2018). The theoretical model presented in Chapter 2 of this book, however, suggests that an expansion of the formal economy augments both the traditional and modern nonfarm sectors, along with modern farming activities, through the contraction of traditional farming. This theoretical model proposed the following specific conjectures:

1. There is a movement and/or diversification of the workforce away from traditional agriculture into both the advanced segments of agriculture and the advanced and especially petty segments of the rural nonfarm economy (RNFE).
2. The urban–rural modern formal sector triggers both the push and pull effects (working on the traditional agricultural workforce) and thereby induces this dual movement/diversification process.
3. The formal sector expansion not only boosts this spread of dualism but also deepens the divide between the modern and traditional agricultural segments, especially within the RNFS across its petty-modern sections (by increasing the inter-sectoral productivity gaps).

Given these positions, let us look into the relevant Indian data. However, in this chapter, our primary focus will be on the nonfarm sector. Chapter 6 looks into the issue of agricultural sector in greater detail.

As mentioned earlier, an analysis of the Indian condition could be taken as a representative study, given the country's sheer size; given the recent experiences of the Indian economy regarding growth, employment generation, sectoral characteristics, and dynamics, etc.; and most importantly, given the proliferation of old dualism (farm–nonfarm) and the creation of the new forms of heterogeneities (intra-farm and intra-nonfarm), despite a consistently high rate of growth for a decade or so. Finally, an analysis of the Indian sub-national states has a unique advantage; the states are so large and diverse that they could tentatively project a multi-country scenario. We have chosen India to study the RNFS especially for the following reasons.

First, in India, the RNFS (the main focus of our analysis) is vast and contributes significantly to both income and employment generation. According to the Periodic Labour Force Survey (2018), around 50 per cent of the rural workers in India are engaged in the RNFS. In the case of income generation, within the rural areas, the nonfarm sector contributes around 80 per cent.[38]

Second, the nonfarm sector of India consists of both the formal (modern) and informal segments (akin to other developing countries and the developed world), where the latter can further be categorized as modern and traditional informal sectors according to the existing literature (Ranis and Stewart, 1993; Chakrabarti, 2013). As stated in Chapters 1 and 2, the modern nonfarm sector is considered to be a part of the 'accumulation economy' (thus an extended part of the overall rural–urban formal sector) as it lies within the circuit of global capital. Thus, some modern informal firms may have a complementary relationship with this (rural–urban) formal sector of the economy, and they expand as this formal economy grows. The traditional nonfarm sector (essentially, the traditional informal sector), on the other hand, lies outside the circuit of capital (as in Sanyal, 2007). As theorized by Ranis and Stewart (1993), in India, too, the traditional nonfarm activities (i.e. the traditional informal segments) are involved in the production of low-quality products by individual households on a very small scale. Perhaps smaller firms, in most instances, lack adequate capital and sophistication required for producing goods that have a demand in the 'accumulation economy'. The formal sector, on the other hand, generally faces a higher transaction cost when it deals with such tiny enterprises owing to the absence of economies of scale; hence, the formal sector prefers the modern nonfarm segment.

[38] Income figures can be obtained by adding up the gross value added of different sectors.

For all these reasons, we pick up the RNFS of India to address our earlier theoretical propositions.

In this chapter, we intend to test the theoretical propositions of Chapter 2 empirically, using the secondary databases of India. Such an empirical analysis is difficult to carry out at the global level owing to the unavailability of data in greater detail.

In order to address our objectives, we make a comparison of the state of the rural economy of India across two time periods, viz. 1999–2000 and 2015–2016. We explore how the farm and nonfarm sectors of India have performed over the past two decades in terms of employment, output, and investment. We then try to capture and map the relationship of the RNFS with other sectors of the economy, specifically with the formal sector and agriculture. The data sets used in this chapter primarily include unit-level Annual Survey of Industries (ASI) data (Central Statistical Office (CSO), Government of India), unit-level Employment and Unemployment Surveys, Periodic Labour Force Surveys, and Enterprise Surveys data, Debt and Investment Surveys and Situation Assessment Survey of Farmers data, all by the National Sample Survey Office (NSSO, Government of India). Brief descriptions of these data sets are provided in the Appendix (see Appendix A.5.1).

Our chapter is subdivided into the following sections. Section 5.1 provides a comparison of the state of the rural economy between 1999–2000 and 2015–2016 using descriptive statistics. Here, we see descriptively how different subsectors of the rural economy in general, and the nonfarm economy in particular, have grown over the years. Section 5.2 presents a regression analysis to explore the factors that have augmented the changes in the RNFS. Results are discussed in section 5.3 and a conclusion is presented in section 5.3.

5.1 The state of the rural economy of India: Spatial and temporal changes

A majority of India's population lives in rural areas. According to the 2011 census (Government of India), around 68 per cent of the total population of India lives in rural areas, and the 2017–2018 Periodic Labour Force

Survey shows that the share of rural areas in total employment is 71 per cent.[39]

Even though the share of rural areas in total employment and population is very high, certain changes are taking place at a fast pace, which bears a resemblance to the global economy as well. Table 5.1, which provides information on employment, unemployment, and labour force across rural and urban areas for the past two decades, shows that total employment in rural areas has declined from 286 million in 1999–2000 to 265 million in 2017–2018 (Table 5.1). Thus, in the context of India, not only do we observe a reduction in rural employment share vis-à-vis urban employment but also an absolute fall. This is indeed significant, given the fact that the overall population is increasing; despite a population explosion, rural employment falls (this is clearly visible at least until the COVID-19 pandemic of 2020/2021). During the same time period, one also observes an expansion of employment in the urban sector and an increase in unemployment in rural areas (Table 5.1). This might indicate a process of transition from rural to urban; thus, with the growth of the urban economy, the rural segment is contracting, and it might be a mark of a progressive transformation. However, this picture of apparent smooth change might be misleading. Let us investigate further to understand this issue.

While overall rural employment has shown a declining trend, the trend is not uniform across different sectors of the rural economy. Table 5.2 shows the contribution of different sectors of the rural economy to overall employment for the years 1999–2000 and 2015–2016. The rural economy is subdivided into the agricultural sector, formal manufacturing sector, construction, own account enterprises (self-employment, mostly informal/unorganized), and establishments (unorganized/informal firms with hired labour).

In the above subdivision, agriculture, forestry, and fishing are broadly classified as agriculture. The formal manufacturing sector includes registered factories involved in manufacturing. Own account enterprises (OAEs) are informal or unregistered firms that satisfy the characteristics of the traditional nonfarm sector. They use family labour and are located

[39] The higher share of rural areas in total employment vis-à-vis that of its share in total population is mainly because of the lower unemployment rate in rural areas.

Table 5.1 Distribution of employment, unemployment, and labour force across rural and urban areas (in Lakhs)

Year	Sector	Total employment	Unemployment	Labour force
1999–2000	Rural	2,865.407 (78.42)	42.98 (1.48)	2,908.394
	Urban	788.332 (21.58)	39.27 (4.75)	827.602
	Total	**3653.739 (100)**	**82.26 (2.20)**	**3,735.996**
2011–2012	Rural	2,783.401 (72.18)	65.7 (2.30)	2,849.101
	Urban	1,073.018 (27.82)	42.898 (3.84)	1,115.916
	Total	**3,856.419 (100)**	**108.598' (2.73)**	**3,965.017**
2017–2018	Rural	2,658.788 (71.35)	150.085 (5.34)	2,808.874
	Urban	1,067.41 (28.65)	90.86 (7.84)	1,158.27
	Total	**3,726.198 (100)**	**240.945 (6.07)**	**3,967.144**

Note: Figures in parentheses corresponding to the total employment column provide information on the share of the rural/urban sector in total employment. The figures in parentheses corresponding to unemployment represent the unemployment rate.

Sources: Computed using the Employment and Unemployment Survey, NSSO, GOI.

mostly within household premises.[40] Establishments, on the other hand, are informal firms that use at least one hired worker.[41] Mostly, they generate a surplus. While smaller establishments may have similar characteristics to that of an OAE, larger establishments are expected to generate a meaningful surplus, and hence, they can be considered to have the characteristics of the modern/formal nonfarm sector. Due to the presence of surplus, they can tune themselves to the needs of the accumulation

[40] Using unit-level enterprise survey data we found that around 56 per cent of OAE enterprises were located within household premises and 24 per cent of OAEs had a fixed premises and a permanent structure outside the household. The remaining OAE enterprises were either operating without any fixed premises or were operating from a temporary structure outside the household.

[41] Around 60 per cent of the establishments were located outside the household in fixed premises with a permanent structure.

economy and, hence, are mostly linked directly and/or indirectly to this accumulation economy.

The sources of data for these different sectors are as follows. Construction and agricultural employment data are taken from the employment and unemployment round of the NSSO and Periodic Labour Force Survey (PLFS), respectively (both government data), formal manufacturing data is taken from ASI (CSO, Government of India), and OAE and establishment data are computed from enterprise surveys of the NSSO. The states are sorted in descending order based on their net state domestic product (NSDP) for the year 2015–2016, that is, the developed state is placed on top, and the least developed state (measured in terms of NSDP) is placed at the bottom of the table.

It is important to mention here that the employment and unemployment round of the NSSO was not available for the year 2015–2016. Therefore, in Table 5.2, agriculture and construction sector employment was interpolated for the year 2015–2016 using the 2011–2012 employment unemployment round of NSSO and 2017–2018 PLFS data. The interpolated figures for employment (L) were obtained using the following formula:

$$L_{2015-16} = L_{2011-12} + \frac{(2016-2012)}{2018-2012}\left(L_{2017-18} - L_{2015-16}\right).$$

Let us now see how different sectors have grown in terms of employment in rural areas over time.

A careful examination of Table 5.2 leads us to certain interesting results. First, spatial differences in development (defined in terms of NSDP per capita) have a limited role in shaping the sectoral composition of employment in rural areas when we consider sectors in a broader sense. It is observed that there is less difference between developed, middle-performing, and less developed states in terms of share of the agricultural sector in overall employment. Second, from Table 5.2, we find that in rural areas, overall agricultural employment has declined, and nonfarm sector employment has increased in all the states (considered here). For instance, if we divide total employment into farm and nonfarm employment, we see that the share of the farm sector in total employment has reduced from 76.3 per cent in 1999–2000 to 63.5 in 2015–2016 and that of

Table 5.2 State-wise employment in different sectors of rural India (in Lakhs)

States	Year	Agriculture	OAE	Establishment	Construction	Formal manufacturing	Total
Maharashtra	1999–2000	217.8 (82.6)	19.38 (7.3)	3.91 (1.5)	6.14 (2.3)	4.32 (1.6)	263.8
	2015–2016	186.2 (79.9)	22.77 (9.8)	6.39 (2.7)	11.71 (5)	8.93 (3.8)	233.1
Haryana	1999–2000	32.5 (68.6)	4.02 (8.5)	0.52 (1.1)	3.1 (6.5)	0.68 (1.4)	47.4
	2015–2016	25.01 (50.4)	3.8 (7.7)	2.8 (5.6)	7.84 (15.8)	2.35 (4.7)	49.62
Gujarat	1999–2000	120.1 (79.8)	9.86 (6.6)	2.28 (1.5)	4.06 (2.7)	3.33 (2.2)	150.4
	2015–2016	87.39 (76.1)	11.8 (10.4)	4.35 (3.8)	6.9 (6.1)	7.19 (6.3)	113.7
Tamil Nadu	1999–2000	129.2 (67.9)	22.8 (12)	6.3 (3.3)	7.7 (4)	5.5 (2.9)	190.2
	2015–2016	70.8 (49.8)	17.5 (12.3)	9.8 (6.9)	26.2 (18.4)	10.8 (7.6)	142.3
Kerala	1999–2000	37.7 (48.3)	10.6 (13.5)	6.2 (7.9)	7.3 (9.4)	2.3 (2.9)	78.1
	2015–2016	18.8 (34.5)	9.7 (17.8)	8.7 (16)	12.5 (22.9)	1.8 (3.4)	54.31

Punjab	1999–2000	43.1 (72.5)	4.9 (8.2)	1.3 (2.3)	3.1 (5.3)	0.8 (1.3)	59.4
	2015–2016	23.96 (52.3)	6.02 (13.1)	2.3(5)	8.7 (19.1)	2.7 (5.9)	45.8
Karnataka	1999–2000	140.9 (82.2)	15.2 (8.8)	5.2(3)	2.6 (1.5)	1.1 (0.6)	171.5
	2015–2016	97.8 (71.8)	19.9 (14.6)	6.57 (4.8)	7.4 (5.4)	2.4 (1.7)	136.2
Andhra Pradesh and Telangana	1999–2000	220 (78.9)	32.7 (11.7)	3.9 (1.4)	6.3 (2.3)	3.0 (1.1)	279
	2015–2016	165.6 (72.8)	35.1 (15.4)	10.0 (4.4)	20.0 (8.7)	6.5 (2.9)	227.6
West Bengal	1999–2000	128.8 (63.6)	44.9 (22.2)	4.3 (2.1)	4.4 (2.2)	1.0 (0.5)	202.4
	2015–2016	114.7 (53.6)	67.3 (31.5)	14.3 (6.7)	24.0 (11.2)	1.8 (0.8)	213.8
Rajasthan	1999–2000	122.5 (77.6)	11.9 (7.5)	1.6 (1)	12.5 (7.9)	0.7 (0.5)	157.7
	2015–2016	107.5 (63.8)	14.5 (8.6)	5.2 (3.1)	29.3 (17.4)	2.1 (1.2)	168.4
Madhya Pradesh and Chhattisgarh	1999–2000	237.4 (87.1)	18.7 (6.9)	1.6 (0.6)	4.9 (1.8)	1.2 (0.4)	272.4
	2015–2016	221.1 (74.3)	25.42 (8.5)	5.76 (1.9)	29.9 (10)	1.9 (0.6)	297.4

(continued)

Table 5.2 Continued

States	Year	Agriculture	OAE	Establishment	Construction	Formal manufacturing	Total
Orissa	1999–2000	95.8 (78.2)	23.4 (19.1)	1.2 (1)	3.9 (3.2)	0.5 (0.4)	122.4
	2015–2016	68.2 (63.6)	19.7 (18.4)	3.98 (3.7)	18.4 (17.2)	1.5 (1.4)	107.2
Assam	1999–2000	45.6 (67.7)	7.6 (11.2)	1.03 (1.5)	1.2 (1.8)	0.9 (1.4)	67.4
	2015–2016	42.2 (55.4)	8.3 (10.9)	3.4 (4.4)	6.96 (9.1)	1.7 (2.3)	76.21
Uttar Pradesh and Uttarakhand	1999–2000	337.45 (76.2)	63.4 (14.3)	9.3 (2.1)	14.4 (3.3)	2.1 (0.5)	442.6
	2015–2016	274.1 (65)	65.6 (15.6)	20.8 (4.9)	62.95 (14.9)	5.41 (1.3)	421.9
Bihar and Jharkhand	1999–2000	217 (80.6)	31.9 (11.8)	1.7 (0.6)	5.98 (2.2)	0.8 (0.3)	269.1
	2015–2016	157.1 (57.9)	42.9 (15.8)	8.5 (3.1)	43.6 (16.1)	1.2 (0.5)	271.2
India	**1999–2000**	**2,186.2 (76.3)**	**329.4 (11.9)**	**53.3 (2)**	**93.8 (3.3)**	**30 (1)**	**2,865**
	2015–2016	**1,714.1 (63.5)**	**381.3 (14.1)**	**117.4 (4.3)**	**331.5 (12.3)**	**143.0 (5.3)**	**2701**

Sources: Computed using ASI, Employment and Unemployment Survey (NSSO), PLFS and Enterprise Survey (NSSO). The figures in the parentheses show the shares of each sector in total employment. Note: The total may not add to 100 due to the use of different data sets.

the residual (i.e. the nonfarm sector) has increased. During the same time period, we also notice an increase in urban employment and the labour force (Table 5.1). Stated otherwise, with the decline in agricultural employment, two simultaneous developments are happening, viz. growth of the urban sector and expansion of the rural nonfarm employment. This is something we have also observed in Chapter 3, and it is a unique experience in most developing countries we are observing. Unlike the experience of most of the advanced countries, where with overall growth, there was a shift of the labour force from rural to urban locations, in India and other developing countries, we see that the growth of the economy is also causing growth in rural nonfarm employment (along with urban expansion), a feature that is referred to as unique to India's rural transformation (Binswanger-Mkhize, 2012). Thus, the simplistic observation derived from Table 5.1 is questioned by the stylized facts of Table 5.2.

Next, if one delves into the RNFS further, one finds that employment has increased manifold in the rural formal manufacturing sector, construction, and establishment. On the other hand, employment in OAEs has marginally increased. In fact, OAE employment has reduced in states like Tamil Nadu, Orissa, and Kerala (Table 5.2).

From Table 5.2, the first impression that comes to mind is that the rural economy is slowly becoming integrated within the global circuit of capital. This is because the formal sector is growing, and within the informal sector, the establishments (which primarily generate surplus and thus can hire workers) are developing faster. OAEs, which, to a large extent, satisfy the characteristics of a traditional sector (due to their tiny size and locations mostly within household premises), are either decreasing or their growth is marginal.

However, developing conclusions by observing aggregate data of a sector may not be correct. If we segregate the rural informal sector (i.e. OAEs and establishments) further, in terms of the number of workers they employ, we get additional interesting insights.

Table 5.3 provides information on employment in rural enterprises (OAEs and establishments) having one to two workers, three to five workers and above five workers, respectively. It is observed that OAE employment has increased largely for enterprises that employ one to two workers, but

Table 5.3 Employment in rural own-account enterprises and establishment in terms of the number of workers employed by each sector

States	Year	OAE employment				Establishment employment			
		1–2	3–5	Above 5	Total	1–2	3–5	Above 5	Total
Maharashtra	1999–2000	87	11.9	1.1	100	28.9	30.3	40.7	100
	2015–2016	93.5	5.7	0.8	100	24	35.8	40.2	100
Haryana	1999–2000	92.2	5.3	2.6	100	26.8	26.4	46.8	100
	2015–2016	95.3	4.6	0.1	100	15.1	23.8	61	100
Gujarat	1999–2000	89.1	10.1	0.8	100	17.6	32.3	50.1	100
	2015–2016	91.7	8.3	0.1	100	15.3	22	62.7	100
Tamil Nadu	1999–2000	81.5	16.4	2.2	100	14.1	31.3	54.5	100
	2015–2016	94	6	0	100	17.4	30.9	51.7	100
Kerala	1999–2000	88.5	10.5	1	100	23.7	42.2	34.1	100
	2015–2016	89.7	7.2	3.1	100	25.4	38.5	36.1	100
Developed total	**1999–2000**	**86**	**12.5**	**1.5**	**100**	**21**	**34.6**	**44.4**	**100**
	2015–2016	**92.8**	**6.4**	**0.8**	**100**	**20.4**	**32.1**	**47.5**	**100**
Punjab	1999–2000	95	5	0	100	26.9	39.8	33.3	100
	2015–2016	97.6	2.3	0.2	100	45.4	29.2	25.4	100
Karnataka	1999–2000	86.1	13.3	0.6	100	12.4	27.8	59.8	100
	2015–2016	89.6	9.3	1.1	100	21.9	31.1	47	100
Andhra Pradesh	1999–2000	81.8	17	1.2	100	15.5	53.5	31	100
	2015–2016	91.3	7.7	1	100	14.2	29.5	56.2	100

West Bengal	1999–2000	82.7	16.2	1.1	100	17.2	43.6	39.2	100
	2015–2016	88.1	11.1	0.8	100	18.9	35.9	45.1	100
Rajasthan	1999–2000	88.5	11.1	0.4	100	20.7	51.2	28.2	100
	2015–2016	92.6	7.4	0	100	17.2	26.1	56.7	100
Middle Performing	**1999–2000**	**84.1**	**15**	**0.9**	**100**	**16.4**	**41.4**	**42.2**	**100**
	2015–2016	**89.9**	**9.3**	**0.8**	**100**	**19.6**	**31.7**	**48.7**	**100**
Madhya Pradesh	1999–2000	85.1	13.8	1	100	19.7	38.9	41.4	100
	2015–2016	83.4	14.8	1.8	100	14.5	28.2	57.3	100
Orissa	1999–2000	79.2	19.9	0.9	100	29.9	51.4	18.7	100
	2015–2016	81.7	14.8	3.4	100	30.5	38.7	30.9	100
Assam	1999–2000	94.4	5.5	0.1	100	28.4	48.7	22.9	100
	2015–2016	94.4	5.6	0	100	45	31.9	23	100
Uttar Pradesh	1999–2000	84	12.6	3.4	100	17.2	32.7	50	100
	2015–2016	86.1	13.2	0.8	100	17.9	25.4	56.7	100
Bihar	1999–2000	85.4	13.7	0.9	100	17.9	61.3	20.8	100
	2015–2016	93.3	6.3	0.4	100	35.2	37.1	27.7	100
Less Developed	**1999–2000**	**84.2**	**13.8**	**2**	**100**	**19.4**	**39.3**	**41.4**	**100**
	2015–2016	**87.4**	**11.4**	**1.1**	**100**	**24.3**	**29.9**	**45.9**	**100**
India	**1999–2000**	**84.7**	**13.9**	**1.5**	**100**	**19.6**	**38.4**	**42**	**100**
	2015–2016	**89.5**	**9.6**	**0.9**	**100**	**22.3**	**31**	**46.6**	**100**

Source: Computed using unit-level 55th and 73rd rounds of the Enterprise Survey (NSSO).

for larger enterprises, it has reduced.[42] On the other hand, for establishments, employment growth is higher for firms that employ more than five workers. If we compare this transformation across developed, less developed, and middle-performing states, we see that growth in employment of OAEs with one or two workers is marginally higher among the developed states compared to that of less developed and middle-performing states.

Thus, rural areas of India are experiencing an uneven transformation, where growth in employment is happening for the formal sector and the larger informal units with simultaneous growth of smaller informal units. This transformation also has certain other implications, particularly with respect to migration. It is seen that apart from rural-to-urban migration (Table 5.1), this transformation is causing a migration of workers from urban to rural areas, particularly for workers who are skilled. This is because rural areas are experiencing growth in the formal sector, which requires a skilled workforce. Sixty-fourth-round NSSO data on migration reveals that in the year 2007–2008, while 55 million people migrated from rural to urban areas, there were also around 16 million individuals in urban areas who migrated to rural areas. Also, a majority of such migration was as a result of employment-related factors (NSSO, 2010).

Tables 5.4 and 5.5 provide certain additional insights. Both tables provide information on the type/nature of rural employment. In both Tables 5.4 and 5.5, employment is segregated as self-employment, regular salaried job, and casual employment. Table 5.4 concentrates largely on spatial/interstate differences in the status of jobs observed in two time periods (i.e. 1999–2000 and 2015–2016), while Table 5.5 provides information on temporal changes that are observed at the national level with information even for the intermediate periods.

From both Tables 5.4 and 5.5, it is seen that there has been an expansion of regular salaried jobs over time (an indicator of expansion of the modern sector). Table 5.4 also shows that apart from Assam, relatively developed states have a higher share of regular salaried jobs. However, as far as spatial and temporal changes in self-employment and casual

[42] It might have happened that, due to income squeeze, the household labour force of the larger OAEs have been compelled to diversify and thereby larger firms have given way to multiple smaller OAEs. The other alternative could be that while the larger firms have experienced involution (due to income squeeze), the smaller OAEs have appeared due to the migration/diversification of the stressed agrarian population. Whatever the process, this should be an outcome of push, either from the larger OAEs or from petty agriculture.

Table 5.4 Distribution of rural employment by type of employment across different states (%)

States	1999–2000				2015–2016			
	SE	RS	CE	Total	SE	RS	CE	Total
Maharashtra	44.3	7.3	48.4	100	55.0	10.8	34.2	100
Haryana	66.4	12.4	21.2	100	53.2	21.7	25.1	100
Gujarat	54.2	6.3	39.5	100	60.7	13.0	26.3	100
Tamil Nadu	36.7	11.8	51.5	100	33.0	18.6	48.3	100
Kerala	42.9	13.7	43.4	100	38.0	24.2	37.8	100
Punjab	65.5	13	21.5	100	51.9	20.7	27.4	100
Karnataka	50.2	5.3	44.5	100	53.9	12.9	33.1	100
Andhra Pradesh	45.8	5.9	48.3	100	48.8	9.5	41.7	100
West Bengal	52.2	7	40.8	100	47.8	11.7	40.5	100
Rajasthan	79.9	4.9	15.2	100	69.5	10.3	20.2	100
Madhya Pradesh	56.6	3.5	39.9	100	63.1	6.7	30.2	100
Orissa	48.7	4.2	47.1	100	60.7	9.3	30.0	100
Assam	58.2	16.6	25.2	100	61.8	19.0	19.2	100
Uttar Pradesh	72.7	5.6	21.7	100	67.4	8.3	24.3	100
Bihar	52.3	3.5	44.2	100	57.4	8.5	34.0	100
India	55.8	6.8	37.4	100	57.1	11.5	31.4	100

Note: SE—self-employment, RS—regular salaried employment, CE—casual employment.

Source: Estimated, using the 55th and 68th rounds of the Employment and Unemployment Survey (NSSO) and PLFS (2017–2018).

Table 5.5 Distribution of rural workers and the status of their employment during the National Sample Survey 38th round (1983) to 68th round (2011–2012) and Periodic Labour Force Survey (2017–2018) (%)

NSSO rounds	Male			Female		
	Self-employed	Regular salaried	Casual labour	Self-employed	Regular salaried	Casual labour
PLFS (2017–2018)	57.8	14.0	28.2	57.7	10.5	31.8
68th (2011–2012)	54.5	10.0	35.5	59.3	5.6	35.1
66th (2009–2010)	53.5	8.5	38.0	55.7	4.4	39.9
61st (2004–2005)	58.1	9.0	32.9	63.7	3.7	32.6
55th (1999–2000)	55.0	8.8	36.2	57.3	3.1	39.6
50th (1993–1994)	57.7	8.5	33.8	58.6	2.7	38.7

Source: Annual Report 2017-2018 (PLFS), GOI.

employment are concerned, there is no definite trend. We can see that the share of workers engaged in self-employment activity experienced a decline between 2004–2005 and 2009–2010 and an increase afterwards (Table 5.5). It seems that there is a high degree of occupational mobility (probably horizontal) prevailing across self-employment and casual employment activities, particularly in the lower segment. This is because self-employed individuals engaged in big and sophisticated business activity may face higher social and economic transaction costs of shifting; for the petty ones, such costs are much less. An increase in the number of OAEs employing just one to two workers has made occupational movement in the lower segments more explicit (Table 5.3).

There are other types of changes too within the RNFS. For instance, Table 5.6 presents rural informal manufacturing employment and its share in aggregate employment of the rural informal sector and in aggregate employment of the rural manufacturing sector. It is seen that within the RNFS, share of informal manufacturing has declined while formal manufacturing has gone up. This might have happened due to an urban-to-rural shift in the formal sector. Table 5.6, on the other hand, shows that in many states (particularly the developed ones), informal manufacturing employment has either stagnated or has reduced in absolute terms as well. Thus, there is a change in the nature of the RNFS in terms of manufacturing and non-manufacturing activities. It seems that rural informal manufacturing has given way to rural petty services (like petty trading); thus, the condition might have deteriorated (expecting that the productivity in manufacturing is higher than that in the petty/rudimentary service sector). A deeper understanding could be gained in this regard through our subsequent analysis.

The movement of factors of production across different sectors is generally guided by the return obtained from that sector. Table 5.7, in this context, provides information on the gross value added per worker (an indicator of return from a sector) across different sectors and states of rural India. We have computed the gross value added per worker at 2011–2012 prices (based on the Consumer Price Index for agricultural workers).

Table 5.7 reveals that gross value added (GVA) per worker has increased in real terms for all the sectors and for all the states between

Table 5.6 Rural informal manufacturing sector employment and its share in aggregate rural informal sector employment and in aggregate employment in the rural manufacturing sector

States	Year	Rural informal manufacturing employment in Lakhs	Share of rural manufacturing employment within the rural informal sector (%)	Share of rural informal manufacturing in total rural manufacturing employment (%)
Maharashtra	1999–2000	9.21	39.5	68.1
	2015–2016	9.22	31.6	50.8
Haryana	1999–2000	1.23	27.1	64.4
	2015–2016	1.9	28.8	44.7
Gujarat	1999–2000	5.34	44.0	61.6
	2015–2016	4.91	30.4	40.6
Tamil Nadu	1999–2000	16.44	56.5	74.9
	2015–2016	11.78	43.2	52.2
Kerala	1999–2000	6.53	38.9	74.0
	2015–2016	4.98	27.1	73.5
Punjab	1999–2000	1.85	29.8	69.8
	2015–2016	2.39	28.7	47.0
Karnataka	1999–2000	10.54	51.7	90.5
	2015–2016	10.57	39.9	81.5
Andhra Pradesh and Telangana	1999–2000	14.71	40.2	83.1
	2015–2016	18.97	42.1	74.5
West Bengal	1999–2000	29.2	59.3	96.7
	2015–2016	49.5	60.7	96.5
Rajasthan	1999–2000	6.05	44.8	89.6
	2015–2016	5.44	27.6	72.1
Madhya Pradesh and Chhattisgarh	1999–2000	10.31	50.8	89.6
	2015–2016	11.44	36.7	85.8
Orissa	1999–2000	15.13	61.5	96.8
	2015–216	6.96	29.4	82.3
Assam	1999–2000	2.34	27.1	72.2
	2015–2016	3.03	25.9	64.1
Uttar Pradesh and Uttarakhand	1999–2000	29.09	40.0	93.3
	2015–2016	27.13	31.4	83.4

(continued)

Table 5.6 Continued

States	Year	Rural informal manufacturing employment in Lakhs	Share of rural manufacturing employment within the rural informal sector (%)	Share of rural informal manufacturing in total rural manufacturing employment (%)
Bihar and Jharkhand	1999–2000	13.6	40.5	94.4
	2015–2016	14.88	28.9	92.5
India	**1999–2000**	**175.84**	**45.9**	**85.4**
	2015–2016	**188.03**	**37.7**	**56.8**

Source: Informal manufacturing employment is computed using a unit-level enterprise survey, and ASI data is used for formal manufacturing employment.

1999–2000 and 2015–2016. However, unevenness exists between regions (i.e. developed, less developed, and middle-performing states) and also between sectors. Developed states, for instance, have a higher GVA per worker compared to that of the less developed and middle-performing states.

While comparing across sectors, it is found that the formal sector has a higher GVA per worker[43] compared to that of other sectors of the rural economy. In the informal sector, GVAs per worker are higher in establishments and lower in OAEs. We also found that the gap between OAEs and establishments has increased over time in terms of GVA per worker.

Additionally, Table 5.8 measures the difference between OAE and Establishment in terms of GVA per worker for each year. The table shows that the difference in GVA per worker (between OAE and Establishment) has increased over time (see the last column, Table 5.8). It is also observed that the increase is higher for the developed and middle-performing regions (which have a higher presence of the formal sector) compared to that of less developed states. Thus probably, the presence of formal sector enterprises augments the gap between the modern informal firms and the traditional informal sector.

[43] Information on construction sector GVA per worker was not available for individual states, so it was computed at the national level. At the national level, GVA per worker for construction sector was above agriculture, OAEs, and establishments and below that of the formal sector (Kundu et al., 2021).

Table 5.7 Gross value added per worker (in Indian rupees) in 2011–2012 prices

State	Year	OAEs	Establishment	Formal manufacturing	Agriculture
Maharashtra	1999–2000	36,282.23	80,021.53	644,537.07	32,166.8
	2015–2016	52,808.68	130,692.01	1,288,634.67	47,337.6
Haryana	1999–2000	39,892.7	68,431.23	296,052.82	92,941.9
	2015–2016	69,817.43	101,780.21	632,533.84	139,923.64
Gujarat	1999–2000	35,271.92	53,420.38	741,795.2	25,575.36
	2015–2016	46,014.25	182,104.03	1,875,912.58	85,406.37
Tamil Nadu	1999–2000	24,552.83	42,938.16	252,172.72	29,513.5
	2015–2016	44,671.03	84,715.09	556,178.44	61,496.03
Kerala	1999–2000	40,968.31	60,128.36	199,632.19	63,470.89
	2015–2016	68,032.81	121,040.59	341,785.45	100,573.6
Punjab	1999–2000	47,332.61	56,002.23	452,178.27	109,607.5
	2015–2016	63,863.34	87,064.81	391,669.06	188,317.07
Karnataka	1999–2000	23,736.08	44,373.73	338,706.31	39,573.8
	2015–2016	49,779.66	101,510.83	1,116,772.05	46,474.81
Andhra Pradesh	1999–2000	18,331.92	36,919.46	282,090.75	28,572.7
	2015–16	35,508.76	79,392.47	691,701.69	48,294.7
West Bengal	1999–2000	24,784.77	34,427.53	180,667.91	53,611.0
	2015–2016	51,827.8	92,964.73	401,025.72	66,729.4
Rajasthan	1999–2000	33,775.13	48,492.61	840,357.98	36,698.0
	2015–2016	53,032.67	90,179.47	842,951.21	66,245.6
Madhya Pradesh	1999–2000	21,160.55	55,027.38	558,308.16	22,965.3
	2015–2016	27,221.73	66,155.64	1,142,943.68	39,128.2
Orissa	1999–2000	13,008.51	50,984.74	233,232.43	23,125.4
	2015–2016	27,054.72	64,612.18	918,258.66	35,127.74
Assam	1999–2000	38,124.49	39,210.88	203,289.41	48,577.7
	2015–2016	55,922.6	58,407.74	309,164.1	59,994.57
Uttar Pradesh	1999–2000	23,948.93	38,252.22	305,405.84	52,686.7
	2015–2016	35,136.32	54,449.7	931,256.76	66,729.42
Bihar	1999–2000	25,278.36	38,582.55	258,954.47	18,322.1
	2015–2016	48,520.54	75,498.98	308,522.39	29,221.4

Source: Authors' computation based on various databases.

Table 5.8 Difference in gross value added per worker between own account enterprises and establishment and its change over time

State	Year	OAEs	Establishment	Difference between OAE and establishments in 1999–2000 and 2015–2016	Difference in differences
Maharashtra	1999–2000	36,282.23	80,021.53	43,739.3	34,144.03
	2015–2016	52,808.68	130,692.01	77,883.33	
Haryana	1999–2000	39,892.7	68,431.23	28,538.53	3,424.25
	2015–2016	69,817.43	101,780.21	31,962.78	
Gujarat	1999–2000	35,271.92	53,420.38	18,148.46	117,941.32
	2015–2016	46,014.25	182,104.03	136,089.78	
Tamil Nadu	1999–2000	24,552.83	42,938.16	18,385.33	21,658.73
	2015–2016	44,671.03	84,715.09	40,044.06	
Kerala	1999–2000	40,968.31	60,128.36	19,160.05	33,847.73
	2015–2016	68,032.81	121,040.59	53,007.78	
Punjab	1999–2000	47,332.61	56,002.23	8,669.62	14,531.85
	2015–2016	63,863.34	87,064.81	23,201.47	
Karnataka	1999–2000	23,736.08	44,373.73	20,637.65	31,093.52
	2015–2016	49,779.66	101,510.83	51,731.17	
Andhra Pradesh	1999–2000	18,331.92	36,919.46	18,587.54	25,296.17
	2015–2016	35,508.76	79,392.47	43,883.71	
West Bengal	1999–2000	24,784.77	34,427.53	9,642.76	31,494.17
	2015–2016	51,827.8	92,964.73	41,136.93	
Rajasthan	1999–2000	33,775.13	48,492.61	14,717.48	22,429.32
	2015–2016	53,032.67	90,179.47	37,146.8	
Madhya Pradesh	1999–2000	21,160.55	55,027.38	33,866.83	5,067.08
	2015–2016	27,221.73	66,155.64	38,933.91	
Orissa	1999–2000	13,008.51	50,984.74	37,976.23	−418.77
	2015–2016	27,054.72	64,612.18	37,557.46	
Assam	1999–2000	38,124.49	39,210.88	1,086.39	1,398.75
	2015–2016	55,922.6	58,407.74	2,485.14	
Uttar Pradesh	1999–2000	23,948.93	38,252.22	14,303.29	5,010.09
	2015–2016	35,136.32	54,449.7	19,313.38	
Bihar	1999–2000	25,278.36	38,582.55	13,304.19	13,674.25
	2015–2016	48,520.54	75,498.98	26,978.44	

Source: Computed using the unit-level 55th and 73rd rounds of the Enterprise Survey (NSSO).

Going back to Table 5.7, we get certain additional (and very crucial) information. It is observed that for most states, GVA per worker is lower in OAEs compared to that of the agricultural sector.

OAEs are expected (hypothesized) to have a higher GVA per worker compared to that of the agricultural sector. This is because, for the past two decades, the agricultural sector has observed a decline in employment, and in OAEs (particularly for OAEs having one to two employees), employment has increased. Thus, we could think of a situation where the surplus labour of agriculture was moving towards the OAEs in search of a better income. However, Table 5.7 shows a different situation, where the agricultural population is migrating/diversifying towards the OAE segment despite the fact that the average income there is less than that of agriculture. This result signifies a possibility of a 'push effect' from agriculture to smaller-sized OAEs; the distressed surplus labour of agriculture is pushed towards the OAE segment. There may also be the possibility that workers are getting 'locked in' in the OAEs so that they are finding it difficult to get out of the sector. These aspects require further exploration.

Push effects from agriculture to the nonfarm sector may happen because of factors that are endogenous to agriculture (such as poor irrigation, lack of access to credit, higher cost of cultivation, inadequate market access, non-remunerative output price, etc.), or they may happen due to certain exogenous factors (such as climate change or a transformation in agriculture induced by the growth of another sector). While we deal with agriculture in detail in Chapter 6, at present, we focus more on nonfarm enterprises.

As far as OAEs are concerned, the locked-in status of employment in OAEs may arise if there exists an absence of access to credit or capital or a lack of certain skills among firms and employees of OAEs. Such inadequacies may obstruct the firms involved in the sector from aligning with the global circuit of capital or restrict the employees from leaving the sector.

While GVA per worker shows the present economic status, it sheds less light on the growth prospects of firms and their social implications. In order to look at this aspect, we have also computed a table on the additions to assets/capital stock per OAEs and establishments (Table 5.9). It can be seen that while there have been improvements in a net addition to

Table 5.9 Percentage of firms having net addition to capital stock Rs 5,000 and above at 2015–2016 prices

State	Year	OAEs	Establishment	Difference	Difference in differences
Maharashtra	1999–2000	3.73	9.04	5.31	2.99
	2015–2016	5.3	13.6	8.3	
Haryana	1999–2000	8.26	16.33	8.07	5.13
	2015–2016	7.4	20.6	13.2	
Gujarat	1999–2000	2.7	9.54	6.84	16.86
	2015–2016	6.4	30.1	23.7	
Tamil Nadu	1999–2000	2.33	7.86	5.53	0.27
	2015–2016	7.3	13.1	5.8	
Kerala	1999–2000	5.07	8.94	3.87	9.73
	2015–2016	11.8	25.4	13.6	
Punjab	1999–2000	2.27	8.64	6.37	2.33
	2015–2016	6.1	14.8	8.7	
Karnataka	1999–2000	1.23	6.1	4.87	7.63
	2015–2016	4.6	17.1	12.5	
Andhra Pradesh	1999–2000	1.6	8.3	6.7	1.2
	2015–2016	3.9	11.8	7.9	
West Bengal	1999–2000	0.86	5.43	4.57	10.13
	2015–2016	2.5	17.2	14.7	
Rajasthan	1999–2000	2.94	18.77	15.83	−3.43
	2015–2016	5	17.4	12.4	
Madhya Pradesh	1999–2000	1.34	7.71	6.37	4.03
	2015–2016	2.6	13	10.4	
Orissa	1999–2000	0.27	4.16	3.89	10.91
	2015–2016	2.8	17.6	14.8	
Assam	1999–2000	0.2	1.3	1.1	−0.5
	2015–2016	0.2	0.8	0.6	
Uttar Pradesh	1999–2000	2.05	10.14	8.09	7.21
	2015–2016	4.3	19.6	15.3	
Bihar	1999–2000	0.8	6.4	5.6	−1.1
	2015–2016	0.9	5.4	4.5	
India	1999–2000	1.91	8.37	6.46	5.34
	2015–2016	3.8	15.6	11.8	

Source: Computed using the unit-level 55th and 73rd rounds of the Enterprise Survey (NSSO).

assets for both types of enterprises, in the case of establishment, a larger percentage of firms are able to generate assets above 5,000 Indian rupees. It is also observed that the gap between OAEs and establishments is rising as well, which may well have implications for rural inequality in future. This, in a way, indicates the possibility of deepening dualism within the nonfarm sector and thereby corroborates our theoretical conjecture.

5.2 Employment generation in rural establishments and own account enterprises: Identification of factors causing its growth

Section 5.1 discussed in detail the transformation/changes that the rural Indian economy has undergone. Specifically, we have seen that the rural economy has experienced an expansion of the OAEs (the smaller units) as well as of the larger establishments simultaneously, and the gaps between these two sectors in terms of value addition and net investment have increased. Thus, we have identified a clear tendency for the spreading and deepening of the duality within the RNFE of India, especially the rural informal sector. Further, we have identified other forms of heterogeneities as well; thus, we have identified a deepening formal–informal dualism across rural India, too. In this section, we explore the factors determining such a dualism, that is, such simultaneous expansions of employment in both these sectors—OAE and Establishment—using an econometric model. Given the theoretical framework presented in Chapter 2, using regression, we specifically try to see whether or not an expansion of the formal sector causes an expansion of the modern and traditional segment in the rural nonfarm segment. There are other covariates, too, in our regression model. We now explain the model in greater detail.

Our econometric analysis is based on cross-sectional data. In the absence of compatible time-series data, inferences are drawn using cross-sectional econometric techniques. Specifically, our regression analysis explores the impact of variations of the explanatory variables across the NSSO defined regions on the size of different sectors (modern, traditional, and also unemployment). In this context, one should note that the NSSO categorizes India into many regions to facilitate its data collection. In most instances, these territories are smaller than states but larger than sub-state districts. Utilizing NSSO regions as a unit of analysis provides sufficient information about different covariates that can be used in regression, which may not be possible when we considered districts (since the number of individuals surveyed was much less). On the contrary, considering state as a unit of observation in cross-sectional analysis reduces the sample size to below thirty. Each NSSO region largely corresponds to an agro-climatic region within a state. For example, the state of Andhra Pradesh comprises three regions: Coastal Andhra Pradesh, South Western Andhra Pradesh, and Inland Andhra Pradesh. Geographically and agro-climatically, these exhibit distinct characteristics that also have an impact on the farm as well as the nonfarm sector.

In our analysis, the variable representing formal sector growth is one of the primary independent variables. It is regressed on different segments of the rural economy that has significant contributions to the workforce. We have considered five segments of the rural economy that the formal sector can impact. These are the modern nonfarm segment, traditional nonfarm segment, traditional agriculture, modern agriculture, and unemployment. Our regression analysis helps us in identifying the determinants of the size of these segments. It is essential to recognize that due to the presence of several equations, what we need is an estimation of a system of linear equations. Further, the dependent variable of one equation becomes an explanatory variable of another equation. In other words, we have the problem of endogeneity. Considering both these aspects, we have considered a three-stage least squares (3SLS) model for identifying the determinants of different rural sectors and unemployment.

5.2.1 The econometric model

The 3SLS approach was developed by Zellner and Theil (1962). It is a method of estimating a system of linear equations that consists of endogenous variables as regressors. The method is an application of the seemingly unrelated regression (SUR) model on a system of linear equation models estimated first using the two-stage least square approach. As expected, there are three stages in this method of estimation. The first stage consists of estimating the reduced form of all equations in the model.

In other words, it involves regressing each endogenous variable on all exogenous variables. In stage 2, the predicted values from the first stage are utilized to replace the endogenous variables in the structural equations. This step is similar to 2SLS. The third stage consists of estimating the transformed equations using a SUR model, which was introduced by Arnold Zellner for the estimation of multiple regression equations. In the SUR model, the error terms across the different equations are assumed as correlated. Correlations among equations provide additional information that is not available when one considers each equation in isolation, as is the case with ordinary least squares (OLS). The SUR model incorporates this additional information in parameter estimation via a generalized or a feasible generalized least squares approach.

A brief explanation of the 3SLS model is provided below.

Suppose the ith equation in the set of five equations is

$$y_i = X_i\beta_i + u_i, \qquad i = 1, 2, 3, 4, 5.$$

Where y_i in the present context is an 88×1 vector of observations on the dependent variable, X_i is a $88 \times k$ matrix[44] of observations on explanatory variables, β_i is a $k \times 1$ vector of coefficients; and u_i is the vector of disturbances. The initial steps include replacing all the endogenous explanatory variables by its instrument (using 2SLS) so that the disturbance term is uncorrelated with the explanatory variables. After replacing each endogenous variable by its instrument using 2SLS, one can now think of the following set of equations in matrix form, which do not have any endogenous explanatory variables:

$$\begin{pmatrix} y_1 \\ y_2 \\ \cdots \\ y_5 \end{pmatrix} = \begin{pmatrix} X_1 & \cdots & 0 \\ \vdots & \ddots & \vdots \\ 0 & \cdots & X_5 \end{pmatrix} \begin{pmatrix} \beta_1 \\ \beta_2 \\ \cdots \\ \beta_5 \end{pmatrix} + \begin{pmatrix} u_1 \\ u_2 \\ \cdots \\ u_5 \end{pmatrix}.$$

This can be written as $Y = X\beta + u$.

[44] There are eighty-eight NSSO regions under consideration.

The variance covariance matrix for u of this model is given by

$$\sum = E(uu') = \begin{pmatrix} E(u_1u_1') & \cdots & E(u_1u_5') \\ \vdots & \ddots & \vdots \\ E(u_5u_1') & \cdots & E(u_5u_5') \end{pmatrix}.$$

In the above matrix, each term in the principal diagonal is an 88 × 88 variance covariance matrix and each off-diagonal term is the contemporaneous covariance between disturbances from a pair of equations.

Assuming $E(u_iu_j') = \sigma_{ij}I$; $i, j = 1, 2, 3, 4, 5$; one can write the matrix of $E(uu')$ as

$$E(uu') = \begin{pmatrix} \sigma_{11}I & \sigma_{1M}I \\ \sigma_{M1}I & \sigma_{MM} \end{pmatrix} = \Sigma \otimes \mathrm{I} = \Psi.$$

In the formulation presented above, the symbol ⊗ denotes the Kronecker product operator. $\Sigma = (\sigma_{ij})$ is a positive definite symmetric matrix indicating absence of linear dependencies among the disturbances in the M equations.

If σ_{ij} is observable and Σ is known, the generalized least squares (GLS) approach can be used. The estimator of β using GLS is given by

$$\hat{\beta} = \left[X'\left(\Sigma^{-1} \otimes I_n\right)X\right]^{-1} X'\left(\Sigma^{-1} \otimes I_n\right)Y\cdot$$

However, since σ_{ij} is unobservable, Σ is unknown. Therefore, instead of GLS, the model is often estimated with the feasible generalized least squares (FGLS) method. Zellner and Theil, (1962) suggested a two-stage procedure in which the initial step involves running an ordinary least squares regression for each equation. The residuals from this regression are then utilized to estimate the components of the matrix S (as provided below).

$$\mathrm{S} = \begin{bmatrix} \hat{\sigma}_{11} I_n & \cdots & \hat{\sigma}_{1M} I_n \\ \vdots & \ddots & \vdots \\ \hat{\sigma}_{M1} I_n & \cdots & \hat{\sigma}_{MM} I_{Tn} \end{bmatrix}$$

where $\hat{\sigma}_{ij}$ is the estimator of σ_{ij}.

The FGLS estimator of β is

$$\hat{\beta}_F = \left[X'\left(S^{-1} \otimes I_n\right)X\right]^{-1} X'\left(S^{-1} \otimes I_n\right)Y \cdot$$

The variables selected for doing this analysis are explained in section 5.2.2. We additionally performed the Durbin–Wu–Hausman endogeneity test for the presence of endogeneity among other variables. However, the test showed absence of endogeneity.

5.2.2 Variables selected for the analysis

The model comprises five equations with five dependent variables, namely, rural modern nonfarm sector employment, rural traditional nonfarm sector employment, employment in the traditional farm sector, employment in the modern farm sector, and unemployment.

Employment in OAEs in rural areas of each NSSO region has been utilized as an indicator of the size of the rural traditional nonfarm sector for previously stated reasons. Individuals working in a household enterprise (self-employed) either as a worker, employer, helper, or unpaid family worker is considered as employed in the OAE employment category. Next, the regular salaried employment in proprietary or partnership enterprises in rural areas of each NSSO region is included for representing the modern rural sector. Enterprises hiring regular salaried employees naturally need higher investments, and they are expected to generate a surplus required for hiring workers. Both the above employment figures at the regional level were computed using the PLFS 2018–2019.

The third dependent variable denotes the traditional agricultural sector. We have included the number of marginal farmers to capture it. Farmers cultivating less than 1 hectare of land are classified as marginal farmers. Apart from this, we classify semi-medium, medium, and large farmers as modern farmers, specifically those who cultivate land over 2 hectares.

Marginal farmers are regarded as representatives of traditional agriculture, while large farmers are associated with modern agriculture for the following reasons.

The marginal farmers for cultivating smaller-sized land typically produce a low marketable surplus, resulting in fewer opportunities to engage with the formal sector. The formal sector typically engages with larger farms to use the benefits of economies of scale. Engaging in business with marginal farmers raises their transaction costs. Additionally, the formal sector may express interest in acquiring commercial or cash crops. Larger farmers typically cultivate multiple crops, including commercial varieties, and can therefore be classified as modern farmers. Data regarding the number of marginal farmers and that of modern farmers were obtained from the unit-level 77th round of the Situation Assessment Survey of Farmers data provided by the NSSO.

The dependent variable in the last equation is unemployment. Unemployment figures were computed from the PLFS 2018–2019. An equation on unemployment was kept in the analysis due to the fact that a push effect is expected to create unemployment as well. The variable unemployment was also used as a covariate in the regression equation having own account employment as the dependent variable to see whether regions characterized by high unemployment also increases own account employment or not. If the coefficient of unemployment is positive and significant, it would imply that the OAE employment is a residual employment.

Now let us consider the explanatory variables.

Our main covariate in the regression analysis is the formal sector employment in a given NSSO region, which is again computed using PLFS data. Higher formal sector employment in a region implies higher formal sector growth. Individuals working in government, public-sector enterprises, autonomous bodies, public/private limited companies, co-operative societies, or in a trust or other non-profit institution were considered as employed in the formal sector.

The other covariates used in the regression analysis are explained below.

Since the size of the NSSO region may vary in terms of population, the size of the workforce was used as an explanatory variable in all the equations under consideration.

The third variable that is considered in all the regression equations (apart from workforce and formal sector employment) is incidence of indebtedness. Incidence of indebtedness, defined as the percentage of households having outstanding loans at a given date (here 30 June 2018) is used to capture the access to credit of a region. Higher access to credit is expected to augment the employment of both farm and nonfarm sectors. Further, it is expected to also reduce unemployment. The data was computed using the 77th round of the All India Debt and Investment Survey of the NSSO.

Since a section of workers may require skill in the modern nonfarm sector, we have included the number of individuals who received any vocational/technical training in a region as one of the explanatory variables in the regression that identifies the determinants of the size of the rural modern nonfarm sector. An individual has been considered as a trained individual if they have received a formal or informal vocational or technical training. Even individuals who have received training from family, through self-learning, or getting training while on the job or any other means have also been considered as a trained individual. The variable is also incorporated into the regression equation determining unemployment, since an expansion of the skilled workforce is likely to reduce unemployment.

We have also captured the farm nonfarm interlinkage in our regression model. A large section of literature argues that expansion of the farm sector augments the nonfarm sector. To capture its impact, we have included the volume of marketable surplus generated by marginal farmers and volume of marketable surplus generated by medium and large farmers as covariates in the model. A surplus by marginal farmers is expected to increase demand for the traditional sector goods. On the other hand, large farmers are expected to have linkage with the modern nonfarm sector. Marketable surplus is computed by the sale value of the farmers. In the regression equations with regular salaried employment and OAE employment as dependent variables, we have also included the Crop Diversification Index as a regressor. Simpson's Index (defined as 1-H, Herfindahl Index) is used to compute the Crop Diversification Index (CDI). Literature suggests that crop diversification augments the modern sector and reduces the size of the traditional nonfarm sector. The CDI was computed using the 77th round of SAS data.

Apart from this, the nonfarm sector (i.e. OAE and regular salaried) was included as the covariates in the farm sector equations.

The summary of the variables is presented in Tables 5.10 and5.11 below. This is followed by the regression results and discussion.

Table 5.10 Definition of the variables used in the regression model

Variable	Definition
Regular salaried	Regular salaried employment in proprietary or partnership enterprises in rural areas of each NSSO region
OAE employment	Total employment in OAEs in rural areas of each NSSO region
Marginal farmer	Number of farmers cultivating land below 1 hectare in rural areas of each region
Large and medium farmers	Number of farmers cultivating land above 2 hectares
Unemployment	Number of unemployed individuals according to UPSS
Rural workforce	Size of the workforce in each NSSO region
Rural formal	Employment in government, public sector enterprises, autonomous bodies, public/private limited company, cooperative societies, or in a trust or other non-profit institution
Rural vocational	Number of individuals with vocational or technical training
IOI	Incidence of indebtedness
Medium large sale	Total volume of sales by farmers cultivating land above 2 hectares
Marginal sale	Total volume of sales by farmers cultivating land below 1 hectare
CDI	Crop Diversification Index
Area irrigated	Area irrigated in each NSSO region
Area unirrigated	Area unirrigated
Sale per land	Ratio of total sales done by farmers and total cultivated land

Note: UPSS—Usual Principal and Subsidiary Status

Source: Authors' computation. .

Table 5.11 Mean standard deviation and maximum and minimum values of the variables used in the regression analysis

Variable	Observations	Mean	Std. Dev.	Minimum	Maximum
Regular salaried	89	156,263.4	150,851.4	0	734,388.4
OAE employment	89	426,510.8	433,195.0	4.485	2,464,671
Marginal farmer	88	464,598.9	744,879.2	8	5,507,764
Large and medium farmer	88	256,470.1	273,958.5	0	1,277,797
Unemployment	89	160,672.4	202,564	0	1,397,981
Rural workforce	89	3,181,882	2,830,330	4,551.827	1.57E + 07
Rural formal	89	258,738.3	218,201.5	1,288.783	1,452,541
Rural vocational	89	528,199	811,053.8	0	5,123,727
IOI	88	0.31183	0.160483	0.030757	0.696535
Medium large sale in lakhs	87	262,743.8	302,505.2	6.6475	1,465,661
Marginal sale in lakhs	88	177,557.7	193,919.8	9.30656	1,213,395
CDI	89	0.514181	0.26843	0	0.907951
Area irrigated	88	1,130,165	1,346,285	0	7,595,306
Area unirrigated	88	1,014,335	1,401,596	0	7,258,548
Sale per land	88	27,061.82	20,633.9	3,674.382	155,844.6

Source: PLFS 2018–2019, Situation Assessment Survey of Farmers (NSSO), All India Debt and Investment Survey (NSSO).

5.3 Results

Table 5.12 above presents the regression results. Model 1 displays the complete regression analysis, in which all the covariates are considered simultaneously. Model 2 illustrates the robustness of the regression results, specifically the regression equations pertaining to the nonfarm sector. Due to identification problems, we could not drop variables from other equations while we checked for robustness.

Our results show that formal sector employment augments the growth of modern nonfarm sector employment and unemployment. Both models 1 and 2 yield this conclusion. Thus, the formal sector generates both push and pull effects.

Table 5.12 Three-stage least squares regression model identifying the factors affecting employment across various rural sectors and the overall rural unemployment

Regression equation	Model 1					
	Observation	Parameters	RMSE	R Sq	Chi sq	P
Regular salaried	87	7	89,406.1	0.64	165.27	0
OAE employment	87	7	144,199.3	0.89	727.03	0
Marginal farmer	87	7	946,724.3	–0.62	125.4	0
Large and medium farmer	87	7	243,868.6	0.199	480.22	0
Unemployment	87	5	107,958.4	0.722	223.03	0
	Model 2					
Regular salaried	88	2	89,735.04	0.64	157.77	0
OAE employment	88	2	187,355	0.81	378.06	0
Marginal farmer	88	7	572,069.1	0.40	345.53	0
Large and medium farmer	88	7	170,744.5	0.607	1,525.65	0
Unemployment	88	4	109,229.8	0.708	218.41	0

	Model 1				Model 2			
Variables	**Coefficients**	**S.E.**	**Z**	**P > Z**	**Coefficients**	**S.E.**	**Z**	**P >Z**
Equation 1 Regular salaried								
Rural workforce	0.030	0.006	5.41	0	0.037	0.004	9.14	0
Rural formal	0.138	0.054	2.57	0.01	0.131	0.052	2.52	0.012
Rural vocational	−0.005	0.006	−0.76	0.448	–	–	–	–
IOI	58,433.4	71,731.9	0.81	0.415	–	–	–	–
Medium large sale	0.055	0.032	1.69	0.092	–	–	–	–
Marginal sale	0.051	0.056	0.91	0.361	–	–	–	–
CDI	−31,148.8	32,501.1	−0.96	0.338	–	–	–	–
Constant	2,738.4	25,129.03	0.11	0.913	6,335.063	16,029.77	0.4	0.693
Equation 2 OAE employment								
Rural workforce	0.072	0.018	4.05	0	0.136	0.008	16.28	0
Rural formal	0.083	0.095	0.87	0.382	0.052	0.108	0.48	0.633
IOI	172,389.8	113,492	1.52	0.129	–	–	–	–
Medium large sale	−0.168	0.063	−2.66	0.008	–	–	–	–
Marginal sale	0.654	0.136	4.81	0	–	–	–	–
CDI	−145,048.2	61,847.4	−2.35	0.019	–	–	–	–
Unemployment rural	0.507	0.251	2.02	0.043	–	–	–	–
Constant	44,384.5	41,650.6	1.07	0.287	−19,671.5	33,468.1	−0.59	0.557

(continued)

Table 5.12 Continued

	Model 1				Model 2			
Variables	Coefficients	S.E.	Z	P > Z	Coefficients	S.E.	Z	P >Z
Equation 3 Marginal farmers								
Rural workforce	0.208	0.184	1.13	0.258	−0.10	0.26	−0.38	0.706
Rural formal	0.258	0.458	0.56	0.574	−0.78	0.54	−1.44	0.151
Area irrigated	0.142	0.058	2.44	0.015	0.06	0.11	0.53	0.596
Area unirrigated	−0.084	0.067	−1.25	0.211	−0.07	0.11	−0.63	0.527
IOI	−11,730.6	549,332.9	−0.02	0.983	−742,845.2	373,625.5	−1.99	0.047
OAE employment	2.251	0.974	2.31	0.021	2.76	2.08	1.33	0.185
Regular salaried	−8.511	2.378	−3.58	0	−0.82	3.71	−0.22	0.825
Constant	32,428.8	164,988	0.2	0.844	161,153.7	100,687.5	1.6	0.109
Equation 4 Large medium								
Rural workforce	−0.031	0.045	−0.69	0.49	0.02	0.05	0.29	0.768
Rural formal	−0.245	0.109	−2.24	0.025	−0.08	0.11	−0.75	0.453
Area irrigated	0.101	0.013	7.59	0	0.12	0.02	5.53	0
Area unirrigated	0.133	0.016	8.21	0	0.14	0.02	6.54	0
IOI	−62054.290	135,348.9	−0.46	0.647	65,488.01	73,678.8	0.89	0.374
OAE employment	−0.440	0.247	−1.78	0.075	−0.57	0.41	−1.4	0.163
Regular salaried	2.365	0.549	4.31	0	1.27	0.73	1.75	0.08
Constant	6,258.03	40,870.7	0.15	0.878	−23,240.2	22,832.5	−1.02	0.309

Equation 6 Unemployment rural								
Rural workforce	0.061	0.005	11.6	0	0.06	0.01	11.23	0
Rural formal	0.157	0.064	2.46	0.014	0.15	0.06	2.42	0.016
Rural vocational	−0.054	0.014	−3.82	0	−0.05	0.01	−3.75	0
IOI	−114,810.1	77,854.8	−1.47	0.14	–	–	–	–
Sale per land	1.016	0.544	1.87	0.062	0.14	0.47	0.29	0.774
Constant	−36,406.7	31,274.1	−1.16	0.244	−39,430.3	23,687.8	−1.66	0.096

The impact of the formal sector on traditional employment is not statistically significant; however, the regression results show that higher unemployment augments the OAE sector. On the one hand, this implies a disjointed relationship between the formal and traditional sectors. The traditional nonfarm sector may be considered a residual sector that expands with an increase in rural unemployment. Even dropping the endogenous covariates in the three SLS regressions or performing an OLS regression yields the aforementioned results.

There are other important results, too. The sale volume of farmers cultivating land above 2 hectares positively influences employment generation in the modern nonfarm sector. On the other hand, the sales volume of marginal farmers has a positive impact on the traditional nonfarm sector. The sales volume of relatively larger farmers has a negative impact on OAE employment. The above two results may be due to the possibility of demand-side linkages between marginal farmers and OAEs.

The results show that crop diversification reduces OAE employment. However, its impact on the modern sector is negligible.

Results from the agricultural sector show that as the formal sector expands, the number of larger farmers declines. This may happen due to a reduction in land availability in regions with dominance of the formal sector. The results show that the number of farmers above 2 hectares increases with an increase in both irrigated and unirrigated land. We observe a decrease in the number of marginal farmers as unirrigated land increases. It is possible that unirrigated land increases production costs, which may make production by marginal farmers unviable.

Similar to the regression equation for nonfarm sectors, the regression equation for the farm sector also shows a strong linkage with the nonfarm sector. As anticipated, the employment of OAE negatively impacts large and medium farmers, whereas it positively impacts the traditional farm sector. Conversely, the modern nonfarm sector enhances modern farming while diminishing traditional farming.

The regression equation on unemployment displays interesting results as well. As already stated, unemployment increases with formal sector expansion. It is possible that a much larger decrease in informal employment may accompany the increase in formal sector employment. One also finds that unemployment decreases with the expansion of vocational and technical training in a region. It is observed that unemployment increases with agricultural productivity. Higher sales per hectare in a region are known to increase unemployment. This may be due to increased farm mechanization.

The coefficient for the variable incidence of indebtedness is found to be statistically insignificant (about 10 per cent) in the equations for the modern nonfarm sector and the farm sectors (both marginal and large). Nevertheless, it substantially decreases unemployment and enhances job creation in the OAE sector. Existing research indicates that the credit flow to the agricultural sector in most regions of India has less disparity due to priority sector lending norms of the Reserve Bank of India. Hence, the disparities in regional credit access are mostly due to variations in credit availability for the non-agricultural sector. Moreover, in the nonfarm sector, access to credit mostly affects the lower strata, such as OAEs or the unemployed; larger nonfarm entities are expected to possess sufficient savings to finance their operations.

5.4 Conclusion

In this chapter, we have tried to understand the nature of the transformation that the rural economy of India has experienced over the past two decades. Our focus was primarily on the RNFS. We found that overall agricultural employment has declined and that of the nonfarm sector has expanded. The chapter shows that the expansion of nonfarm employment has happened in two definite directions.

Thus, we have observed a simultaneous expansion of the modern nonfarm sector and of the traditional nonfarm economy. We have also looked into the per capita output/income and investments in both these sectors and found that though both the sectors have observed an expansion in output and investment, the gap between traditional and modern nonfarm sectors (in terms of per capita output/income) has been increasing over the years. Furthermore, the modern nonfarm sector is able to accumulate more than its traditional counterpart. Thus, we observe a phenomenon of the proliferation of a dual structure in the rural economy of India. Finally, we could also show that, tentatively, this dualism has been induced by the expansion of the formal sector. While there might have been a pull effect on the modern part of the nonfarm economy originating from an expansion of the formal sector and associated activities, the traditional nonfarm sector and unemployment experience a push effect, and thereby it expands. More precisely, we could provide some empirical support in favour of the following propositions:

1. There is a movement and/or diversification of the workforce away from traditional agriculture into both the advanced segments of agriculture and the advanced and especially petty segments of the RNFE.
2. The urban–rural modern formal sector triggers both the push and pull effects (working on the traditional agricultural workforce) and thereby induces this dual movement/diversification process.
3. The formal sector expansion not only boosts this spread of dualism but also deepens the divide between the modern and traditional agricultural segments, especially within the RNFS, across its petty-modern sections (by increasing the intra-sectoral productivity gaps).

The regression analysis highlighted some useful linkages existing between farm sector, nonfarm sector, and unemployment. We observed that the traditional farm sector is associated with the traditional nonfarm sector and unemployment, while the modern farm sector is associated with the modern nonfarm sector.

A.5 Appendix

A.5.1 Brief notes on the data sets used in this chapter

1. The Employment and Unemployment Survey was a comprehensive survey on employment and unemployment related indicators. The first survey was in 1972, and thereafter it was conducted quinquennially (every five years). The last round of employment and unemployment was carried out in 2011–2012 (68th round). Thereafter it was replaced by the PLFS.
2. The PLFS is conducted by the NSSO in India, and it was launched in April 2017. The objective of this survey is to provide annual data on employment and unemployment and other related factors. The

survey is conducted on more than 1 lakh households, and information is collected regarding each individual member of the households. In this survey, rural and urban areas have different sampling design. A rotational panel sampling design has been used in urban areas. In this rotational panel scheme, each selected household in urban areas is visited four times, in the beginning with a 'First Visit Schedule' and thrice periodically later with a 'Revisit Schedule'. In urban areas, samples for a panel within each stratum were drawn in the form of two independent subsamples. The scheme of rotation ensures that 75 per cent of the first-stage sampling units (FSUs) are matched between two consecutive visits. There was no revisit in the rural samples. For rural areas, samples for a stratum/substratum were drawn randomly in the form of two independent subsamples. For rural areas, in each quarter of the survey period, 25 per cent of the FSUs of annual allocation were covered.

3. The All India Debt and Investment Survey (AIDIS) is conducted by the National Sample Survey Office. The data set is collected once every ten years. The AIDIS has been conducted six times so far, starting from 1971–1972. The latest survey was carried out during the period January–December 2019 as part of the 77th round of the NSS. The data set provides detailed information on household credit, its terms and conditions, and asset accumulation.
4. We have also used Situation Assessment Survey (SAS) of Farmers data. The Situation Assessment Survey of Agricultural Households provides comprehensive data on various aspects of agricultural households, including land holdings, livestock ownership, income, productive assets, farming practices, and indebtedness. To date, there have been three rounds of the survey, starting from 2002–2003 onwards. The latest survey was conducted in 2019.

6

The State of the Agricultural Sector and Its Implications for the Rural Nonfarm Economy

In our earlier chapters, we have shown that there is migration and/or diversification of the workforce away from traditional agriculture into both the advanced segments of agriculture and the advanced and especially petty segments of the rural nonfarm economy. This is particularly true in the case of India, along with some other countries of the Global South. Further, we have claimed that the urban–rural (modern) formal sector triggers both the push and pull effects (working on the traditional agricultural workforce) and thereby induces this dual migration/diversification process.

Now, the analysis of this movement of the workforce towards the different segments of agriculture and non-agriculture remains grossly incomplete if we do not clearly understand the source(s) of these diversifications or migrations. Stated otherwise, the analysis of the source gives us an idea about the nature of this movement: whether it is push-driven or pull-induced. Some heuristic understanding could be developed by looking at the pattern of the diversifying/migrating population, but a comprehensive picture could only be derived through a multi-pronged study: studying the movement, studying the destination, and, of course, studying the source. Given that, as in the present context, the source of migration/diversification is the traditional agricultural segment, an analysis of this crucial part of the economy becomes essential.

We need to understand the structure and dynamics of the traditional agricultural subsector of India and, most importantly, to identify the factors that are responsible for the specific pattern of changes that are happening in this traditional agricultural segment. We know, and we have

The Nonfarm Economy. Manojit Bhattacharjee, Saumya Chakrabarti, and Meenakshi Rajeev,
Oxford University Press.
DOI: 10.1093/9780198972013.003.0006

also touched on this in our earlier chapters, that Indian agriculture is reeling under an acute crisis. Now, our first question is whether and how this crisis is related to the movement of the workforce away from this sector; whether and how this crisis could be a cause of this migration/diversification of labour. Second, we ask the crucial question of whether and how this agrarian crisis is related to the nature and dynamics of the rest of the Indian economy; whether and how the very nature and dynamics of growth of the modern formal sector could cause distress in traditional agriculture. With these issues in mind, we now enter into the analysis of Indian agriculture.

As far as the Indian agricultural sector is concerned, a substantial transformation has been observed over the past few decades. Akin to the experiences of the developed world, with the growth of the economy, India's agricultural sector observed a decline in its share in the gross domestic product. For instance, the farm sector had a share of around 41 per cent of the gross domestic product (GDP) in 1972–1973, but by 2011–2012, it had come down to 14 per cent. However, this structural shift (as observed in the case of output) was not visible in the employment pattern. While, with the growth of the economy, there was a significant decline in the employment share of the agricultural sector, the decline was not proportional to the decline observed in the sectoral output share. Recent data shows that the sector still employs 59 per cent of India's rural population and 44 per cent on aggregate (Periodic Labour Force Survey (PLFS), 2017–2018). The lack of association between sectoral employment and income is one crucial problem that the Indian economy is experiencing, and a large body of literature has paid attention to this issue (Bardhan, 2010; Chowdhury, 2011; Binswanger-Mkhize, 2013).

However, it is important to note that academic discourse has not paid much attention to a related issue. As observed in Chapter 4, in recent years, the decline in farm sector employment (both in absolute and relative terms) has been accompanied by an increase in jobs in two distinct sectors of the nonfarm economy, namely, the modern rural enterprises (such as larger size establishments) and own account enterprises. It is worth noting that, among these enterprises, the latter sector, on average, generates less value added per worker than agriculture (see Table 5.7). This means that a part of the nonfarm employment that has grown in recent years is made up of a sizeable portion of the workforce displaced/ diversified from agriculture, which was generating a higher value addition in agriculture than in its present activity.

While workforce movement from low productive sectors to higher productivity (from agriculture to the modern nonfarm industry) is a common phenomenon, the opposite (i.e. movement of workers from a higher value-added sector such as agriculture to a less remunerative sector, say nonfarm self-employment) is a bit unusual. Even if we assume that this is done to maximize household income by adding some extra cash flow, not hampering the original activities (i.e. essentially, an employment diversification rather than a movement away from the age-old professions altogether), this obviously marks an inherent phenomenon of distress. Stated otherwise, such movements primarily happen if there are push factors operating in traditional agriculture. Since the agricultural sector of India is observing both the push- and pull-driven outflow of the workforce (to both the modern and traditional nonfarm segments) simultaneously, it is worth exploring the underlying causes. The theoretical framework presented in Chapter 2 considers the expansion of the formal sector as an important reason behind the outmigration of the workforce from agriculture towards both traditional and modern nonfarm sectors. Our objective in this chapter is to understand this movement of workers in greater detail. This is because Chapter 5 relates the growing duality within the nonfarm sector to the movement of workers from the farm sector.

We specifically address two issues here. First, we understand the reasons behind falling agricultural employment and its implications for other rural sectors. We also explore the role of formal sector expansion in the overall employment dynamics in rural India (as stated above).

Given this background, the chapter is subdivided into the following sections. We start in section 6.1 by focusing on the changing composition of employment within the agricultural sector to identify the activities that are reducing within agriculture over time. Section 6.2 then explore the reasons behind the transitions happening in agriculture. After this, section 6.3 discusses the implications of the changes on the rural nonfarm sector. Sections 6.4 and 6.5 contains a crucial discussion on the role of the formal sector in inducing this change. Finally, section 6.6 ends with a conclusion.

6.1 Understanding the composition of agricultural employment

The agricultural sector in most states of India has observed a decline in employment both in absolute terms and in terms of the share of individuals engaged in the sector vis-à-vis that of other sectors. In order to understand this declining trend, we have first tried to explore the employment subcategories that are declining within agriculture.

Table 6.1 illustrates the changing nature of employment within the agricultural sector. The table provides certain important insights into falling agricultural employment. In Table 6.1, we have segregated rural employment into cultivators, agricultural workers, and plantation workers.[45] The figures are in percentage terms, and the residual employment, which has not been shown, indicates employment in the nonfarm sector. The table shows that between 2001 and 2011, there has been an increase in the share of agricultural workers and a fall in the number of cultivators (see also Gupta, 2016). For example, while, in 2001, around 43 per cent of workers were engaged in the agricultural sector as cultivators, this reduced to around 36 per cent in 2011. During the same period, the share of agricultural workers in total rural employment increased from 26.65 to 33.06 per cent.

One gets a similar picture while exploring how the source of income of households engaged in the farm sector has changed over the years (Table 6.2). It can be seen that even within a farm household, the share of wage income has increased and income from cultivation has reduced (Table 6.2). For instance, the share of income from cultivation for an average farm household declined from 47.95 per cent in 2012–2013 to 37.17 per cent in 2019–2020. During the same period, the share of wage income increased from around 32 per cent to 40 per cent. This means that more and more members of farm households are engaging in wage activities (in both farm and nonfarm sectors) by reducing engagement in cultivation.

It seems that the reduction in agricultural employment, which is stated in our previous chapters, is happening primarily because of the fall in the

[45] Only main workers were considered, that is, workers who were employed for more than six months in a year.

Table 6.1 Share of cultivators, agricultural workers, and plantation workers in total workers in the age group (15–59) in India

Age group	2001				2011			
	Cultivators	Agricultural workers	Plantation and livestock	Total	Cultivators	Agricultural workers	Plantation and livestock	Total
15–19	37.08	35.05	4.2	100	27.38	44.3	2.45	100
20–24	40.11	28.8	3.61	100	30.66	37.01	2.09	100
25–29	40.14	27.47	3.61	100	32.27	33.58	2.21	100
30–34	40.98	26.78	3.75	100	34.5	32.45	2.33	100
35–39	42.23	26.4	3.93	100	36.38	32.18	2.55	100
40–49	45.61	24.36	3.98	100	39.81	30.96	2.85	100
50–59	50.64	22.31	3.6	100	44.11	29.3	2.98	100
Total	**42.87**	**26.65**	**3.8**	**100**	**36.17**	**33.06**	**2.54**	**100**

Note: The residual employment share (i.e. the gap between total employment and agricultural employment share) is the employment share of the nonfarm sector (not shown here).

Source: Computed using census data (2001) and (2011).

Table 6.2 Share of different sources in farm household's average income for each size class of land (ha)

	Land size	Wage income	Cultivation	Animals	Business	Total income
2012–2013	< 0.01	63.63	0.66	25.89	9.80	100
	0.01–0.40	57.47	16.55	14.96	11.05	100
	0.41–1.00	38.33	40.88	11.99	8.81	100
	1.01–2.00	23.52	57.28	11.13	8.07	100
	2.01–4.00	15.44	68.58	10.82	5.16	100
	4.01–10.00	10.34	77.62	7.64	4.38	100
	10.00 +	3.17	86.22	6.34	4.28	100
	All sizes	32.23	47.95	11.87	7.97	100
2015–2016	< 0.01	57.43	14.81	18.60	9.16	100
	0.01–0.40	59.70	12.99	15.45	11.86	100
	0.41–1.00	45.58	31.31	15.58	7.54	100
	1.01–2.00	31.86	46.03	16.12	6.00	100
	2.01–4.00	21.59	57.39	15.52	5.50	100
	4.01–10.00	15.10	69.44	12.20	3.26	100
	10.00 +	6.49	71.76	18.88	2.87	100
	All sizes	39.76	37.17	15.48	7.58	100

Source: Computed using the 70th and 77th rounds of the NSSO Situation Assessment Survey of Farmer's data.

number of cultivators.[46] In other words, the expansion of nonfarm employment is happening most probably because of the movement of cultivators to nonfarm activities and may not be due to the movement of the causal workers, as one generally presumes.

Several questions arise in this context.

1. Why is there a reduction in the share of cultivators and not agricultural workers?
2. If the number of agricultural workers is rising, how are they getting accommodated within agriculture when there is a fall in the number of cultivators, given that the sector also faces the constraint of limited resources, primarily land?

[46] Decline in number of cultivators here means that cultivation is no longer a major activity for the shifted individuals.

3. Does the formal or urban sector have any role in these processes of change in the agricultural sector of India, and does it thereby affect the phenomenon of the proliferation of the rural nonfarm sector as well (as the theoretical framework introduced in Chapter 2 presumes)?

In this chapter, we try to provide answers to these questions.

6.2 The distress of cultivators: Possible causes

One of the factors that may change the composition of employment within agriculture is demography. One should note that owing to demographic changes, between 2001 and 2011, individuals in the younger age group have gone up proportionately more than that of individuals in the older age groups in India. Since, during the same period, additional lands were also not brought under cultivation (Table 6.3), one can expect that the younger workers have mostly joined the workforce as workers and not cultivators. Table 6.1 also supports this. More precisely, when we compare the share of cultivators across different age groups, it is observed that the decline in the share of cultivators is more among younger age groups as compared to that of older age groups (Table 6.1). Thus, demographic changes, to some extent, explain the reduction in the share of cultivators vis-à-vis agricultural workers.

Interestingly, however, not only has the number of cultivators declined in relative terms vis-à-vis agricultural workers, but also there is an absolute fall in the number of cultivators. Census data shows that the number of cultivators declined from 87.29 million to 78.39 million between 2001 and 2011. This happened in spite of the fragmentation of agricultural land holdings and a natural phenomenon of an increasing number of cultivators[47] owing to an increase in population and division

[47] The Food and Agricultural Organization (FAO, 1995) defines an agricultural operational holding as 'all land which is used wholly or partly for agricultural production and is operated as one technical unit by one person alone or with others without regard to title, legal form, size or location'. The concept of agricultural operational holdings that has been adopted in India includes those holdings that are operating only agricultural activities and are not occupied exclusively for livestock, poultry, and fishing activities.

Table 6.3 Operated area under agriculture according to the size of land holdings

Sl.	Size of groups	Operated area (in '000 ha)									
		1970–1971	1976–1977	1980–1981	1985–1986	1990–1991	1995–1996	2000–2001*	2005–2006*	2010–2011	2015–2016
1	Marginal (0–1ha)	14,599	17,509	19,735	22,042	24,894	28,121	29,814	32,026	35,908	37,923
2	Small (1–2 ha)	19,282	20,905	23,169	25,708	28,827	30,722	32,139	33,101	35,244	36,151
3	Semi-medium (2–4 ha)	29,999	32,428	34,645	36,666	38,375	38,953	38,193	37,898	37,705	37,619
4	Medium 4–10 ha	48,234	49,628	48,543	47,144	44,752	41,398	38,217	36,583	33,828	31,810
5	Large (10 +)	50,064	42,873	37,705	33,002	28,659	24,160	21,072	18,715	16,907	14,314
	All sizes	162,178	163,343	163,797	164,562	165,507	163,354	159,435	158,323	159,592	**157,817**

Source: Computed from the Agricultural Census (2015–2016).

arising from the inheritance of the paternal property (Niroula and Thapa, 2005).[48]

There are a number of reasons that can cause this. First, the total operational holding or land area used for agricultural activities has reduced in India from 163.35 million hectares in 1995–1996 to 157.82 million hectares in 2015–2016. The All India Report on Agriculture Census (2015–2016) considers the utilization of agricultural land for urbanization and non-agricultural uses such as housing, industry, and infrastructure as the main reasons behind the reduction in operated holdings. The recent changes in the Land Acquisition Act might have accentuated the problem further (Hoda, 2018).[49]

It is important to note that the Indian Parliament passed a radical Act in 2013 pertaining to land acquisition (Hoda, 2018). The Right to Fair Compensation and Transparency in Land Acquisition, Rehabilitation and Resettlement Act (LARR) 2013 replaced the colonial Land Acquisition Act of 1894, and it put an end to forcible acquisitions. The LARR (2013) increased the compensation of the landowners and had provisions for resettling the displaced families. The Act also granted greater decision-making powers to the Gram Sabhas (village councils) in land acquisition. However, this Act was diluted soon after, through an ordinance, following a change in government at the centre following the elections in 2014. The new ordinance allowed the government to acquire land for defence, rural infrastructure, affordable housing, and industrial projects without conducting a social impact assessment and taking consent. The ordinance (though it could not be passed in the Upper House of Parliament) paved the way for several individual states to implement their own Acts by replicating the Ordinance. This is because Article 254(2) of the Indian Constitution allows the states to pass legislation on

[48] Table A.6.1 shows the number of holdings across different size groups and its change over time. It is observed from the table that there has been an increase in the number of land holdings from 119.9 million in 2001 to 138.3 million in 2011 (see also Table 5.2) at the aggregated level. Decrease in number of cultivators, even in the presence of land fragmentation, means that the actual exodus of cultivators to other activities is higher than the decrease in the number of cultivators, as observed in the data on employment.

[49] This issue is extremely important, as it is, in a way, related to our third question, as above, that is, the role of modern sector expansion and urbanization in inducing an expansion of the rural nonfarm sector.

subjects provided in the concurrent list.[50] As per media reports, forcible acquisition of land and converting land from agriculture to other activities have increased following these changes.[51] Obviously, this will have an impact on the number of cultivators and the average size of the operational holdings they cultivate.

The second reason behind the fall in the number of cultivators could be a decline in the size of land holdings per cultivator. This might have happened owing to a decline in land used for agricultural activities and the distribution of paternal property among descendants. Table 6.4, in this context, provides information on the average size of land holdings across different size groups of farmers. It can be seen that the average size of land holdings in India has reduced in the aggregate and also across all size groups. In fact, when we compare the number of holders across different size groups of land holdings (see Table A.6.1 in the Appendix), it is observed that for medium and large farmers, the number of holdings has reduced, while for the marginal and small farmers, it has increased considerably. Not much change is observed for semi-medium farmers.

It is possible that the reduction in the size of land holdings accompanied by an increase in the number of cultivators in the marginal farmers' group has caused unviable-sized land holdings for many cultivators. In fact, a large number of studies have also considered unviable-sized holdings as the prime reason behind the crisis in agriculture (Nadkarni, 2018, 2022). Sharma and Malik (2021) provide a detailed account of the proliferation of holdings of lower-sized farm categories. They pointed out that between 1982 and 2013, the average size of land holdings below half a hectare and below one hectare decreased continuously for a majority of the states in India, such as Assam, Bihar, Jammu and Kashmir, Kerala, Odisha, Uttar Pradesh, and West Bengal. For other states, the average size of holdings up to half a hectare has remained unchanged or has registered a marginal increase. They also found that the average size of landholdings for holdings below half a hectare is 0.06 ha in Punjab and around 0.26 ha in Karnataka and Maharashtra.

[50] For instance, Andhra Pradesh, Maharashtra, Gujarat, Haryana Tamil Nadu, and Telangana have already made the amendments in the LARR Act 2013 and, thus, can now acquire land in their respective states without consent and social impact assessment requirements.

[51] One can understand the extent of land conversion from traditional uses to commercial purposes from one of the disclosures of the Indian Government to Parliament in which the government reported that nearly 60,000 hectares of forest land have been diverted for commercial purposes over the past three years (News18, 2024).

Table 6.4 Average size of land holdings according to size class

Size groups	**Average (in ha)**									
	1970–1971	**1976–1977**	**1980–1981**	**1985–1986**	**1990–1991**	**1995–1996**	**2000–2001***	**2005–2006***	**2010–2011**	**2015–2016**
Marginal (0–1 ha)	0.40	0.39	0.39	0.39	0.39	0.40	0.40	0.38	0.39	0.38
Small (1–2 ha)	1.44	1.42	1.44	1.43	1.43	1.42	1.42	1.38	1.42	1.40
Semi-medium (2–4 ha)	2.81	2.78	2.78	2.77	2.76	2.73	2.72	2.68	2.71	2.69
Medium 4–10 ha	6.08	6.04	6.02	5.96	5.90	5.84	5.81	5.74	5.76	5.72
Large (10 +)	18.10	17.57	17.41	17.21	17.33	17.20	17.12	17.08	17.38	17.07
All sizes	2.28	2.00	1.84	1.69	1.55	1.41	1.33	1.23	1.15	1.08

Source: Computed from the Agricultural Census (2015–2016).

6.3 The distress of cultivators: Possible effects

Extremely small-sized land holdings are considered unviable.[52] This is because smaller-sized land holdings may not produce the output required for the sustenance of a household. Apart from the inability to produce apt quantities, smaller-sized holdings also face a higher (average) cost for procuring inputs for agricultural production. The United Nations Development Programme (UNDP, 2006), in its *Human development report*, for instance, envisaged an erosion of entitlements to water for small farmers due to the presence of powerful constituencies over time. In fact, the report states that such phenomena are indeed happening in water-stressed districts of India, where wealthy farmers are crowding out smallholders by using irrigation pumps and extracting water for an entire day. Such factors evidently push up the cost of accessing water for smaller farmers.

To gain a glimpse of the cost of cultivation, we have computed a table on the average monthly expenses incurred by households for producing crops according to their size class (Table 6.5). In the table, the lowest size class possesses a land holding that is 100 times lower than the wealthiest category of cultivators. However, if we compare the monthly expenditure on different items, it can be seen that the cost borne per unit of land is much higher for smaller holders. For example, while cultivators with land holdings below 0.10 hectares pay around 234 Indian rupees monthly on average for irrigation, cultivators holding land above 10 hectares pay only around 331 Indian rupees. In this context, one should note that smaller holders lack several pieces of equipment and machinery required for agricultural production, which they generally borrow from larger cultivators and thus face additional expenses (Bhattacharjee, 2012; Bhattacharjee and Rajeev, 2014).

Apart from the above-mentioned factors, it is also worth pointing out that smallholders have lower access to information and government schemes (see Table A.6.2 in the Appendix), and also, they avail themselves of loans primarily for unproductive purposes and thus incur additional

[52] The size of land holdings that can be considered as unviable changes with change in technology and climatic and other institutional factors.

Table 6.5 Average monthly expenses (both paid out and imputed) for crop production per agricultural household reporting crop production by size class of land possessed during July 2018–June 2019 (in Indian rupees)

Land size (ha)	Irrigation	Fertilizer	Repair and maintenance	Diesel	Electricity	Human labour	Animal labour	Other expenses	Total
<0.01	234	750	59	117	50	890	25	1,288	3,413
0.01–0.40	101	258	11	23	12	455	19	411	1,290
0.41–1.00	131	520	22	53	41	896	53	3,602	5,318
1.01–2.00	146	916	49	112	98	1,462	104	1,757	4,644
2.01–4.00	180	1,630	111	247	172	2,459	189	3,447	8,435
4.01–10.00	253	2,937	214	804	283	4,216	295	7,235	16,237
10.00+	331	7,515	586	2,602	864	10,709	596	29,356	52,559

Source: NSSO report no. 587: Situation Assessment of Agricultural Households.

expenditure in the form of interest rate to money lenders (Table A.6.3 in the Appendix).

The higher cost of cultivation is expected to have implications on the income of farmers. Table 6.6, in this regard, provides the average monthly income per farm household during 2012–2013 and 2019–2020 from different sources for different-sized classes. From the table, it can be seen that as land size increases, there is an exponential rise in income from cultivation for each period.

Further, in addition to the above-mentioned factors, smaller holdings reduce the ability of farmers to pursue lucrative crop diversification. If the size of land holdings is small, a household may concentrate on the

Table 6.6 Average monthly income per farm household in Indian rupees during 2012–2013 and 2019–2020 from different sources for different size classes of land possessed (ha) (in 2019–2020 prices)

Year	Size class	Wage income	Cultivation	Farming of animals	Business	Total income
2012–2013	<0.01	4,232.08	43.75	1,722.29	651.87	6,649.99
	0.01–0.40	3,479.58	1,001.87	905.62	669.37	6,056.44
	0.41–1.00	2,932.71	3,128.12	917.29	673.75	7,651.87
	1.01–2.00	2,520.00	6,138.12	1,192.92	864.79	10,715.83
	2.01–4.00	2,416.46	10,731.87	1,693.12	807.92	15,649.37
	4.01–10.00	2,961.87	22,229.37	2,188.96	1,255.62	28,635.82
	10.00+	1,911.87	52,040.61	3,823.75	2,581.25	60,357.48
	All sizes	3,020.21	4,493.12	1,112.71	746.67	9,372.71
2019–2020	< 0.01	6,435	1,660	2,084	1,026	11,205
	0.01–0.40	4,491	977	1,162	892	7,522
	0.41–1.00	3,906	2,683	1,335	646	8,570
	1.01–2.00	3,647	5,269	1,845	687	11,448
	2.01–4.00	3,548	9,432	2,551	904	16,435
	4.01–10.00	4,273	19,645	3,451	923	28,292
	10.00 +	3,943	43,599	11,473	1,743	60,758
	All sizes	4,063	3,798	1,582	775	10,218

Note: We have used CPI for Agricultural labour for computing the figures in 2019–2020 prices.

Source: Computed using the 70th and 77th rounds of the NSSO data on the Situation Assessment Survey of Farmers data.

production of fewer crops and, thus, may face frequent shocks arising from price fluctuations and/or risks posed by climate factors. Frequent loss reduces their savings and ability to invest in various capital goods. Larger farmers, on the other hand, can minimize their risk by diversifying production across various crops.

Table 6.7 provides information on crop diversification across various sizes of land holdings. Crop diversification basically means the simultaneous production of several crops. To capture diversification, we have used Simpson's Index. This index is defined as $1\text{-}H^2$, where H is the Herfindahl Index, that is, the sum of squares of the proportion of land used for each crop in the region. A value of 0 means that only one crop is produced in the region, and a value of 1 means that an infinite number of crops are produced. Table 6.7 shows that marginal farmers have a low value of crop diversification as compared to larger farmers. For instance, the Crop

Table 6.7 Crop Diversification Index based on the size class of land holding in 2015–2016

Size class (ha)	Crop diversification index ($1-H^2$)	Share of gross cropped area
Below 0.5	0.776	11.4
0.5–1.0	0.839	14.2
Marginal	0.813	25.6
1.0–2.0	0.887	22.7
Small	0.887	22.7
2.0–3.0	0.898	14.5
3.0–4.0	0.906	8.9
Semi-medium	0.901	23.4
4.0–5.0	0.903	6.7
5.0–7.5	0.915	8.8
7.5–10.0	0.916	4.5
Medium	0.912	19.9
10.0–20.0	0.917	5.5
20.0 and above	0.918	2.9
Large	0.919	8.4
All classes	0.888	100

Source: Computed using agricultural census data.

Diversification Index of farmers cultivating land below 0.5 hectares was 0.776, while large farmers (having cultivated land above 20 hectares) had an index value of 0.919. Thus, the larger farmers are in a better position to manage risk.

We have already pointed out in our earlier chapters, and at the beginning of the current chapter, that these traits and trends pertaining to agriculture are expected to affect the rural nonfarm sector in a number of ways. The nonfarm sector is linked to the farm sector through different forms of linkages, viz., production linkage, consumption linkage, factor market linkage, and productivity linkage (Haggblade, 2007).[53] Each of these linkages will cease to exist if cultivation gets squeezed, which in turn is expected to adversely affect the nonfarm sector. For instance, the nonfarm sector depends on the agricultural sector for inputs as well seeing the agricultural sector as its final market. Apart from this, a section of workers who are losing jobs in the agricultural sector is expected to land up in the nonfarm sector. If more people migrate from the farm to the nonfarm sector, the sector will observe an increase in disguised unemployment and a reduction in value added per worker.[54] Thus, we see that there is a deep interdependence between the farm and nonfarm segments, and if one is adversely affected, the other has to bear its effects. If we focus on the enterprise surveys of the National Sample Survey Office (NSSO), providing information about the status of enterprises, one can see that over time, an increased number of enterprises are observing stagnation or decline in the rural nonfarm sector (see Table A.6.4 in the Appendix). Since the agricultural sector has a sizeable impact on the nonfarm economy, agrarian distress could be a major reason for the proliferation of rural nonfarm activities and their immiseration.

[53] Production linkage mainly includes either forwards linkage from agriculture to nonfarm sector or backwards linkage from nonfarm to farm sector. Consumption linkage comprises consumption of locally produced nonfarm goods and services by farm households. Factor market linkage includes farm–nonfarm linkage in the background of seasonal change in demand for labour/other inputs. Farm and nonfarm linkage may also influence productivity of workers. This aspect is known as productivity linkage. For instance, a rise in food price may adversely affect the nutritional status of nonfarm workers. All these linkages are expected to be affected due to a decline in the number and size of the cultivators. Generally, small and marginal farmers purchase locally produced nonfarm goods, and also the petty producers depend on locally produced farm products.

[54] The chance of small and marginal farmers carrying out better nonfarm activities and generating higher income is contingent on several factors, such as access to credit, social networks, access to insurance, and information (Rajeev and Bhattacharjee, 2017).

6.4 What determines an increase in employment for agricultural workers despite distress for the cultivators?

Apparently, this issue may seem to be rather unrelated to the fundamental problem of this book, that is, the phenomenon of the expansion of the rural nonfarm economy. However, as we proceed, we find that the reason for the sizeable increase in the number of agricultural workers is actually related to our third and crucial question: what is the role of the formal sector in the whole process of expansion of the rural nonfarm economy? With this perspective, we turn to the present issue.

Smaller or unviable-sized land holdings generally push households out of agriculture to other activities. Table 6.6, for instance, shows that the share of earnings from wages was higher for households cultivating lesser-sized land holdings (Table 6.6). In fact, when we compare the two time periods (i.e. 2012–2013 and 2015–2016), we observe that for most size classes, the share of income from wages was rising.

Let us now consider how the agricultural sector is generating jobs in the agricultural labour market, even though there is a decline in the average size of holdings.

Employment pattern in agriculture varies crop-wise and also according to the size class of holdings. Certain crops require more agricultural workers per unit of land. Labour employment also depends on the size of the land, as larger land size dissociates owner and worker. For marginal and small farms, the cultivators and their family members may themselves be engaged as workers, but that may not happen for larger cultivators.

Table 6.8 provides information on the distribution of employment within agriculture in terms of crops or activities. Table 6.8 is computed using national industrial classification codes from employment and unemployment rounds of the NSSO. The table shows that of the total agricultural employment, employment has declined for individuals engaged in cereals production but has increased in all other crops.[55] For example,

[55] The table is computed using a unit-level employment and unemployment survey of the NSSO. Information on crop is obtained from National Industrial Code, while employment figures are obtained based on Usual Principal and Subsidiary Status.

Table 6.8 Distribution of employment in agriculture in terms of the type of crop or activities

Crop/activities	1999–2000	2011–2012	Difference
Cereals plus pulses (food grains)	180,344,404	135,182,165	-45,162,239
Oilseeds	3,286,874	8,373,293	5,086,419
Sugarcane, tobacco, cotton, jute, etc.	9,714,926	23,592,849	13,877,923
Fruits, spices, vegetables, beverages	6,069,940	6,519,491	449,551
Other activities	19,205,512	24,490,064	5,284,552
Total	**218,621,656**	**198,157,862**	**-20,463,794**

Source: Computed using the unit-level 55th and 68th rounds of the NSSO data on employment and unemployment.

between 1999 and 2011–2012, employment in the production of cereals declined by 45 million, while that of all other crop categories increased. This, to some extent, indicates that agricultural workers are primarily being accommodated in the production of non-food grains that include food crops such as fruits or vegetables and also non-food crops such as cotton, tobacco, etc.

A number of factors can be cited as reasons behind the decline in employment in cereals and the increase in employment in other crops. First, cereals are primarily land-intensive crops, while horticultural products (such as fruits and vegetables) are labour-intensive.

The fact that cereals require fewer labour hours can be established from the data obtained from the Cost of Cultivation Survey. Table 6.9 shows the labour required per unit of land (defined in hectares) is higher for sugarcane, cotton, onions, and potatoes compared to paddy, wheat, and other food crops.

Second, in the past two decades, more land has been brought under non-food grains compared to food grains. Table 6.10 provides information on gross cropped area under different crops. Table 6.10 shows that at the national level, the gross cropped area under cereals has declined, while the area under fruits and vegetables, spices, and other food crops has increased. While comparing across different size groups (Table 6.10), it is observed that the reduction in area under cereals has mainly happened in the case of farmers cultivating land above 1 hectare. For the marginal farmers, there is an increase in the area under cereals. Thus,

Table 6.9 Simple average of human labour requirement per unit (ha) of different crops

Crop	Human labour (hours)
Paddy	676.58
Wheat	360.33
Sugarcane	1,437.06
Cotton	826.90
Moong	324.70
Sunflower	380.64
Aarhar	537.51
Groundnut	644.32
Rape seed and mustard	403.14
Onion	1,312.39
Potato	847.05

Source: Computed using the cost of cultivation survey, Directorate of Economics and Statistics.

agricultural employment is being generated from relatively larger farms. Since marginal farmers are largely own account enterprises, it is obvious that they will not generate additional employment, and also they produce crops required only for their own sustenance.

In summary, we could say that a section of the distressed agrarian population is either moving towards the nonfarm economy or being engaged as day labourers on larger farms, mostly practising crop diversification.

6.5 Can urbanization/formal sector growth induce such a transformation?

Now, we come to a crucial question posited earlier. In the previous sections, we have discussed the issue of agrarian distress and the intra-farm sector and farm–nonfarm sector movement of the workforce. Here, we pick up our third question, as enlisted earlier, that is, the role of modernization and urbanization in these processes of migration and/or employment diversification.

The changes that are happening in agriculture can be attributed to the formal sector expansion via large-scale capital accumulation and

Table 6.10 Percentage area under different crops in gross cropped area

	Cereals		Pulses		Fruits and vegetables		Spices and other food crops		Oil seeds		Other non-food	
Area	1995–1996	2015–2016	1995–1996	2015–2016	1995–1996	2015–2016	1995–1996	2015–2016	1995–1996	2015–2016	1995–1996	2015–2016
Below 0.5	69.1	72.7	7.1	6.1	5.6	5.7	3.9	3.3	8.2	6.7	6.1	5.5
0.5–1.0	66.9	64.9	8.8	8.4	4.1	4.7	4.1	4.0	8.8	10.0	7.4	8.0
Marginal	67.8	68.4	8.1	7.4	4.7	5.1	4.0	3.7	8.5	8.5	6.9	6.9
1.0–2.0	61.1	55.4	9.7	10.6	3.5	4.4	4.0	4.3	11.6	14.2	10.1	11.1
Small	61.1	55.4	9.7	10.6	3.5	4.4	4.0	4.3	11.6	14.2	10.1	11.1
2.0–3.0	59.0	53.1	10.2	11.6	3.0	3.7	3.8	4.3	12.9	15.4	11.2	11.9
3.0–4.0	56.8	51.9	10.9	12.4	2.7	3.6	3.7	4.4	13.9	15.9	12.0	11.7
Semi-medium	58.1	52.6	10.5	11.9	2.9	3.7	3.8	4.4	13.3	15.6	11.5	11.8
4.0–5.0	55.5	52.6	11.1	12.4	2.4	3.4	3.5	4.1	14.3	15.4	13.1	12.2
5.0–7.5	51.6	48.5	12.1	13.5	2.0	3.1	3.1	3.7	16.1	15.9	14.9	15.3
7.5–10.0	50.0	49.3	13.0	13.7	1.8	3.1	2.8	3.7	17.1	15.7	15.2	14.5
Medium	52.4	50.0	12.0	13.2	2.1	3.2	3.2	3.8	15.8	15.7	14.4	14.1
10.0–20.0	47.7	47.7	14.3	13.4	1.6	2.9	2.4	3.5	16.4	13.5	17.8	19.0
20.0 and above	46.9	46.1	13.7	10.2	1.6	3.0	1.8	3.3	11.2	9.9	24.8	27.5
Large	47.4	47.1	14.1	12.3	1.6	3.0	2.2	3.4	14.6	12.2	20.2	21.9
All classes	57.8	56.3	10.7	10.7	3.0	4.1	3.5	4.0	12.8	13.2	12.2	11.7

Source: Computed using agricultural census data (1995–1996) and (2015–2016).

urbanization. In the previous sections, we have already discussed the issue of land conversion for urbanization and modern sector expansion and its adverse impacts on the cultivators, pushing them towards rural nonfarm activities. Thus, the direct role of formal sector expansion in inducing a rural transformation in general, and in the process of proliferation of the rural nonfarm sector in particular, has been discussed. Now, we look at a somewhat indirect role, which has not been discussed sufficiently in the literature.

In sections 6.3 and 6.4, we discussed the issue of crop diversification and its probable effects on the nonfarm economy of rural India. Here, we take up the next stage of analysis, that is, the influence of modernization–urbanization on crop diversification and, hence, on the nonfarm economy. In this context, it is important to note that non-food grains have higher demand in urban areas and in agro-based industries. With the growth of the economy and with urbanization, one expects a steady decline in the area under food grains and thus a fall in the level of employment in these crops.

Further, a higher rate of urbanization induces higher crop diversification and/or production of non-food grains. This, in turn, may push up agricultural wages,[56] which may be faced equally by small and large farms, and thus smaller farmers may find it unprofitable to continue production of crops and thus might migrate to other activities such as non-agricultural jobs. For instance, Table A.6.5 in the Appendix shows that states having higher crop diversification have higher agricultural wage rates. Thus, the growth of non-food grains as induced by higher urbanization may reduce agricultural employment (particularly among cultivators) not only directly by reducing operational holdings but also indirectly by forcing holders to go for crop productions that are not feasible for smaller farms to carry out.

In this context, Table 6.11 provides an important insight. The table shows that as land size increases, a household spends more on leasing in land. On the other hand, for the small and marginal farmer category,

[56] When one compares general agricultural and non-agricultural wages data from the Labour Bureau of the Government of India, one finds that the gap has reduced/has not widened over the years. Government employment schemes such as the Mahatma Gandhi National Rural Employment Guarantee Act (MNREGA) might also play an important role in reducing the gap by setting a critical wage rate below which wage rates may not actually reduce.

Table 6.11 Expenditure and earnings per household in Indian rupees from land leasing in and leasing out in rural India

Land size(ha)	Expenditure on leasing in land	Earnings from leasing out land
<0.01	80	254
0.01–0.40	27	189
0.41–1.00	71	76
1.01–2.00	132	74
2.01–4.00	467	146
4.01–10.00	1,430	451
10.00+	13,757	581

Source: Computed using the 77th round of the NSSO data on the Situation Assessment of Agricultural Households.

earning from leasing out of land is higher than expenditure on leasing in the land.

Finally, our theoretical model in Chapter 2 has highlighted an important channel through which formal sector accumulation can cause a push effect from traditional agriculture. Formal sector accumulation can push up prices of several goods (modern nonfarm goods) and, thus, can reduce the real income of people engaged in agriculture. Let us reconsider Table 6.6, which provides the income of an average agricultural household from different sources during 2012–2013 and 2019–2020.

One can see from Table 6.6 that between 2012–2013 and 2019–2020, although farm households observed a marginal increase in overall income owing to engagement in wage-related work, an average farm household observed a decline in real income from cultivation in 2019–2020 prices. For instance, while the overall income for farmer households on an average increased from 9,371 to 10,218 Indian rupees, income from cultivation reduced from 4,493 to 3,798 Indian rupees. It is interesting to note that such a reduction in income from cultivation is observed for all size classes.

We also computed average real income (i.e. in 2019–2020 prices) from cultivation per hectare of land for 2012–2013 and 2019–2020 using the Consumer Price Index (CPI) for agricultural workers. It was observed that the average real income from cultivation per hectare of land also declined from 4,282 Indian rupees in 2012–2013 to 4,162 Indian rupees in 2019–2020. Since, during the same period, there was no decline in productivity, a decline in net receipt per hectare of land implies an adverse movement of terms of trade against the cultivators. In other words, this means that the price that a cultivator receives has performed poorly compared to the prices of other commodities that a farmer purchases.

6.6 Conclusion

This chapter had three main objectives. The first was to provide an in-depth study of the transformations of Indian agriculture. Next, we focused on whether and how these transformations could affect the rural nonfarm economy of India. Finally, we have seen how far formal sector expansion, infrastructure development, and urbanization (i.e. the overall modernization of the economy) could affect the processes of transformation in agriculture and thereby influence the phenomenon of the proliferation of nonfarm activities.

Thus, although this chapter may apparently seem to be slightly out of place, it happens to be a major building block for this book. This is because the basic theoretical argument of the book is that the process of modernization of the economy squeezes the agricultural sector and triggers a push-driven outmigration or employment diversification from it. Now there are two destinations for this immiserated population: a small but networked part, having access to a variety of assets and resources, could reap the benefits of modernization through diverse linkages with the modern sector and thereby enter into the modern nonfarm sector; the other part of the distressed population, which is much larger but asset- and resource-poor and not that much connected socio-economically, has no option but to throng the petty nonfarm segment. In this broad theoretical framework, agriculture plays a crucial role: its transformation, the role of the formal sector in the process of this transformation, and finally the effects of this transformation on the rural nonfarm economy are all that constitute this book project. Given the broad contribution of this chapter, if we look at the specific issues, we get the following outcomes.

Employment in agriculture is falling, primarily because of a reduction in the number of cultivators as compared to that of casual workers, contrary to the usual belief. We found that the reduction is driven by several factors. First, due to urbanization, industrialization, and infrastructure development (i.e. modernization of the economy), the overall agricultural area has reduced. The process of acquiring land for industrialization or infrastructural development has been augmented in recent years owing to changes in land acquisition laws in different states of India. Second, the land is becoming fragmented, which in turn is leading to unviable-sized land holdings. Unviable-sized landholders earn less income (even though they may be more productive) due to low crop production, and they also face a higher cost of cultivation. One of the important factors inducing the increasing cost of cultivation is agricultural wages, which have moved up more in recent years due to higher production of commercial crops, which have a higher demand from the urban sector.

Government intervention in the agricultural wage market (via minimum wage regulation, the MNREGA, etc.) may also have played a role in increasing the wage rate.

Third, overall real income from cultivation has reduced over time owing to higher inflation in other sectors of the economy. This might have also happened due to formal sector accumulation, as envisaged in our theoretical model.

Owing to unviable land holdings, loss of land, and reduction in real income, smaller-sized landholders are primarily shifting to labouring activities within agriculture or are moving towards the nonfarm sector. If these shifted workers are able to find a job in the capital-/urban-linked modern sector, they would acquire higher earnings. On the contrary, if such provisions are absent, they overcrowd the traditional nonfarm sector in which earnings are less. Over time, they also become dependent on government support (such as the MNREGA, subsidized food, etc.) for a livelihood.

A.6 Appendix

Table A.6.1 Number of agricultural holdings in India

Srl	Size of groups	Number of holdings (in '000)									
		1970–1971	1976–1977	1980–1981	1985–1986	1990–1991	1995–1996	2000–2001*	2005–2006*	2010–2011	2015–2016
1	Marginal (0–1ha)	36,200	44,523	50,122	56,147	63,389	71,179	75,408	83,694	92,826	100,251
2	Small (1–2 ha)	13,432	14,728	16,072	17,922	20,092	21,643	22,695	23,930	24,779	25,809
3	Semi-medium (2–4 ha)	10,681	11,666	12,455	13,252	13,923	14,261	14,021	14,127	13,896	13,993
4	Medium (4–10 ha)	7,932	8,212	8,068	7,916	7,580	7,092	6,577	6,375	5,875	5,561
5	Large (10 +)	2,766	2,440	2,166	1,918	1,654	1,404	1,230	1,096	973	838
	All sizes	71,011	81,569	88,883	97155	106,638	115,580	119,931	129,222	138,348	**146,454**

Source: Computed from agricultural census report (2015–2016).

Table A.6.2 Number per 1,000 agricultural households with access to different facilities/schemes

Land size class (ha)	Bank account	Membership in a registered farmer's organization	Kisan credit card	Crop insurance under PMFBY	MNREGA job card	Got work under the MNREGA	Soil health card	Adopted the recommendations from the soil health card	Animal health card
<0.01	939	1	17	20	265	135	11	11	24
0.01–0.40	976	31	97	15	420	227	7	2	4
0.41–1.00	977	38	194	56	441	237	14	4	4
1.01–2.00	987	50	264	120	436	232	23	10	9
2.01–4.00	989	62	332	185	406	216	25	11	9
4.01–10.00	991	66	409	246	337	171	38	20	14
10.00+	983	42	487	307	330	143	63	25	38
All sizes	980	41	191	71	426	228	15	6	6

Source: Computed using the 77th round of the NSSO data on the Situation Assessment of Agricultural Households.

Table A.6.3 Per 1,000 distribution of the amount of loan outstanding by the purpose for which the loan was taken for different size classes of land possessed (ha)

Land size class (ha)	Capital expenditure in farm business	Revenue expenditure in farm business	Nonfarm business	Housing	Marriages and ceremonies	Education	Medical	Other consumption expenditure	Others	All
(1)	(2)	(3)	(4)	(5)	(6)	(7)	(8)	(9)	(10)	(11)
<0.01	26	42	41	25	128	2	420	191	124	1,000
0.01–0.04	138	152	57	215	98	22	92	142	84	1,000
0.41–1.00	203	257	46	149	77	24	39	111	93	1,000
1.01–2.00	289	336	38	99	58	15	27	88	52	1,000
2.01–4.00	340	376	24	66	46	10	19	72	47	1,000
4.01–10.00	311	452	35	39	53	5	13	62	30	1,000
10.00 +	341	488	16	33	4	64	0	35	19	1,000
All sizes	259	316	39	112	64	18	36	94	62	1,000

Source: Computed using the 77th round of the NSSO data on the Situation Assessment of Agricultural Households.

Table A.6.4 Status of nonfarm enterprise in the past three years (percentage)

Type of enterprise	2010				2015			
	Expanding	Stagnant	Contraction	Other	Expanding	Stagnant	Contraction	Other
OAE	31.3	41.8	8.5	14.4	26.8	46.3	11.2	15.7
Establishment	41.8	34.5	6.4	17.3	40.2	33.5	8.0	18.4

Note: Others primarily include enterprises that have started their operation in the past three years.

Source: Computed using the Enterprise Survey (NSSO).

Table A.6.5 Agricultural wages (in Indian rupees) and Crop Diversification Index across different states of India 2015–2016

States	Average wage rate of field agricultural workers (male)	Average wage rate of field agricultural workers (female)	Crop Diversification Index (1–H^2)
Andhra Pradesh	295.35	199.82	0.86
Assam	244.89	200.06	0.48
Bihar	215.05	202.65	0.67
Chhattisgarh	180.80	133.96	0.47
Gujarat	175.88	155.58	0.88
Haryana	388.24	321.52	0.71
Himachal Pradesh	276.30	252.47	0.73
Jharkhand	181.56	169.66	0.64
Karnataka	272.31	244.95	0.94
Kerala	576.47	427.03	0.87
Madhya Pradesh	213.09	183.75	0.83
Odisha	224.43	173.23	0.37
Punjab	373.38		0.63
Rajasthan	299.63	246.62	0.90
Tamil Nadu	334.50	141.84	0.84
Telangana	283.70	184.15	0.79
Tripura	288.02	225.08	0.63
Uttar Pradesh	238.40	216.10	0.71
Uttarakhand	336.46	268.58	0.80
West Bengal	259.40	219.18	0.58

Source: Agricultural wage data is computed from the report Agricultural Wages in India Directorate of Economics and Statistics, Ministry of Agriculture, and crop diversification is computed from the Agricultural Census (2015–2016).

7

The COVID-19 Pandemic and Its Impact on the Rural Economy

The history of pandemics and epidemics is long and complex. Throughout the history of human civilization, one finds evidence of outbreaks of different infectious diseases as well as their devastating impacts. For instance, between 430 and 420 BC, there was an epidemic at Athens that not only annihilated the population but also contributed significantly to the downfall of the city of Athens (Retief and Cilliers, 1998).

In most cases, these outbreaks have occurred due to the zoonotic transfer of viruses from animals to human beings, which in turn got accentuated with increased interactions of human beings with animals, such as through animal husbandry activities, pet trade, and conversion of forest land for human use (Cutler et al., 2010).

Though outbreaks existed throughout human history, the prevalence of disease in larger geographic regions is a result of an increase in human mobility and travel. One therefore finds a higher incidence of pandemics in the period following the Industrial Revolution, which increased interconnectedness among people of different societies.

The world in which we currently live is more connected and complex compared to our known history, including any period following the Industrial Revolution. As mentioned in Chapter 3, in the era of the Industrial Revolution and thereafter, though production and consumption were happening in two distant points on the globe, the production process was largely carried out within a single factory. However, with the advent of the internet and other communication technologies in the 1990s, the production process itself got unbundled, and in this contemporary globalized era, due to advancements in communications, goods

The Nonfarm Economy. Manojit Bhattacharjee, Saumya Chakrabarti, and Meenakshi Rajeev,
Oxford University Press.
DOI: 10.1093/9780198972013.003.0007

are manufactured by sourcing inputs from many locations worldwide, increasing interconnectedness. Thus, in today's world, if modern capital accumulation and globalization are realities, so is the prevalence of pandemics/epidemics.

In the preceding chapters of this book, we have concentrated on highlighting the effects of accumulation on various sectors of the rural economy. We have shown that accumulation creates a dichotomy (through both push and pull effects) in rural agricultural and nonagricultural economies. Owing to accumulation, parts of both farm and nonfarm sectors modernize and integrate with the formal economy, enjoying the benefits of growth, while a large part is either pushed or stays tied to traditional household activities that haven't changed much. Consequently, over time, the gap between both these segments expands.

In this chapter, we try to answer a related question. We try to see what happens to this (dualistic) developmental trajectory (as mentioned above) if we incorporate the possibility of a pandemic in which there is a cessation/slowing down of capital accumulation. Specifically, our objective is to look at how the break in the accumulation process affected the employment formation and income generation in the traditional and modern segments of the rural farm and nonfarm economy during and after the COVID-19 pandemic of 2020/2021 and what implications it holds for future.

To study this objective, this chapter primarily uses the annual unit-level Periodic Labour Force Survey (PLFS) data of the Indian National Sample Survey Office, International Labour Organization (ILO) data, data published by the Press Information Bureau (PIB), and All India Debt and Investment Survey Reports.

In this context, it is essential to acknowledge that the COVID-19 pandemic ended just three years ago, which makes it challenging to comprehensively assess its effects on rural development. Therefore, in this chapter, we shall focus on the developments that have been noticed so far and, based on these advancements, attempt to outline the potential future trajectory.

One should also note that even though this chapter mainly draws conclusions from the COVID-19 pandemic, its implications can have wider applications in contexts or situations in which the economy experiences a slowdown.

The chapter has the following sections. Section 7.1 presents a brief review of existing literature on the pandemic and its impact specifically on the rural economy. This is followed by sections 7.2–7.6 on data analysis and our observations. We end the chapter with policy implications and conclusions in section 7.7.

7.1 The pandemic and its implications: Review of existing studies

Akin to several epidemics and pandemics of the past, the impact of the COVID-19 pandemic is multidimensional. One can segregate these impacts into short-term, medium-term, and long-term impacts. Since the pandemic ended very recently, existing studies have primarily documented the short-term impact, which we briefly delineate below.

The virus that caused the COVID-19 pandemic was first identified in the city of Wuhan in China at the beginning of 2020. It was observed that a new species of coronavirus, initially called SARS-CoV-2 and later renamed COVID-19, was causing the infection. The virus quickly spread to other parts of the globe.

Akin to other crises led by epidemics and pandemics, the COVID-19 pandemic first caused production losses owing to the deaths and illnesses of workers. Subsequently, as the number of infections grew, governments across the globe initiated measures such as social distancing, local containment, and nationwide lockdowns.[57] All these measures caused the disruption of economic activities, which subsequently resulted in job loss.

According to the estimates made by the ILO, globally, the loss of working hours in 2020 was equivalent to 255 million full-time jobs and \$3.7 trillion in labour income, compared to the pre-pandemic situation (World Economic Forum, 2021). As far as India is concerned, based on

[57] India observed a complete lockdown in four phases from 24 March to 31 May 2020, after which phase-wise unlocking of the country took place between 1 June and the end of November. Each phase had higher relaxation in the unlocking period than the earlier one. In 2021, India observed the second wave of COVID-19 that resulted in a state-wide lockdown from April to June.

an estimate provided by the Centre for Monitoring Indian Economy, the unemployment rate rose to around 24 per cent in the month of April and 22 per cent in the month of May after the introduction of the lockdown (Sharma and Rai, 2024).

Prior to the pandemic, there was evidence of an effective demand problem. Lockdown measures led to supply inelasticity and made the economies more vulnerable (Dasgupta and Rajeev, 2020; Sharma and Rai, 2024). Due to retrenchment and panic arising from lockdown and death, many countries also experienced migration of workers on a large scale (World Bank, 2020b). In India, for instance, a nationwide lockdown initially caused massive outmigration of contractual workers from bigger cities to villages (World Bank, 2020b). This caused an expansion of the workforce and overall population in the rural sector.

Rural areas also reported declining jobs due to movement disruption during the lockdown. Using FAS–PARI data, an editorial in the Review of Agrarian Studies (2020) stated that about 45 per cent of non-agricultural wage jobs, which were created outside of villages, prior to the pandemic, were adversely affected owing to the problems with movement during the pandemic. Baldwin (2020) explained the macroeconomic impact of the loss of jobs and disruption in household income. According to him, disruption in income reduced consumption and saving at the individual level, which in turn reduced investment and aggregate output at the macro level. A reduction in aggregate output thus hurts the labour income itself. In other words, in Baldwin's framework, labour is the most adversely affected factor of production.

Akin to Baldwin, other studies examining the impact of the crisis across different classes have also posited that the pandemic has disproportionately affected the vulnerable segment of society most (ILO, 2020; Braam et al., 2021; Kundu et al., 2021).

Few studies have summarized the effects of the pandemic on sectoral output and employment. The World Bank (2021), for instance, published its findings obtained from a telephone survey conducted among rural Indian households during the COVID-19 pandemic. The survey showed that the pandemic caused an increase in agricultural employment as well as the area under cultivation. As far as the production of crops was concerned, it was found that a substantial percentage of farmers shifted towards traditional crops such as cereal production. Further, a large fraction of the households covered in the survey reported receiving monetary relief from the government in June 2020 as a direct cash transfer.

Aneja and Ahuja (2021), based on their review of different articles amidst the pandemic, found that compared to other sectors, the manufacturing sector was most affected owing to the global supply chain disruptions. The service sector experienced a temporary halt in the tourism and hospitality segment due to restrictions on mobility. They also observed in their study that the agricultural sector, with the exception of segments like horticulture and poultry, experienced the least impact.

Certain studies have documented both the effect and the rate of recovery in different sectors in the post-pandemic period. Sharma and Rai (2024), for example, using data from the National Sample Survey Office (NSSO) and the Centre for Monitoring Indian Economy (CMIE), found that services, real estate, construction, and manufacturing were all hard hit by COVID-19 and had a slow rate of recovery. On the other hand, not only was agriculture the least affected sector, but it also provided more employment in the post-COVID-19 period.

While these studies have documented several impacts of the pandemic that were observed, there is less information about the issue that the present book is addressing, that is, how the crisis affected the traditional and modern segments of the rural farm and nonfarm economy and how these sectors recovered in the post-COVID-19 period. This chapter therefore delves into this issue.

Now, before studying and analysing the impact on the rural economy of India, we first present the impacts of this crisis on employment and earnings for individuals across different regions of the globe. Such a comparison would provide us with an understanding of the differential impact of the crisis in the developed and the developing world, particularly in countries that have experienced the generation of dualism with accumulation.

7.2 The pandemic and employment: Impact across the globe

Table 7.1 provides information on full-time jobs lost in 2020 and 2021 compared to the jobs available during the fourth quarter of 2019.[58] The table is based on the ILO's estimation, which assumes that a full-time job in a week is equivalent to forty-eight hours of work.

Table 7.1 shows that most regions across the globe experienced significant losses in jobs. However, the loss is comparatively higher in the developing world (South Asia, North Africa, and Sub-Saharan Africa) vis-à-vis the developed regions (Northern Europe, North America, or East Asia). For instance, Southern Asia's share in the global aggregate employment (mostly formal) was around 19.8 per cent in 2019. However, its share in the aggregate job loss in 2020 and 2021 was 34.1 and 38.5 per cent, respectively. The figures are much lower in Northern Europe, East Asia, and Northern America.

It is worth mentioning that in developing countries, a significant number of jobs are of a casual or temporary nature, and a large number of employees may be employed for less than forty-eight hours in a week.[59] Therefore, in the context of developing countries, a full-time job loss, as defined by the ILO, may imply that the actual loss of jobs is even greater than the one captured by the ILO.

In addition to a higher loss of jobs, Table 7.1 shows that, in absolute terms, the share of the developing world's aggregate job loss was higher in 2021 compared to 2020. In other words, the developed world observed not only a lesser impact but also a faster recovery vis-à-vis the developing world.

Figure 7.1 provides a better illustration of the recovery from the loss of jobs. The figure shows that low-income and lower-middle-income

[58] In the full-time equivalent method, hours worked by several part-time and full-time employees are aggregated and expressed as hours worked by full-time employees. The ILO provides estimation based on both forty and forty-eight hours of work per week.

[59] For instance, in India, as per the Periodic Labour Force Survey data for 2018–2019, around 24.1 per cent of employed individuals who were working as casual wage labourers actually worked an average of 43.7 hours per week.

Table 7.1 Jobs lost due to the COVID-19 crisis expressed as the number of full-time equivalent (FTE) jobs (in thousands) based on forty-eight hours of work per week and annual employment in 2019 for individuals above fifteen years

Region	Number of FTE jobs lost		Annual employment above fifteen years in 2019
	2020	2021	
Northern Africa	5,790.1 (2.2)	3,696.9 (2.9)	6,3937 (1.9)
Sub-Saharan Africa	23,098.7 (8.9)	16,503.9 (13.1)	389,617 (11.9)
Latin America and the Caribbean: Upper-middle income	36,320.8 (14)	13,445.9 (10.7)	282,819 (8.6)
Northern America	13,242.1 (5.1)	6,444.1 (5.1)	180,125 (5.5)
Eastern Asia	34,557.2 (13.4)	2,045.3 (1.6)	906,352 (27.6)
South East Asia	22,174.3 (8.6)	20,473.5 (16.3)	324,412 (9.9)
Southern Asia	88,194.2 (34.1)	48,363.2 (38.5)	650,911 (19.8)
Northern Europe	3,505.8 (1.4)	1,446.1 (1.1)	52,478 (1.6)
Western Asia	4,847.7 (1.9)	1,348.1 (1.1)	40,870 (1.2)
India	68,647.8 (26.55)	34,725.4 (27.61)	457,262 (14)
World	258,535.5 (100)	125,751.5 (100)	3,287,296 (100)

Note: Figures in parenthesis show the percentage share of each country in the global aggregate.
Source: Computed from ILO model estimates.

countries have a slower recovery than high-income and upper-middle-income countries.

As far as India is concerned, Table 7.1 shows that the loss of jobs is considerable. India's share in global employment was 14 per cent in 2019, whereas her share in global job loss was 26.55 per cent.

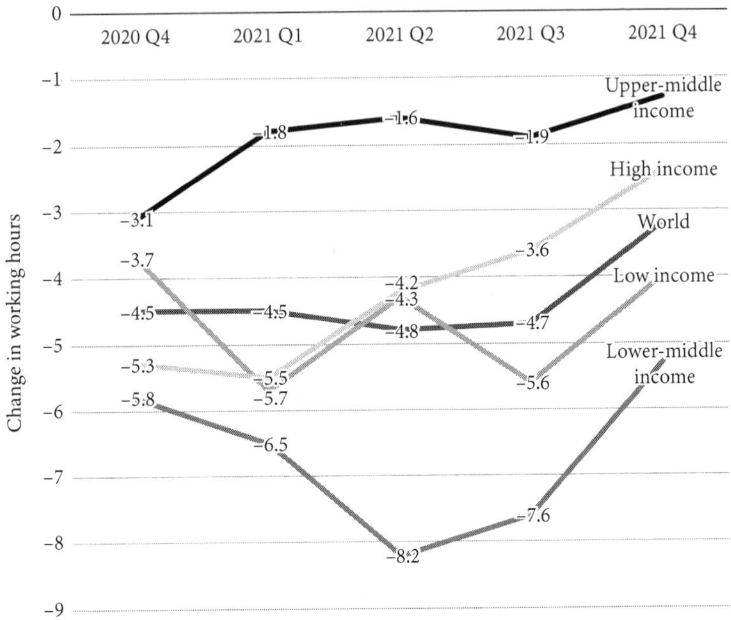

Figure 7.1 Change in working hours relative to 2019 Q4
Source: Computed based on ILO-modelled estimates.

7.3 COVID-19 and its impact on rural employment, unemployment, and recovery: Evidence from Indian data

Let us now turn our attention to the Indian economy. Our objective is to understand how the crisis affected the traditional and modern segments of the rural farm and nonfarm economy and also the process of duality generation. Studying these aspects would also help us understand why developing countries are experiencing a slower recovery.

Table 7.2 provides information on the distribution of the total workforce in terms of employment and unemployment in both rural and urban areas. The table portrays several intriguing results. From the table, one observes that the pandemic primarily led to job loss in the urban areas. Between 2019–2020 and 2020–2021, both urban employment and the workforce observed a decline. During this time (amidst the pandemic and thereafter), rural employment and the workforce observed a rise, possibly due to the movement of labour from urban to rural areas.

The table also shows that the recovery was slow. Both urban employment and the workforce reached the 2019–2020 level again in 2023–2024. This implies that many workers who moved to rural areas have not returned. Studies have reported that such outmigration and delayed return created an acute shortage of workers in cities; on the other hand, it caused overcrowding in rural areas. Bhattacharya and Menon (2021), for instance, argued that due to outmigration, larger companies in cities involved in manufacturing, e-commerce, logistics, construction, and real estate had faced an acute shortage of labour (about 20–25 per cent). The reasons behind such delayed return could be the absence of savings among households required for movement or the possibility of getting locked-in some rural works. In this context, one should note that in many places in rural India, there exists an advance payment system in which rural farmers, or, in some cases, casual workers, receive money from an agent (say, for example, a trader or landlord) in advance against the promise or obligation to sell their future produce or labour services (Taufique and Hoque, 2017). Such a system generally creates a locked-in effect and can hamper the free movement of labour.

While Table 7.2 provides information on aggregate employment or change of workforce during the pandemic, from the table one does not get information about what kind of employment is generated in rural areas. In other words, based on the above table, one may not understand whether the farm sector accommodated the excess workers or the nonfarm sector. Therefore, we looked into Table 7.3, which provides information on employment across farm and nonfarm sectors in rural and urban areas.

From Table 7.3, one finds that as the workers moved from the urban areas to the rural areas, both farm and the nonfarm sector observed an increase in employment (in absolute terms). However, when one looks into the relative contribution of each sector, one finds that the percentage increment in employment was much higher in the nonfarm sector as compared to the farm sector. In fact, the nonfarm sector's share in employment in rural areas showed a sustained rise, even in the period following the pandemic when lockdown and other restrictions were not in place.

Table 7.2 Distribution of total workforce into employment and unemployment across rural and urban areas

Year	Rural			Urban			Workforce (rural plus urban)
	E	U	W	E	U	W	
2019–2020	304.7	12.6	317.3	122.04	9.1	131.2	448.4
	(67.9)	(2.8)	(70.8)	(27.2)	(2.0)	(29.2)	(100)
2020–2021	322.2	10.9	333.2	115.3	8.3	123.6	456.8
	(70.5)	(2.4)	(72.9)	(25.2)	(1.8)	(27.1)	(100)
2021–2022	340.1	11.4	351.6	119.0	7.96	126.96	478.5
	(71.1)	(2.4)	(73.5)	(24.9)	(1.7)	(26.5)	(100)
2022–2023	380.4	9.5	389.9	122.2	6.9	129.2	519.09
	(73.3)	(1.8)	(75.1)	(23.5)	(1.3)	(24.9)	(100)
2023–2024	389.5	9.9	399.4	136.3	7.3	143.6	543.04
	(71.7)	(1.8)	(73.5)	(25.1)	(1.3)	(26.5)	(100)

Note: E, U, and W imply employment, unemployment, and workforce, respectively. The figures in parenthesis reflect the percentage with respect to total workforce (rural plus urban). Employment data are based on the usual principal and subsidiary status of individuals.

Source: Computed using the unit-level PLFS data (2019–2020, 2020–2021, 2021–2022, 2022–2023, and 2023–2024).

Several factors may contribute to the proportionately higher rise in nonfarm jobs compared to farm jobs in rural areas during and after the pandemic. First, the existence of unviable-sized holdings in rural areas, as mentioned in Chapters 6, may have contributed to this higher increase in employment in the nonfarm sector compared to the farm sector. Second, the World Bank (2021) showed that during the pandemic, and even after that, a large number of farmers shifted to traditional crop cultivation. Since traditional crop has a lower return and is not labour intensive, it is possible that such cultivation may not have generated sufficient demand for hired workers. Finally, if the push effect is the reason for migration from farm to nonfarm work, as stated in the theoretical framework (presented in Chapter 2) and also established in subsequent analysis, then it is not feasible for a worker to re-engage in the agricultural sector.

Table 7.4 in this regard provides useful information on the type of employment that the farm and the nonfarm sector generated during the pandemic.

Table 7.3 Distribution of employment across farm and nonfarm sectors in rural and urban areas (usual principal and subsidiary status)

	Sector	Rural		Urban	
		employment (in millions)	Percentage	employment (in millions)	Percentage
2019–2020	Farm	187.4	61.5	6.97	5.7
	Nonfarm	117.3	38.5	115.07	94.3
	Total	304.7	100	122.04	100
2020–2021	Farm	195.8	60.8	7.48	6.5
	Nonfarm	126.4	39.2	107.83	93.5
	Total	322.2	100	115.31	100
2021–2022	Farm	200.7	59	8.03	6.7
	Nonfarm	139.4	41	110.97	93.3
	Total	340.1	100	119.00	100
2022–2023	Farm	222.2	58.4	7.82	6.4
	Nonfarm	158.2	41.6	114.41	93.6
	Total	380.4	100	122.23	100
2023–2024	Farm	233.1	59.8	9.17	6.7
	Nonfarm	156.4	40.2	127.14	93.3
	Total	389.5	100	136.31	100

Note: Employment data are based on the usual principal and subsidiary status of individuals.
Source: Computed using unit-level PLFS data (2019–2020, 2020–2021, 2021–2022, 2022–2023, and 2023–2024).

In Table 7.4, we have divided total employment in terms of employment within own account enterprises, regular salaried jobs, and casual workers. The table displays the following results.

One can see from the table that the pandemic has reduced the number of hired workers (such as regular salaried employees and casual labourers), and it has created an expansion of own account employment. Before the pandemic, the percentages of own account jobs, regular salaried jobs, and casual labour jobs were, respectively, 59.8 per cent, 12.5 per cent, and 26.6 per cent in 2019–2020. In 2020–2021, they were 61.3 per cent, 12.1 per cent, and 25.4 per cent, respectively. An increase in own account employment and a decrease in hired workers imply a reduction in the number of businesses that are linked to the modern sector. This is because firms associated with the modern sector have the

Table 7.4 Type of employment in the farm and nonfarm segment of rural areas in percentage terms

Year	Sector	Own account worker				Regular salaried employee	Casual wage labour		Total
		Worker	Employer	Helper	Total		Public worker	Others	
2019–2020	Farm	42.3	1.9	30.1	74.4	1.7	0	23.9	100
	Nonfarm	31.4	1.2	3.9	**36.4**	29.8	2.9	30.9	100
	Total	38.1	1.7	20	59.8	12.5	1.1	26.6	100
2020–2021	Farm	42.3	2	32.1	76.3	1.3	0.1	22.3	100
	Nonfarm	32.3	1.3	4.5	**38.1**	28.8	2.8	30.2	100
	Total	38.3	1.7	21.3	61.3	12.1	1.2	25.4	100
2021–2022	Farm	42.9	2.3	33.2	78.4	0.8	0.1	20.8	100
	Nonfarm	31.2	1.7	4.4	**37.3**	29.5	3	30.2	100
	Total	38.1	2	21.4	61.5	12.5	1.3	24.6	100
2022–2023	Farm	44.2	2.6	33.9	80.7	0.8	0.2	18.2	100
	Nonfarm	30.5	2.3	5.4	**38.1**	28.1	2.1	31.7	100
	Total	38.5	2.5	22	63	12.2	1	23.8	100
2023–2024	Farm	43.3	2.8	36.1	82.3	0.9	0.2	16.6	100
	Nonfarm	30.9	2.4	5.2	**38.5**	30.5	2.4	28.6	100
	Total	38.4	2.7	23.7	64.7	12.7	1.1	21.4	100

Note: Employment data are based on the usual principal and subsidiary status of individuals.

Source: Computed using unit-level PLFS data (2019–2020, 2020–2021, 2021–2022, 2022–2023, and 2023–2024).

ability to generate surplus, which in turn leads to the employment of hired workers.

Second, the pandemic resulted in an increased demand for public works. For instance, in 2019–2020, the percentage of workers engaged in casual wage labour in public work was 1.1 per cent; it increased to 1.2 per cent in 2020–2021 and to 1.3 per cent in 2022–2023. Though the percentage figures may reflect marginal change, in absolute terms, they are high. It is also important to note that the employment status here indicates the individual's usual employment status, meaning that their engagement in this activity was for a major part of the year. In reality, there are more individuals who took up employment as casual wage labourers, working for fewer days. Section 7.4 provides a detailed account of the temporary/short-term increase in demand for public work during the pandemic.

Third, one also finds in Table 7.4 that there has been an increase in unpaid family workers (helpers) in both the farm and nonfarm segments. An increase in unpaid family workers, on the one hand, may be an indicator of disguised employment generation. On the other hand, it may indicate the expansion of unviable-sized or highly vulnerable farm and nonfarm businesses in the traditional segment, which could not accommodate full-time workers.

An alternative way of understanding the generation of vulnerable businesses owing to the pandemic is to look into the distribution of employment across different firm size. This is provided in Table 7.5 in the context of nonfarm businesses.

The table shows that the pandemic has increased employment in own account enterprises (OAEs) and also the smaller-sized firms generating employment for between one and five workers. Comparing this result with the results presented in Chapter 5 provides us with an important aspect of the development trajectory of the rural sector of India.

It can be seen that as the economy grows (as observed from the prepandemic data), there is an increase in the number of firms that act like smaller capitalist enterprises generating surplus and employing hired workers. However, Tables 7.4 and 7.5 indicated that these firms are very vulnerable in nature, and their aggregate wealth is not enough to bear a

Table 7.5 Distribution of employment in terms of the enterprise size in the nonfarm businesses of rural areas

Year	Type of activity	Number of workers					
		1–5	6–9	10–19	Greater than 20	Not known	Total
2019–2020	CW	57.2	20.4	6.4	9.9	6	100
	OAE	93.5	3.1	0.7	0.8	1.9	100
	RS	38	18.6	11	26.6	5.8	100
	All	64.7	13.6	5.7	11.6	4.4	100
2020–2021	CW	59.2	20.1	7.5	10.2	3	100
	OAE	94	3.1	0.9	1.2	0.8	100
	RS	38.7	16.7	11.1	30	3.5	100
	All	66.3	12.6	6	12.6	2.5	100
2021–2022	CW	53.9	21.8	8.5	12.2	3.6	100
	OAE	93.8	3.7	0.8	0.8	0.8	100
	RS	36.4	16	11.9	31.5	4.1	100
	All	63.6	13.4	6.6	13.6	2.7	100
2022–2023	CW	51.8	30.8	6.4	9.8	1.2	100
	OAE	96.5	2.2	0.5	0.5	0.3	100
	RS	36.8	17.6	12.4	31.2	2	100
	All	64.7	16.2	5.8	12.2	1.1	100
2023–2024	CW	63.8	18.1	6.1	10.8	1.1	100
	OAE	97.7	1.5	0.4	0.3	0.1	100
	RS	37	15.7	12.3	33.8	1.2	100
	All	68.7	11	5.8	13.7	0.8	100

Note: 1. CW means casual workers, regular salaried job is denoted as RS, and OAE stands for own account enterprises.2. Employment data are based on the usual principal and subsidiary status of individuals.

Source: Computed using unit-level PLFS data (2019–2020, 2020–2021, 2021–2022, 2022–2023, and 2023–2024).

shock and sustain them in the same capitalist segment for long or grow much bigger. These firms are largely liquid and may shift back to the traditional segment in the presence of an external shock. This implies that the limited transformation that the Indian economy has experienced is still unstable.

7.4 Other implications of the pandemic

Overcrowding and an increase in vulnerable jobs have other implications as well. First, they led to increased demand as well as provision of state support. For instance, the Government of India had to launch the Pradhan Mantri Garib Kalyan Anna Yojana (PMGKAY) in March 2020 to address the hardships faced by the poor due to the COVID-19 pandemic. About 80 crore people who were eligible got 5 kg of food grains for free, on top of what they were already entitled to under the National Food Security Act (NFSA). The initial plan was settled for April–June 2020; however, the programme was continued even after that and was finally merged with the NFSA programme in January 2024.

Apart from the public distribution system, there was also increased demand for the government's employment generation programme. One can understand this from data on demand for work under the Mahatma Gandhi National Rural Employment Generation Act (MNREGA), a state-supported job generation programme. Figure 7.2 shows that the demand for work under the MNREGA has remained high in 2020 and 2021 compared to 2019.

Second, since the pandemic pushed back people from the urban economy to their villages during the lockdown and post-lockdown periods, it is expected to have affected the flow of remittances. It is

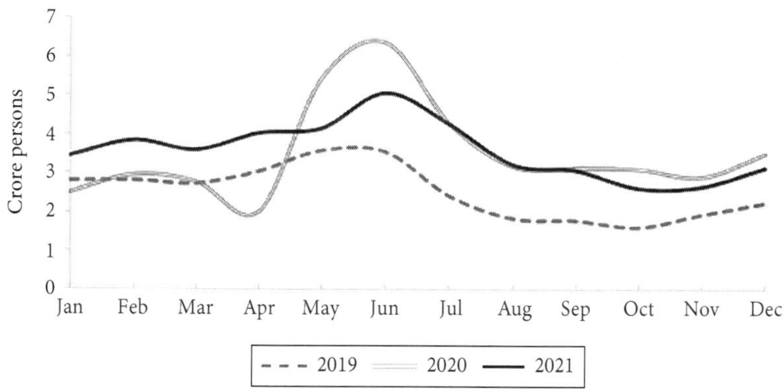

Figure 7.2 Persons demanded work under the Mahatma Gandhi National Rural Employment Guarantee Act (in 10 millions)

Source: Economic Survey (2022), Government of India, Ministry of Finance, Department of Economic Affairs.

Table 7.6 Annual gross value added per establishment for 2021–2022 across different types of enterprise (market establishment) in Indian rupees

	Rural			Urban		
	OAE	HWE	All	OAE	HWE	All
Manufacturing	62,900	802,697	103,375	97,275	870,619	254,916
Trade	123,136	605,027	153,645	195,850	878,579	367,383
Other services	100,314	983,327	175,913	142,288	991,100	328,967
All	96,073	811,811	144,570	152,220	913,645	326,480

Note: HWE stands for hired worker establishment, and OAE means own account enterprises.
Source: Report of the Annual Survey of Unincorporated Sector Enterprises (2021–2022).

important to note that remittances are an essential source of livelihood for families left behind in villages. Apart from the basic needs, it provides a financial buffer to the migrant household (ILO, 2020). Beyond this, remittances also augment transformation by inducing investment and growth in the rural nonfarm sector (Rajeev and Bhattacharjee, 2017). Though there is no recent data on the aggregate size of the internal remittances, micro-level estimates suggest that the size is enormous. For instance, the ILO (2020) reports that a backward community block, Thuamul Rampur of Kalahandi district in Odisha, receives annual remittances of between 300 and 400 million Indian rupees. In addition to remittances received from internal sources, the international flow of remittances was also affected by the pandemic. The World Bank (2020b) projected a decline of global remittances by 20 per cent, and the figure is 22.1 per cent for South Asia. Not only does such remittance flow augment urban development, but also a fraction of it comes to rural areas. A decline would thus reduce overall income and make households more vulnerable.

The third impact of the pandemic is the increased vulnerability arising from the overcrowding of the workforce in the nonfarm sector (particularly the OAEs) and the corresponding decline in their income. The value added per establishment data in Table 7.6 can help one understand the decline in income and the risk that comes with it. It is seen that, largely, OAEs (where overcrowding took place) generate very little value addition annually.

7.5 Pandemic shock: How well were the households prepared?

The above analysis shows the impact of the pandemic on rural Indian households. However, from the analysis, one may not understand how well a household in India is prepared to handle such shocks without an external support (such as the government). To understand it, we examine several other parameters, which are presented below.

First, when individuals become unemployed or they observe a decline in their income, they generally rely on their past savings (such as financial assets owned by them). Therefore, it is important to examine this parameter (financial assets) and determine whether it is sufficient to finance a household's consumption needs, at least in the short term. In this regard, Table 7.7 provides information on the household's average value of financial assets. In the table, the households are categorized into ten asset-holding classes, with class 1 representing the poorest and class 10 representing the richest.

Table 7.7 Average value of financial assets (in Indian rupees) as at 30 June 2018 by occupational category of household and household asset-holding class

Household asset Holding class	Cultivator	Non-cultivator
1	7,226	5,474
2	8,246	10,647
3	12,754	16,434
4	18,176	34,544
5	25,042	53,179
6	39,197	74,150
7	54,051	1,32,548
8	77,332	1,72,251
9	1,17,499	2,40,941
10	2,33,179	4,42,318
All	79,490	63,572

Source: Computed using Table A9R, NSS Report no. 588 (77/18.2).

The table reflects that for a majority of households, the financial assets amount is very low in absolute terms. If one compares this information with consumption (a flow variable), one can understand the problem better. According to the Household Consumption Expenditure Survey for 2023–2024, published by the Ministry of Statistics and Programme Implementation, the average monthly per capita consumption expenditure (MPCE) in rural areas was 4,122 Indian rupees, while in urban areas, it stood at 6,996 Indian rupees at current prices. When one deflates this number and multiplies it by the size of the household, one can observe that the consumption expenditure of households is significantly lower than the average value of financial assets owned by them (particularly for the lower income class).

Second, in the absence of savings, the other factor that may support a household during a time of crisis is access to credit. One of the indicators of measuring access to credit is the incidence of indebtedness (IOI), which is defined as the percentage of households having loans outstanding on any given date. A higher value of IOI is considered an indicator of better accessibility (Bhattacharjee, 2012). From the 77th round of NSSO data (Table 7.8), it is observed that the IOI was 40.3 per cent of the cultivator households and 28.2 per cent of nonfarm households in rural areas, implying the presence of poorer accessibility to credit.

Apart from the IOI, the low value of financial assets (which include gold and other related assets) also indicates poorer accessibility to credit (Table 7.6). This is because the presence of a low value of financial assets implies the absence of collaterals that can be used for availing loans.

7.6 Recovery from the pandemic: Looking into the future

Though it is difficult to predict the future perfectly, one can make specific projections based on the broad contours of different indicators. Our objective here is to map the probable outcomes.

One of the possible trajectories of India's future development is the progress in line with the often-discussed 'K-shaped recovery'. This means that different sections of the economy will experience different growth rates. In other words, it means that in the long run, specific sectors (such

Table 7.8 Incidence of indebtedness (IOI) and the average value of cash loan as of 30 June 2018 in rural India of cultivator and non-cultivator households

Household asset	Cultivator	Non-cultivator	Cultivator	Non-cultivator
Holding class	IOI	IOI	Av. of cash loan	Av. of cash loan
1	27.8	20.5	17,576	15,576
2	27.7	23.4	16,715	16,209
3	30.7	27	21,220	19,476
4	31.1	29.8	22,405	31,087
5	35.6	28.2	33,426	38,139
6	38.1	37	42,974	47,977
7	40.9	37.1	50,583	60,000
8	43.2	31.8	73,468	76,677
9	46.7	39.6	98,570	1,08,893
10	52	35.1	2,04,988	2,43,284
All	40.3	28.2	74,460	40,432

Source: Computed using Tables A8R and A9R, NSS Report no. 588 (77/18.2).

as the formal urban sector and the segment of informal sector linked to it) may experience high growth rates, while others (such as agriculture and the traditional informal sector) may experience lower growth rates. Certain indicators point out the possibility of such a trajectory. We discuss them below.

First, our data showed that even after three years, rural India observed more employment than urban India. It is essential to note that the value added per worker is higher in urban areas than in rural areas, irrespective of job type. Thus, in the post-lockdown period, a substantial number of individuals are experiencing a lower income compared to what they had experienced before.

Further, the employment generated in the formal sector is generally the expansion of jobs of poorer quality. For instance, leading dailies tell us that such jobs are mostly generated in the gig economy in the form of delivery agents. According to the staffing firm Team Lease, the gig economy (such as retail, e-commerce, logistics, and transportation) grew by 8 per cent in 2020 and 30 per cent in 2021 (The Economic Times, 2021). The growth of the gig economy implies increased risk and a lack of autonomy over monetary decisions for workers (Behera, 2020). Further

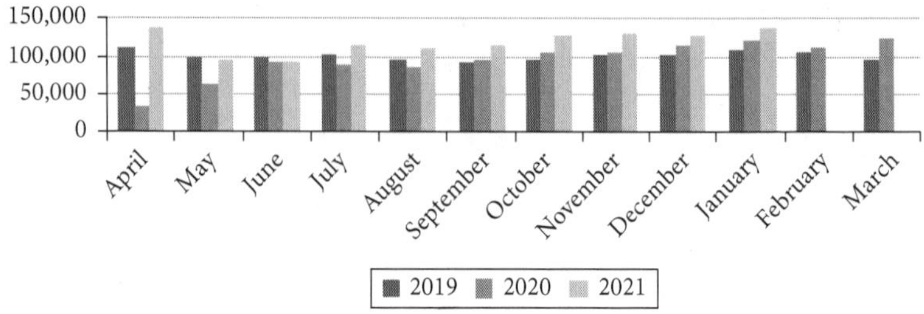

Figure 7.3 GST collection in rupees crores
Source: Computed from data of the Press Information Bureau, Government of India.

these developments can lead to an overall decline in wage income and an expansion of profit income at the aggregate level.

There is also another indicator that suggests unequal recovery. Data on the Goods and Services Tax (GST) shows that even though the economy did not experience significant output and employment growth, during the pandemic, indirect tax such as the GST has observed a steep increase (see Figure 7.3). An increase in GST revenue implies higher formal transactions. Without an expansion of the economy (particularly as observed during the pandemic period), an increase in the GST implies only a redistribution of market share between the formal and informal sectors, where the former is gaining while the latter is losing. In other words, the formal sector, with very few jobs, is crowding out the larger informal economy (including the rural informal nonfarm sector) by taking up its market. This might have happened due to the fact that, during the pandemic, we observed an increase in online transactions replacing traditional transactions or purchases of goods and services from small, informal shops. It will be hard for the traditional sector to regain this space.

Finally, the implication of having less possession of collateralizable assets, as discussed in section 7.5, may have adverse consequences. It possesses the potential to induce qualitative change in society, as we have observed in past pandemics.[60] There is a high chance that a large number of unemployed poor or individuals who migrated out of urban areas may not get access to credit from formal/informal sources to manage their

[60] For instance, some scholars argue that the Black Death, which started in 1348, accentuated the process of the end to feudalism by causing shortage of labour available for cultivating land belonging to landlords (Bagchi, 1982).

livelihood during the pandemic and, therefore, may end up availing loans against nonmarketable collaterals such as future labour service. Such dealings have the potential to slow down the capitalistic development process, particularly if a fraction of households become perpetually indebted. This is because the bonded workers might not be free to move from low-income-generating sectors to higher productivity sectors until their loans are repaid. Such a transformation may inhibit the growth and transformation of the rural nonfarm sector.

7.7 Concluding remarks

The COVID-19 pandemic and the associated lockdown have increased unemployment and exposed millions of workers and their families to hunger and even death (Khan and Mansoor, 2020; Mehta and Kumar, 2020). This chapter primarily focused on the implications of this pandemic in the rural sector in general and the nonfarm sector in particular. In this chapter, we depicted how the pandemic has increased vulnerability among different sections of the economy, specifically the rural poor. It is observed that the pandemic has the potential to strengthen the dualism already existing between the modern and traditional sectors of the economy. We have also observed that the impacts and especially the recovery processes have been distinctly different across the formal and informal sectors. Although the Indian formal sector has been able to absorb the shock to a large extent, the informal sector (be it a farm or nonfarm) is still in bad shape, and there is apprehension that it would really be difficult for this sector to recover fully in the near future. Hence, it could be argued that the formal–informal divide and, more specifically, the modern–traditional duality within the farm and nonfarm sectors have accentuated due to the pandemic.

8

Conclusions and Policy Suggestions

The farm and nonfarm sectors in developing countries are characterized by the presence of dual modes of production, that is, the coexistence of both traditional and modern segments. While the traditional sector produces or sells goods primarily for survival, the modern sector, which includes the formal sector and a segment of the informal sector, produces surplus and is an element in the extended circuit of capital. Mainstream literature has long propounded that higher growth in the economy will eventually pull out the surplus population and transform the traditional sector into a modern one. In other words, with accumulation in the formal segment, the entire economy, including the whole informal sector, will be within the extended ambit of the capitalistic mode of production. It is presumed that such transformation will augment inclusiveness and provide the fruits of high economic growth to all segments of society. However, although several developing nations (particularly India) have observed high rates of economic growth along with slow population growth, diverse modes of production persist simultaneously even today. In fact, our analysis in this book indicates that the size of even the traditional rural nonfarm sector has expanded in the recent period with the growth of the economy.

Against this backdrop, this book attempts to address the following question: is the observed phenomenon of formal sector accumulation and intensification in dualism a spurious relation, or is there an explanation that can link growth and divergence? In order to answer this question, we present a theoretical model in this book that links growth and duality along structuralist lines.

The theoretical model is followed by an in-depth empirical analysis using global data and data from the Indian economy. We used data primarily from the World Bank, International Labour Organization (ILO), and Food and Agriculture Organization (FAO) to understand global changes. For the Indian economy, we used data from the National Sample

The Nonfarm Economy. Manojit Bhattacharjee, Saumya Chakrabarti, and Meenakshi Rajeev,
Oxford University Press.
DOI: 10.1093/9780198972013.003.0008

Survey Office (NSSO) and the Annual Survey of Industries (ASI) at the unit level. The empirical analyses have looked into the changes/evolution/involution of the rural economy in the past two decades, which include the agricultural sector and the rural nonfarm economy. While the book primarily focuses on the rural nonfarm sector, it also includes a separate chapter on the agricultural sector. This is because initial observations indicate that the employment size of the traditional rural nonfarm sector is contingent on the nature and extent of capital accumulation, inducing outmigration from the traditional agricultural sector.

Apart from explaining how the rural economy has changed over the years, this book also provides a chapter on the COVID-19 pandemic and its probable impact on the rural sector. The analysis of the pandemic is critical for understanding the nonfarm economy, since the pandemic and the associated lockdown almost halted the accumulation process, which (according to our observations and analyses) is the source of the accentuation of duality in the recent period. This understanding is crucial, as it could be argued by the main stream discourse that a pandemic-induced shock could trigger a differentiation process in the non-capitalistic segment of the economy, which could eventually (of course, through a torturous path) lead to a comprehensive capitalistic structure. Stated otherwise, the argument could be that a pandemic may have disastrous effects in the short and medium term, but it could ultimately lead to a comprehensive/progressive change in the society in the long term. However, our observations, theoretical conjectures, and the subsequent validation of these conjectures showed some starkly different outcomes. Instead of any kind of grand convergence through post-pandemic recovery, we have, in fact, observed an intensification of structural dualism.

In this context, it is also important to note that the pandemic ended only three years ago, which makes it hard to get a full picture of how it has affected rural development as a whole. We therefore highlight the changes that are observed from available data and try to draw out the future implications. These implications, we believe, can have wider applications in contexts or situations in which the economy observes a slowdown/halt in the capital accumulation process.

Given this background, the chapter is presented as follows. In the next few sections, we summarize our findings. The implications and policy suggestions are discussed subsequently, based on the broad contours of the development process observed during the past two decades and narrated in the earlier chapters.

8.1 Neo dualism in the rural economy: A tale of accumulation and migration

The Global South, in general, and the Indian economy in particular, have experienced substantial transformation over the past few decades. Akin to the experiences of the developed world, with the economy's growth, the share of the agricultural sector in the gross domestic product and that of employment in workforce experienced a decline. However, it is worth noting that in India, the decline in the output share of agriculture was substantially higher than the decline in its employment share. Owing to the higher growth rate in the formal sector of the economy and the lack of adequate opportunity for agricultural workers in this formal segment (particularly due to high capital intensity and also skill shortage), the agricultural sector observed a faster fall in output share as compared to its employment share. Consequently, the economy experienced a widening productivity gap between the agricultural sector and the growth-driving (i.e. modern) sector.

The presence of a high productivity gap has remained a motivating factor for the movement of workers (due to the pull effect) from agricultural to modern nonfarm activities, that is, towards the formal sector and to the linked/advanced informal activities.

However, the movement of workers is not confined only to these two sectors. Additional examination of the agricultural employment data reveals that within the agricultural sector of India, there is an intra-sectoral movement of workers. We found that in the past few decades, employment within agriculture has declined in the traditional segment (i.e. small and marginal farmers engaged in cereals production or other essential food grains), while employment has increased for non-food grains such as fruits or vegetables and non-food crops such as cotton, tobacco, and other crops (i.e. a variety of high-value-crops). It is important to note that these non-food grains or crops have a high linkage with the formal segment of the economy and are produced primarily by larger farmers, who can afford to produce crops beyond basic cereals for owning/leasing in larger-sized land. These non-food grains/crop productions can be clubbed and termed as the modern segment within agriculture. Thus, with accumulation, there is a movement of workers from the traditional farm sector to its modern segment, generating a dichotomy within the farm sector as well.

Apart from the increased employment owing to the pull effect in the modern segments, the rural Indian economy also experienced a substantial increase in jobs in the traditional/petty nonfarm sector with the growth of the economy.

It is worth noting that the traditional nonfarm sector (i.e. the small own account household enterprises), on average, generates less value added per worker than agriculture. Thus, the movement of workers towards this traditional nonfarm sector indicates a push/distress-driven migration/diversification. Perhaps a large part of the population that leaves/diversifies away from traditional agriculture is not fortunate enough to get a job in the remunerative modern farm and nonfarm activities. A fraction of these individuals also loses the opportunity to return and re-engage in traditional agriculture. Hence, a large segment of the migrant/diversifying population is compelled to throng the rural traditional/petty nonfarm segment.

This dual process of capital accumulation and corresponding generation or persistence of structural duality (i.e. the coexistence of structurally modern and traditional segments) is explained using a structuralist theoretical model with micro-foundation in Chapter 2.

Our model begins with a no-migration equilibrium following a Kaleckian-structuralist framework using an extended Harris–Todaro (1970) method of analysis. The no-migration equilibrium is characterized by the equalization of the actual per capita net income from the marketable surplus of traditional agriculture (the source of migration) and the expected per capita real income from all other sectors (the destination/s). In this model, we introduce the process of formal sector accumulation. This accumulation dynamics generates two effects (i.e. push and pull), spreading the heterogeneous rural nonfarm sector and dichotomizing the farm sector too.

In this context, it is important to note that dualism in developing countries is not a new phenomenon. Existing literature considers excess population along with lack of sufficient growth and expansion of the capitalist circuit in developing countries as the primary reason behind the persistence of such a problem. On the contrary, the dualism that we explain is a result of the formal sector capital accumulation process itself. The process we explain is different from the standard Harris–Todaro (1970) (H–T) model as well, and it is also different from the standard Kaleckian (1954/1993) analysis. Our framework actually derives from both: it constructs the macro structure following Kalecki, but uses a modified H–T method. Next, unlike the H–T model, not only do we explicate a demand-pull-driven expansion of the modern sector, but also we highlight the push-driven process (i.e. dispossession) initiated by the modern/capitalistic nonfarm sector growth. In other words, our model incorporates the political-economy discourse of Harvey (2003) (i.e. accumulation by dispossession) in the H–T method of analysis.

Thus, contrary to the dominant literature (Ranis and Stewart, 1993; Marjit, 2003; Fields, 2004; Bardhan, 2009, 2018) that presents a variety of mechanisms through which the formal sector triggers a transition within the heterogeneous rural nonfarm, bringing it close to the formal sector itself and also making it a comprehensive and dynamic whole, our model explicates how the formal sector (rural, in particular) could, in fact, create a division within the farm and nonfarm sectors (across modern and traditional segments) and thereby accentuate the intra-nonfarm and intra-agriculture dualities. Thus, our framework could be a critique of the deterministic narrative of the (all-inclusive) transition from the traditional to the modern.

Our model has implications that can be used to bridge a gap existing in the literature. The theoretical framework explains the process through which formal sector accumulation can generate a disjointed and economically weaker traditional segment. Existing studies (Sanyal, 2007; Agarwala, 2013; Bardhan, 2018) have long indicated that this disjointed segment of the economy is the main contender for government support schemes. Placed in this context, our study can be used to explain the process in which formal sector accumulation, persistence/proliferation of the 'need economy' (Sanyal, 2007), and government support programmes appear as a vicious circle.

Our book also pinpoints the factors apart from accumulation that induce the traditional agricultural workforce to out-migrate.

8.2 Factors inducing push and pull of the agricultural workforce and the limitation of the modern sector

As has been seen in Chapter 6, the movement of cultivators to other sectors is induced by both pull and push factors. While there is no doubt that economic growth has caused a pull-driven movement/diversification of the agricultural workforce towards the modern sector, there are several push factors as well (explained in Chapter 6) that are worthy of pointing out. Thus, our book points out several reasons that are pushing out workers from traditional agriculture. Some of the important factors are listed below.

First, due to the expansion of the real estate business, infrastructure, and the formal manufacturing and services activities in rural areas (possibly due to scarcity of land, higher rents in urban areas, and also a drive from the supply-side economics doctrine), aggregate operational holdings in agriculture have declined, which pushed out several cultivators from the sector. The recent drives towards land acquisition have accentuated this problem further.

The second reason behind the distress-driven movement of cultivators is the increase in the number of unviable-sized land holdings that cannot produce the output required for the sustenance of a household. Unviable-sized land holdings are consequences of a decline in operational holdings (for formal sector and infrastructural expansions and urbanization) and the distribution of paternal property among the increased number of descendants.

Third, higher formal sector accumulation, urbanization, and infrastructural expansion have induced (high-value food-) crop diversification and/or production of non-food grains (through both demand and supply-side drives). This, in turn, has pushed up agricultural wages, which may be faced equally by small and large farms, and thus, smaller farmers may find it unprofitable to continue production of crops and therefore might be compelled to migrate to other activities such as petty non-agricultural jobs (Otsuka et al., 2016; Yamauchi, 2016).

In addition to this, cultivators over time have experienced the movement of terms of trade (the ratio of the index of the price that traditional farmers receive by selling their products and the price index of their consumption basket) in favour of other sectors. Our theoretical model explains that any formal sector expansion inflates the price of modern sector products. Since some of these products also shape the consumption basket of traditional farm workers, they experience a decline in real income, and thus they out-migrate. Empirical data also shows a fall in real income from cultivation per household and also per hectare of land.

All these processes push individuals towards (mostly petty) nonfarm informal activities and thereby generate/sustain a traditional sector that acts as a sink for the unfortunate dispossessed/disadvantaged individuals who are deprived of modern jobs.

A question arises: why can't the modern sector absorb all the pulled and/or displaced workers? We explain some of the several factors that may be responsible. The capital–labour ratio is high in the formal sector compared to that of the traditional sector (Rodrik, 2018). For generating traditional sector equivalent levels of employment, a much higher level of investment and economic growth rate is required, which again may be infeasible owing to the constraints imposed by the scarcity of resources, climatic problems, and also effective demand. In this context, the statement of former Reserve Bank of India (RBI) governor Raghuram Rajan assumes importance. In a lecture organized by the International Monetary Fund (IMF) on globalization and climate change, the former RBI governor pointed out the harmful environmental impact and infeasibility of a growth model based on manufacturing (which is considered the job-generating segment within the formal sector). In his lecture, he largely emphasized the need for service-led growth. However, such a growth strategy also requires investment in skilling the workforce, which is not achievable in the short run. Most crucially, the effective demand problem might be a binding constraint, often missed out in mainstream discussions.

Unemployment could also exist due to the presence of wage rates above the market clearing levels in the capitalist segment. This may happen for a variety of reasons, such as the presence of trade unions, the minimum wages act, efficiency wage criteria, etc. in the formal sector (Fields and Wan, 1989; Ray, 1998; Fields, 1999). Such factors ensure the inability of the capitalist sector to clear the labour market by providing employment to all.

Heterodox scholars have also highlighted how (limited) aggregate demand in a capitalist society can't create full employment (Patnaik,

2016). This primarily happens since higher accumulation reduces the share of wage income, which in turn can adversely affect the aggregate demand in an ex-ante sense. Though the credit market can augment ex-post aggregate demand, however, over-dependence on the credit market increases the possibility of a banking sector crisis. The subprime lending crisis in the United States and the most recent banking crisis in China are examples of recent history in this regard.

There are inherent problems with the migrant workforce as well that may make it difficult for them to get linked to the circuit of capital. These include problems in getting access to credit, the absence of social networking, and adequate access to skill as well as machinery and other related factors.

It is worth noting that even though formal sector accumulation generates dualism in the informal sector and sustains a traditional informal sector, in reality, the economic condition of the workers engaged in the sector may vary across regions. This is primarily because government intervention and welfare policies vary regionally.

In this context, Agarwala (2013) provides useful insights. She argues that informal sector workers organize and demand welfare benefits from the state in the presence of rapid economic growth and an increase in inequalities. However, she points out that workers do not succeed in attaining welfare benefits in all states. States characterized by the presence of competition in politics (such as Tamil Nadu) are better in that respect compared to states characterized by monopoly in politics (such as West Bengal).

8.3 The impact of the COVID-19 pandemic that halted the accumulation process

First, one of the reasons behind the generation of the new form of dualism, as discussed earlier, is accumulation. However, the process of accumulation had been obstructed due to the lockdown and other restrictions imposed during the COVID-19 pandemic of 2020/2021. Therefore, in Chapter 7 of this book, we tried to understand the changes the pandemic introduced into the rural sector. In this context, it is important to note that though the COVID-19 pandemic has ended, since the world which we live in is more connected and complex compared to our known history, problems of epidemics and pandemics may arise frequently in the future.

As far as the recent pandemic is concerned, India observed a complete lockdown in four phases from 24 March to 31 May 2020, after which phase-wise unlocking of the country took place between June and November. Each phase had higher relaxation in the unlocking period than the earlier one. In 2021, India observed a second wave of COVID-19 that resulted in a state-wide lockdown from April to June 2021. Employment and, in some areas, even labour force declined in these lockdown phases, probably due to the disruption of movement.

Our study shows that the lockdown created a reverse movement of workforce from the urban and capitalist segment to rural areas and to the traditional segment. Such reverse movement and delayed return created an acute shortage of workers in cities; on the other hand, it caused overcrowding in rural areas, particularly within the traditional sector. Using data from the Periodic Labour Force Survey, we show that employment in the agricultural sector and the rural nonfarm sector increased enormously owing to the halt in the accumulation process. Since the value added per worker is very low in the traditional nonfarm segment, it can be inferred that an increase in demand for jobs and overcrowding led to a decline in income for the traditional sector. As a result, we found that there was increased demand for work under the Mahatma Gandhi National Rural Employment Act (MNREGA), a state-supported job generation programme.

Second, though the economy did not experience significant output and employment growth during the pandemic, indirect taxes, such as the Goods and Services Tax (GST) collection observed a steep increase. The period also witnessed a frequent boom in the stock market indices. An increase in GST revenue or a boom in the stock market price index implies higher formal transactions or profit by the stock-listed companies.

Without an increase in the growth rate, higher formal transaction/profit implied only a redistribution of market share between the formal and informal sectors, where the formal sector crowded out the larger informal economy (including the rural, informal nonfarm sector) by taking up its market. This might have happened due to increased online transactions arising during lockdown that reduced purchases of goods and services from small informal shops, a trend that persists even in the post-pandemic period.

Third, the decline in employment in cities and in the formal segment during the pandemic implied that employment generated in the modern sector was generally jobs of poorer quality with the absence of social security and tenure. We have shown that such poorer-quality job generation existed even in the post-pandemic period.

Chapter 7 also indicates the possible trajectories of India's future development in the long run. Specifically, we discuss two possibilities, based on the imprints of available data. Since the pandemic, the size of the traditional segment has increased and is still being sustained (owing to some frictions), and the formal sector has largely taken over the informal space, the recovery we are observing is a 'K-shaped recovery'.

This K-shaped recovery is further stimulated by the intensification of the agrarian crisis (especially for the petty farmers), de-globalization owing to geopolitical problems, automation and reversal of the global value chain process, etc.

Chapter 7 also points out the possibility of another trajectory. Our data analyses have shown that workers in the informal sector possess very few collateralizable assets. The absence of collateralizable assets among informal workers creates the potential to induce qualitative change in society. There is a high chance that a large number of unemployed poor or individuals who migrated out of urban areas may not get access to credit and, therefore, may end up availing loans against nonmarketable collaterals such as future labour service. Such dealings have the potential to slow down the capitalistic development process in rural areas and may induce a much larger traditional sector having pre-capitalistic features (such as bonded labour) in rural areas. This may be one of the reasons behind the slow recovery of the economy.

Let us now concentrate on the policy suggestions that can lead to an inclusive transformation of the economy as a whole and can reverse the damage caused by the pandemic and the iniquitous accumulation.

8.4 Policy suggestions

Policy suggestions focusing on the development of the nonfarm sector in the informal space largely depend on the conceptualization of this sector.

One can visualize the informal sector either as a continuum of the capitalist sector or as an excluded/dislocated sector. Both these features can coexist as well within the informal space, as our study shows.

If one conceptualizes the informal sector as a component of the circuit of capital providing flexibility and efficiency to the larger capitalistic sector (such as through subcontracting), then there is little space to suggest policies on transformation, since this sector would be seen as augmenting growth and export. Therefore, studies considering the informal sector within the broader domain of the capitalistic sector have largely suggested drawing the informal workers into the network of state-sponsored welfare programmes (Roychowdhury, 2018). In this context, it is worth pointing out that criticism exists against the welfare programmes that focus on state support without focusing on income generation and the creation of decent workspaces (Roychowdhury, 2018).

A section of these studies also suggests government intervention in terms of raising the minimum wage to improve the living standards of individuals (Kanbur, 2009). However, such studies are less common. Some studies have suggested of developing a closer network between the formal and informal sectors. On the contrary, if we consider the informal sector as an excluded segment of the capitalist sector, policy suggestions can be made beyond the orthodox welfare policy discourse.

Our theoretical and empirical analysis in this book showed a proliferation of the rural nonfarm sector. In this regard, we provide certain policy suggestions that can lead to an inclusive transformation of the sector by combining the opportunities provided by the markets and developing the capabilities of the individuals engaged in the sector.

Nevertheless, the implementation/execution of these policies also depends on two factors: the autonomy of the state under capitalism (Roychowdhury, 2018) and the pressure created by the democratic political framework, that is, the demand of the weaker section of the society for government support (Chatterjee, 2004).

We now explain our policy suggestions, which can be categorized into short-term and long-term suggestions. The short-term policies can concentrate on providing a temporary cushion to the vulnerable households affected by the pandemic that have taken refuge in the traditional sector. The long-term policies can be more concrete.

In the short term, there can be direct government support, such as providing an unconditional cash transfer to the petty producers (Kundu et al., 2021). Such policies seem to be appropriate in this situation because petty commodity producers possess the unique ability to simultaneously expand both production and consumption. Cash injection to the industrial workers, on the other hand, can be inflationary, since they may use it solely for consumption purposes, while such support towards the large entrepreneurs who are net producers can create a glut-like situation. Consequently, direct support by the state should be a necessity during the short and medium term.

In the long term, one needs to think of more constructive policies other than formal sector accumulation and mere government support that can lead to inclusive growth. First, it is important to note that the highly labour-intensive and large traditional nonfarm sector is supposed to have deep linkages with the vast traditional or petty agriculture (Bhattacharjee et al., 2024). Traditional agriculture acts both as a supplier of input and as the final market for rural nonfarm sector products. Modern agriculture, such as floriculture, fruit cultivation, and plantation crop cultivation, on the other hand, primarily has high urban linkage. Therefore, inclusive growth requires sustaining and expanding the vast labour-intensive petty agriculture through government support.

Second, one of the major obstacles to sustaining traditional agriculture is decreasing operational holdings. Studies suggest that the decrease in operational holdings is due not only to forced land acquisition but also to the overall process of increase in the cost of production and unviable land size. Government intervention through the provisioning of land use rights, and not land transfer rights, can address this problem. This is because, in the presence of transfer, a household can sell its land to large agents, who may use the land for unproductive purposes and rent-seeking activities. In addition to this, cooperative farming/cluster formation/land consolidation can be encouraged to reduce the problem of unviable land size. Existing studies have shown that a land consolidation programme has a positive impact on farmer output and income (Gedefaw et al., 2019; Do et al., 2023; Fauziah et al., 2023; Chen et al., 2024).

Third, the petty nonfarm population faces a threat of disintegration; its comprehensive rehabilitation requires product-specific cluster formations (see also Mukherjee et al., 2019; Kundu et al., 2021). This, on the one hand, would generate economies of scale at the industry level (i.e. external economies of scale), strengthen the forward and backward production linkages, and also generate a mechanism through which these units can share tangible–intangible resources and tap large markets. This, in turn, has the potential to foster competitiveness (Cucculelli and Storai, 2018). It has been observed from primary survey-based research in India that micro-unit clusters can help the informal sector to withstand fierce competition by pursuing various innovative methods (Kundu and Chakrabarti, 2008).

In the long run, we are not arguing for the complete removal of government support. There is a need for direct government support that ensures the availability of different resources required by petty producers. Studies have shown that poorer rural households lack capital assets such as machinery and also lack access to credit for purchasing capital goods (Bhattacharjee and Rajeev, 2014). There also exist inequalities in accessing critical inputs, such as water resources (UNDP, 2006), power, etc. Thus, government support and intervention are required to provide seamless access to subsidized loans for purchasing capital goods and cheap raw materials, uninterrupted power supply, access to water, and other necessary inputs. Such measures from the government would help the informal units reap the benefits of agglomeration and economies of scale.

In addition to the above-mentioned supply-side intervention, the government should assist the clusters to have access to output markets directly, such as by creating and providing access to public e-commerce platforms or mobile application services for selling products. This would ensure that small firms reap the entire surplus and reinvest it without sharing it with various intermediaries, which possess better information and access to the global market.[61]

The sustainability of a cluster is crucially dependent on its branding and the corresponding brand value that is acquired over time. The existence and progress of a cluster are conditional upon its acceptance in the broader market, and for that, the government has an important role, especially during the initial years of the cluster.

[61] In this context, it is crucial to emphasize not only that private e-commerce platforms may impose a user fee and exploit indigenous businesses, but also that sellers who sell their products using these platforms encounter additional risks. For instance, Kalra and Stecklow (2021), using internal documents of Amazon, revealed that the company had replicated/copied popular products in India and promoted these copied brands on their own platform. However, these allegations were publicly denied by Amazon.

Clusters could get additional impetus through their linkages with the so-called modern economy. In this respect, the government could play a very important role (as a facilitator of contracts). Thus, providing the clusters with a variety of support (physical and social infrastructure, technology, user rights, branding, information, etc.) and acting as a facilitator for linking them with the long value chain is the crux of the policy bundle that is essential for a cluster-based development model ensuring a job-orientated, inclusive, endogenous, and hence sustainable, growth process.

However, at the present moment, as the vulnerability of the informal sector has increased manifold, there is a higher possibility that these units would be exploited severely by the larger (contracting) firms. Hence, government monitoring should also be present.

Given our theoretical conjectures and empirical analysis of this book, we present our above-mentioned policy discussions (along with some valuable additions) in a more structured way below. For this, we reiterate that we have a fundamental duality in rural India, traditional farm–nonfarm (consisting of petty farming and petty nonfarm sector) versus modern farm–nonfarm (consisting of formal sector, modern informal nonfarm sector, and modernized farming). While a part of the rural economy either constitutes the capitalistic circuit (along with the urban modern sector) or closely interacts with that system, another very large part exists in limbo being functionally unrelated to the capitalist circuit. Given this qualitatively distinct duality, we propose the following:

1. For the modern segments of the rural economy, we propose mainly institutional support so that the linkages between the rural–urban formal sector (mostly nonfarm) and the rural modern informal sectors (farm–nonfarm) are strengthened. This would facilitate formal–(modern) informal interactions and could generate a positive and dynamic multiplier process. On the one hand, this would reduce a variety of costs for the formal segments through subcontracting with the informal segments, and on the other, it would promote technological skill development for the contracting informal units. Thus, ensuring a free market environment along with a proper private property rights structure would be crucial for this part of the dual.

2. For the other segment (i.e. the traditional part of the rural economy—farm–nonfarm), we propose three policy packages/directions:
   a. In times of distress, when demand and supply channels have broken, unconditional cash transfer could induce both supply and demand. This is because, petty commodity production has the unique property of unity between consumption and production. Cash transfer could induce not only demand but also supply, if its flow is maintained over time and a confidence on state and market is reinstated. As already mentioned, for petty commodity production, a cash injection might relax demand immediately with some inflationary pressures, but gradually supply picks up with committed cash flow. Consequently, a noninflationary recovery is possible.
   b. However, this is only a short-to-medium-term measure, and much more fundamental impetus could come from a cluster-based development path involving clustered farm and nonfarm production. For millions of petty farm–nonfarm producers, secluded/individualistic survival and thriving is almost impossible in the context of the dominance of the globalized big capital. Only if such firms and farms are clustered could they negotiate with big capital and even reap the benefits of globalization. This could be a unique opportunity for the micro units, as privately organized firms and farms could enjoy the benefits of a collective preserving individual traits, aspirations, and incentives.
   c. A third and very comprehensive policy paradigm/package for petty commodity production has already been established not only in India but also across the Global South. This is essentially a medium-term endeavour in between the above-mentioned two extremes of cash transfer in the short run and cluster development in the long run. We argue in favour of proper designing and implementation of this third policy package. It has been accepted by a large segment of mainstream academia, policy circle, bureaucracy, and polity that the traditional modernity-centric, capital-centric, market-centric development path of the twentieth century is not providing benefit to the billions of

> petty producers of the Global South. Rather, these productive and survival activities are being marginalized constantly. So, the old pool of outsiders is being expanded by the processes of accumulation and/or development by dispossession. Given this, it has been proposed by the global institutions and global discourses that the problems of underdevelopment of this multitude of outsiders should be addressed directly by the state and its allied institutions (non-governmental organizations, community-based organizations, civil society organizations, and even corporations) beyond the circuit of capitalistic growth. Thus, it is being widely argued that the endowment failures, network failures, and developmental disadvantages of the farm–nonfarm petty producers could be handled with an array of strategies and policies that could be encapsulated as developmentalism or development management (Chakrabarti and Datta, 2024).[62] Through this (mainly) direct management of underdevelopment, it is expected that, the rehabilitation/inclusion of millions of outsiders would be possible, and they would be incorporated into the broad global market, albeit not into the core of the capitalist economy, if proper designing and monitoring of programmes are undertaken (Chakrabarti and Datta, 2024).

However, last but not the least, for all our policy suggestions, we cannot ignore the resistance from the big capital and its allies (generally, the upper-middle-class—the crucial opinion makers). Hence, for all these interventions, perhaps, the political-economic discourses, negotiations, and struggles become the determining factors. All these policy suggestions might seem utopian in a globalized world dominated by big and highly mobile capital, unless we take into consideration the dire necessity of the political-economic contexts, processes, and especially designs and endeavours. Without an appropriate, well-designed, and well-orchestrated political-economic praxis, unfortunately, our three-pronged policy paradigm remains a utopia.

[62] Crucial development management programmes include provisioning of income/food in exchange for work, conditional or unconditional cash/service/goods transfers, etc.

References

Abbott, P., Murenzi, I., & Musana, S. (2012). The role of non-farm household enterprises in poverty reduction, employment creation and economic growth in Rwanda. *Rwanda Journal, 26*, 68–92.

Abduh, M. (2023). Indonesia agricultural transformation: How far? Where would it go? *Journal Perencanaan Pembangunan/Indonesian Journal of Development Planning, 7*(1), 48–82.

Abdulai, A., & Delgado, C. L. (1999). Determinants of nonfarm earnings of farm-based husbands and wives in northern Ghana. *American Journal of Agricultural Economics, 81*(1), 117–130.

Abraham, V. (2016). Agrarian distress and rural non-farm sector employment in India. In P. Kumar & S. Mohanakumar (Eds.), *Indian agriculture: Performance, growth and challenges*. Essays in honour of Ramesh Chand. 273–302.

Abraham, V. (2023). The slow emergence of rural non-farm sector employment in India: Shift or diversification? *Indian Journal of Labour Economics, 66*(3), 661–685.

Abraham, V. (2024). Ruptured rural transformation: From non-farm to mixed households in rural India. *Economic and Political Weekly, 59(50)*, 84–92.

Acheampong, I. K., & Baah-Kumi, B. (2011). The Dutch disease in the context of Ghana's oil and gas find: The plausible economic effects on the Ghanaian economy. *Indian Development Review, 9*(2), 239–254.

Adi, T. W., Prabowo, E., & Prasadjaningsih, O. (2022). Influence of electricity consumption of industrial and business, electricity price, inflation and interest rate on GDP and investments in Indonesia. *International Journal of Energy Economics and Policy, 12*(3), 331–340.

Agarwala, R. (2013). *Informal labor, formal politics, and dignified discontent in India*. Cambridge: Cambridge University Press.

Ahmed, R., Haggblade, S., Hazell, P. B. R., Meyer, R. L., & Reardon, T. (2007). The policy and institutional environment affecting the rural nonfarm economy. In S. Haggblade, P. B. R. Hazell, & T. Reardon (Eds), *Transforming the rural nonfarm economy* (pp. 237–253). Baltimore, MD: Johns Hopkins University Press.

Anang, B. T. (2017, February). Effect of non-farm work on agricultural productivity: Empirical evidence from northern Ghana (World Institute for Development Economics Research (WIDER) Working Paper 2017/38). Helsinki: United Nations University (UNU)-WIDER. Retrieved 11 June 2025, from https://www.wider.unu.edu/sites/default/files/wp2017-38.pdf,

Aneja, R., & Ahuja, V. (2021). An assessment of socioeconomic impact of COVID-19 pandemic in India. *Journal of Public Affairs, 21*(2), e2266.

Asfaw, A., Simane, B., Hassen, A., & Bantider, A. (2017). Determinants of non-farm livelihood diversification: Evidence from rainfed-dependent smallholder farmers in northcentral Ethiopia (Woleka sub-basin). *Development Studies Research, 4*(1), 22–36.

Asumadu, G., Ofori, D., Agyei, J., & Bawa, A. Y. (2021). Ghana's oil discovery and natural resource curse Nexus. *Modern Economy, 12*(12), 1959–1971.

Atamanov, A., & Van Den Berg, M. (2012). Rural nonfarm activities in Central Asia: A regional analysis of magnitude, structure, evolution and drivers in the Kyrgyz Republic. *Europe-Asia Studies, 64*(2), 349–368.

Ayambila, S. N., Osei-Akoto, I., & Ayamga, M. (2017). Determinants of non-farm micro and small enterprise participation in rural Ghana. *British Journal of Economics, Management & Trade, 17*(4), 1–12.

Ayambila, S. N. (2023). Determinants of micro and small enterprises financial performance in the non-farm sector of Ghana: A quantile regression approach. *Cogent Economics & Finance, 11*(2), 2225331.

Azzahra, A., Fatimah, A. F., Boateng, K. A., & Ridzki, M. M. (2024). Analysis of regional minimum wage regulation and it's implementation: A case study of a multinational company. *Eduvest—Journal of Universal Studies, 4*(10), 8499–8507.

Bachewe, F., Berhane, G., Minten, B., & Taffesse, A. S. (2016). Non-farm income and labor markets in rural Ethiopia (Ethiopia Strategy Support Program (ESSP) Research Note 61). International Food Policy Research Institute (IFPRI). Retrieved 11 June 2025, from https://www.fao.org/family-farming/detail/en/c/422266/.

Bagchi, A. K. (1982). *The political economy of underdevelopment.* Cambridge: Cambridge University Press.

Baldwin, R. (2020). *Keeping the lights on: Economic medicine for a medical shock.* VoxEU, Centre for Economic Policy Research (CEPR). Retrieved 11 June 2025, from https://cepr.org/voxeu/columns/keeping-lights-economic-medicine-medical-shock.

Bandyopadhyay, M., & Gupta, M. R. (1995). Development policies in the presence of an informal sector: A note. *Journal of Economics, 61*(3), 301–315.

Bardhan, P. (2009). Notes on the political economy of India's tortuous transition. *Economic and Political Weekly, 44*(49), 31–36.

Bardhan, P. (2010). *Awakening giants, feet of clay: Assessing the economic rise of China and India.* Princeton, NJ: Princeton University Press.

Bardhan, P. (2018). Reflections on Kalyan Sanyal's rethinking capitalist development. *Economic and Political Weekly, 53*(21), 19–22.

Barrett, C. B., Bezuneh, M., & Aboud, A. (2001). Income diversification, poverty traps and policy shocks in Côte d'Ivoire and Kenya. *Food Policy, 26*(4), 367–384.

Basole, A. (2022). Structural transformation and employment generation in India: Past performance and the way forward. *Indian Journal of Labour Economics, 65*(2), 295–320.

Basole, A., & Basu, D. (2011a). Relations of production and modes of surplus extraction in India: Part I—Agriculture. *Economic and Political Weekly, 46*(14), 41–58.

Basole, A., & Basu, D. (2011b). Relations of production and modes of surplus extraction in India: Part II—'Informal' Industry. *Economic and Political Weekly, 46*(15), 63–79.

Basole, A., Basu, D., & Bhattacharya, R. (2015). Determinants and impacts of subcontracting: Evidence from India's unorganized manufacturing sector. *International Review of Applied Economics, 29*(3), 374–402.

Basu, K. (1997). *Analytical development economics: The less developed economy revisited.* Cambridge, MA: MIT Press.

Behera, S. M. (2020). Gig work and platforms during the COVID-19 pandemic in India. *Economic and Political Weekly, 55*(45).

Bernstein, H. (1996). South Africa's agrarian question: Extreme and exceptional? *Journal of Peasant Studies, 23*(2–3), 1–52.

Bernstein, H. (2006). Is there an agrarian question in the 21st century? *Revue canadienne d'études du développement/Canadian Journal of Development Studies, 27*(4), 449–460.

Bezu, S., & Holden, S. (2014). Are rural youth in Ethiopia abandoning agriculture? *World Development, 64*, 259–272.

Bhaduri, A. (1986). *Macroeconomics: The dynamics of commodity production.* Delhi: Macmillan.

Bhaduri, A. (2018). A study in development by dispossession. *Cambridge Journal of Economics*, 42(1), 19–31.

Bhaduri, A., & Banerjee, K. (2025). Land acquisition and economic development: A decolonised view. *World Development, 192*, 107011.

Bhambhri, C. P. (2016). Globalised monopoly capitalism and Indian society. *Social Scientist, 44*(5/6), 65–70.

Bhattacharjee, M. (2012). *Indebtedness in the household sector: A study of selected states in India* (Doctoral dissertation). University of Mysore.

Bhattacharjee, M., & Rajeev, M. (2014). Is access to loan adequate for financing capital expenditure? A household level analysis on some selected states of India (Institute for Social and Economic Change (ISEC) Working Paper No. 315). Institute for Social and Economic Change. Retrieved 11 June 2025, from https://www.isec.ac.in/wp-content/uploads/2023/07/WP-315-Meenakshi-Rajeev-and-Manojit-Bhattacharjee_Final.pdf.

Bhattacharjee, M., Chakrabarti, S., & Rajeev, M. (2024). An inclusive transformation of the rural nonfarm economy: Leveraging farm nonfarm linkages. *Economic & Political Weekly, 59*(15).

Bhattacharya, M., & Mazumdar, M. (2020, 1 October). Can free-trade and corporate farming improve farmer income? *The Hindu Business Line.* Retrieved 10 October 2022, from https://www.thehindubusinessline.com/opinion/can-free-trade-and-corporate-farming-improve-farmer-income/article32745489.ece.

Bhattacharya, R., & Menon, S. (2021, 25 September). They have not returned: How COVID-19 has impacted labour migration in the country. *The Economic Times.* Retrieved 7 February 2022, from https://economictimes.indiatimes.com/news/india/they-have-not-returned-how-covid-19-has-impacted-labour-migration-in-the-country/articleshow/86508788.cms.

Bhattacharya, R., Bhattacharya, S., & Sanyal, K. K. (2013). Dualism in the informal economy: Exploring the Indian informal manufacturing sector. In S. Banerjee & A. Chakrabarti (Eds), *Development and sustainability* (pp. 339–362). Springer India.

Bhattacharya, S., & Kesar, S. (2018). Possibilities of transformation: The informal sector in India. *Review of Radical Political Economics, 50*(4), 727–735.

Binswanger-Mkhize, H. P. (2012, May). India 1960–2010: Structural change, the rural non-farm sector, and the prospects for agriculture. *Stanford Symposium*

Series on Global Food Policy and Food Security in the 21st Century, 1(1), 1–31. Stanford University, Center on Food Security and the Environment.

Binswanger-Mkhize, H. P. (2013). The stunted structural transformation of the Indian economy: Agriculture, manufacturing and the rural non-farm sector. *Economic and Political Weekly, 48*(26/27), 5–13.

Braam, D. H., Srinivasan, S., Church, L., Sheikh, Z., Jephcott, F. L., & Bukachi, S. (2021). Lockdowns, lives and livelihoods: The impact of COVID-19 and public health responses to conflict affected populations—a remote qualitative study in Baidoa and Mogadishu, Somalia. *Conflict and Health, 15*(1), 47.

Breman, J. (2013). *At work in the informal economy of India: A perspective from the bottom up*. New Delhi: Oxford University Press.

Breman, J. (2019). *Capitalism, inequality and labour in India*. Cambridge: Cambridge University Press.

Breman, J., & Mundle, S. (1991). *Rural transformation in Asia*. New Delhi: Oxford University Press.

Bren d'Amour, C., Reitsma, F., Baiocchi, G., Barthel, S., Güneralp, B., Erb, K. H., . . . & Seto, K. C. (2017). Future urban land expansion and implications for global croplands. *Proceedings of the National Academy of Sciences, 114*(34), 8939–8944.

Brueckner, J. K., & Zenou, Y. (1999). Harris–Todaro models with a land market. *Regional Science and Urban Economics*, 29(3), 317–339.

Brünjes, J., & Revilla Diez, J. (2016). Obtaining non-farm wage employment in rural Vietnam. *Asia Pacific Viewpoint, 57*(2), 263–279.

Bui, L. K., & Hoang, H. (2021). Non-farm employment, food poverty and vulnerability in rural Vietnam. *Environment, Development and Sustainability, 23*(5), 7326–7357.

Calvo, G. A. (1978). Urban unemployment and wage determination in LDCs: Trade unions in the Harris–Todaro model. *International Economic Review, 19*(1), 65–81.

Chakrabarti, A., Dhar, A. K., & Dasgupta, B. (2015). *The Indian economy in transition: Globalization, capitalism and development*. Cambridge: Cambridge University Press.

Chakrabarti, A., Dhar, A., & Majumdar, S. (2020). India's transition: A new complex of capitalism and Hindu nationalism. In I. Rossi (Ed.), *Challenges of globalization and prospects for an inter-civilizational world order* (pp. 503–530). Springer.

Chakrabarti, S. (2013). Interrogating inclusive growth: Formal–informal duality, complementarity, conflict. *Cambridge Journal of Economics*, 37(6), 1349–1379.

Chakrabarti, S. (2014a). A critique of inclusive growth: Problems of modernization of agriculture. *World Review of Political Economy, 5*(3), 372–391.

Chakrabarti, S. (2014b). The formal–informal dichotomy: Revisiting the debate on the agriculture–industry linkage. *Economic and Labour Relations Review, 25*(1), 154–178.

Chakrabarti, S. (2016). *Inclusive growth and social change: Formal–informal agriculture relations in India*. New Delhi: Oxford University Press.

Chakrabarti, S., & Datta, P. K. (2024). Development management: A macro political economy perspective. In In B. Chatterjee & J. Sasmal (Eds.), *The Indian economy@75: Success and Challenges* (pp. 99–120). Routledge India.

Chakrabarti, S., & Kundu, A. (2009a). Rural non-farm economy: A note on the impact of crop-diversification and land-conversion in India. *Economic and Political Weekly*, *44*(12), 69–75.

Chakrabarti, S., & Kundu, A. (2009b). Formal–informal sectors' conflict: A structuralist framework for India. *Journal of Economic Development*, *34*(2), 27–67.

Chakrabarti, S., Kundu, A., & Nandi, A. K. (2011). Farm–non-farm linkage in India: A structuralist perspective. *Indian Journal of Agricultural Economics*, *66*(2), 178–197.

Chakravarty, M. (2014, 18 May). Election results a victory for Indian capitalism. *Livemint*. Retrieved 13 April 2025, from https://www.livemint.com/Opinion/rccwjo8IwotZaCbSioNZFP/Election-results-a-victory-for-Indian-capitalism.html.

Chancel, L., & Piketty, T. (2019). Indian income inequality, 1922–2015: From British raj to billionaire raj? *Review of Income and Wealth*, *65*, S33–S62.

Chatterjee, P (2004). *Politics of the governed: Reflections of popular politics in most of the world*. Princeton, NJ: Princeton University Press.

Chatterjee, P. (2008a). Democracy and economic transformation in India. *Economic and Political Weekly*, *43*(16), 53–62.

Chatterjee, P. (2008b). India's divide: Economic growth and marginalized groups. *Brown Journal of World Affairs*, *14*(2), 139–147.

Chatterjee, S., Lebesmuehlbacher, T., & Narayanan, A. (2021). How productive is public investment? Evidence from formal and informal production in India. *Journal of Development Economics*, *151*, 102625.

Chaudhuri, S., & Mukhopadhyay, U. (2002). Economic liberalization and welfare in a model with an informal sector. *Economics of Transition*, *10*(1), 143–172.

Chaudhuri, S., & Mukhopadhyay, U. (2009). *Revisiting the informal sector: A general equilibrium approach*. Springer Science & Business Media.

Chen, X., Xue, Z., Han, G., & Gao, Q. (2024). The impact of land consolidation on farmer income: Evidence from high-standard farmland construction in China. *Frontiers in Sustainable Food Systems*, *8*, 1412095.

Chowdhury, S. (2011). Employment in India: What does the latest data show? *Economic and Political Weekly*, 46(32), 23–26.

Chuong, H. N. (2023). The role of social capital in shaping livelihood for rural Vietnamese households. *PLoS One*, *18*(12), e0295292.

Conley, T., & Udry, C. (2001). Social learning through networks: The adoption of new agricultural technologies in Ghana. *American Journal of Agricultural Economics*, *83*(3), 668–673.

Coppard, D. (2001, November). The rural non-farm economy in India: A review of the literature (Working paper, Natural Resources Institute). University of Greenwich. Retrieved 14 March 2025, from https://gala.gre.ac.uk/id/eprint/11644/1/11644_Coppard_The%20rural%20non%20farm%20economy%20in%20India%20(working%20paper)%202001.pdf.

Corden, W. M., & Findlay, R. (1975). Urban unemployment, intersectoral capital mobility and development policy. *Economica*, *42*(165), 59–78.

CSA (Central Statistical Agency). (2017). Agricultural sample survey 2016/17: Report on area and production of major crops (Private peasant holdings, Meher season). Federal Democratic Republic of Ethiopia, Central Statistical Agency.

Cucculelli, M., & Storai, D. (2018). Industrial districts, district effect and firm size: The Italian evidence. *Cambridge Journal of Economics, 42*(6), 1543–1566.

Cutler, S. J., Fooks, A. R., & Van Der Poel, W. H. (2010). Public health threat of new, re-emerging, and neglected zoonoses in the industrialized world. *Emerging Infectious Diseases, 16*(1), 1.

Dabalen, A., Paternostro, S., & Pierre, G. (2004). *The returns to participation in the non-farm sector in rural Rwanda* (Vol. 3462). World Bank Publications.

Dary, S. K., & Kuunibe, N. (2012). Participation in rural non-farm economic activities in Ghana. *American International Journal of Contemporary Research, 2*(8), 154–161.

Dartanto, T., Yuan, E. Z. W., & Sofiyandi, Y. (2017, October). Structural transformation and the dynamics of income equality in Indonesia: 1996–2014 (Asian Development Bank Institute (ADBI) Working Paper No. 783). ABDI. Retrieved 14 March 2025, from https://www.adb.org/sites/default/files/publication/371316/adbi-wp783.pdf.

Dasgupta, A. (2021). Peasant production in India: How the 'need economy' facilitates accumulation. *Development and Change, 52*(2), 217–240.

Dasgupta, D., & Rajeev, M. (2020). Paradox of a supply-constrained Keynesian equilibrium: The COVID-19 case. *Economic and Political Weekly, 55*(22), 22–27.

Datta, P. K., & Chakrabarti, S. (2024). Problems of globalization of agriculture: A critique of inclusive growth 1. In R. Bhattacharyya & D. Mazumdar (Eds.), *Contemporary issues in international trade* (pp. 263–278). Emerald Publishing Limited.

Davis, B., Di Giuseppe, S., & Zezza, A. (2014, November). Income diversification patterns in rural sub-Saharan Africa: Reassessing the evidence (Policy Research Working Paper No. 7108). World Bank. Retrieved 22 June 2025, from https://documents1.worldbank.org/curated/en/861761468340796327/pdf/Income-diversification-patterns-in-rural-Sub-Saharan-Africa-reassessing-the-evidence.pdf.

Davis, M. (2004). Planet of slums. *New Left Review, 26*, 5.

Deininger, K., Jin, S., & Sur, M. (2007). Sri Lanka's rural non-farm economy: Removing constraints to pro-poor growth. *World Development, 35*(12), 2056–2078.

Dell'Angelo, J., D'Odorico, P., Rulli, M. C., & Marchand, P. (2017). The tragedy of the grabbed commons: Coercion and dispossession in the global land rush. *World Development, 92*, 1–12.

De Mel, S., McKenzie, D., & Woodruff, C. (2012, April). The demand for, and consequences of, formalization among informal firms in Sri Lanka (National Bureau of Economic Research (NBER) Working Paper No. 18019). NBER. Retrieved 12 March 2025, from https://www.nber.org/papers/w18019.

De Silva, L. R., & Kodithuwakku, S. S. (2005). Pluriactivity and socio-economic success of rural households. *Sri Lankan Journal of Agricultural Economics, 7*, 85–108.

De Silva, M., & Kodithuwakku, S. S. (2010). Pluriactivity, entrepreneurship and socio-economic success of rural households (Manchester Business School Working Paper No. 596). University of Manchester. Retrieved 22 June 2025, from https://www.econstor.eu/bitstream/10419/50729/1/656919760.pdf#:~:text=In%20this%20paper%2C%20this%20issue%20is%20investigated%20thro ugh,extent%20of%20socio-economic%20success%20achieved%20by%20farming%20households.

De Soto, H., & Diaz, H. P. (2002). The mystery of capital. Why capitalism triumphs in the West and fails everywhere else. *Canadian Journal of Latin American & Caribbean Studies*, *27*(53), 172.

Do, M. H., Nguyen, T. T., Halkos, G., & Grote, U. (2022). Non-farm employment, natural resource extraction, and poverty: Evidence from household data for rural Vietnam. *Environment, Development and Sustainability*, 1–38.

Do, M. H., Nguyen, T. T., & Grote, U. (2023). Land consolidation, rice production, and agricultural transformation: Evidence from household panel data for Vietnam. *Economic Analysis and Policy*, *77*, 157–173.

Elsevier. (n.d.). Informal sector. In *ScienceDirect*. Retrieved 21 June 2025, from https://www.sciencedirect.com/topics/social-sciences/informal-sector.

FAO (Food and Agriculture Organization). (1995). *Programme for the World Census of Agriculture 2000* (FAO Statistical Development Series No. 5). FAO.

Farooq, S., & Younais, Z. (2022). Do non-farm enterprises offer pathways for upward mobility in rural Pakistan? Evidence from panel dataset. *Pakistan Development Review*, *57*(2), 203–221.

Fauziah, I., Jamhari, & Nugroho, A. D. (2023). The impact of agricultural land consolidation on production and income of rice farming household in Sukoharjo Regency. *Journal of Agribusiness Management and Development*, *2*(1), 42–47.

Fei, J. C., & Ranis, G. (1964). *Development of the labor surplus economy: Theory and policy*. Homewood, IL: Irwin.

Fields, G. S. (1975). Rural–urban migration, urban unemployment and underemployment, and job-search activity in LDCs. *Journal of Development Economics*, *2*(2), 165–187.

Fields, G. S. (1989). On-the-job search in a labor market model: Ex ante choices and ex post outcomes. *Journal of development economics*, *30*(1), 159–178.

Fields, G. S. (1990). Labour market modelling and the urban informal sector: Theory and evidence. Cornell University. Retrieved 22 June 2025, from https://ecommons.cornell.edu/server/api/core/bitstreams/67086a38-fef6-419f-8489-b4cd0db8c227/content.

Fields, G. S. (1999). Employment generation and poverty alleviation in developing economies. Cornell University Industrial and Labor Relations (ILR) Collection. Cornell University, 91-111.

Fields, G. S. (2004). Dualism in the labor market: A perspective on the Lewis model after half a century. *The Manchester School*, *72*(6), 724–735.

Fields, G. S. (2005). A welfare economic analysis of labor market policies in the Harris–Todaro model. *Journal of Development Economics*, *76*(1), 127–146.

Fields, G. S., & Wan Jr, H. (1989). Wage-setting institutions and economic growth. *World Development*, *17*(9), 1471–1483.

Gale, F., & Gooch, E. (2018, 24 April). China's agricultural investment abroad is rising. Amber Waves. US Department of Agriculture, Economic Research Service. Retrieved 22 June 2025, from https://www.ers.usda.gov/amber-waves/2018/april/china-s-agricultural-investment-abroad-is-rising.

Gedefaw, A. A., Atzberger, C., Seher, W., & Mansberger, R. (2019). Farmers' willingness to participate in voluntary land consolidation in Gozamin District, Ethiopia. *Land*, *8*(10), 148.

Ghani, E., Goswami, A. G., & Kerr, W. R. (2012, April). Is India's manufacturing sector moving away from cities? (NBER Working Paper No. 17992). NBER. Retrieved 22 June 2025, from https://www.nber.org/system/files/working_papers/w17992/w17992.pdf.

Ghatak, M., & Mookherjee, D. (2014). Land acquisition for industrialization and compensation of displaced farmers. *Journal of Development Economics, 110*, 303–312.

Government of India, Ministry of Finance, Department of Economic Affairs. (2022). *Economic Survey 2021-22* (with Statistical Appendix). Retrieved from https://www.indiabudget.gov.in/budget2022-23/economicsurvey/doc/echapter.pdf

GRAIN. (2010, 29 March). Land grabbing in Latin America. Retrieved 22 June 2025, from https://www.grain.org/article/entries/3995-land-grabbing-in-latin-america.

Grinols, E. L. (1991). Unemployment and foreign capital: The relative opportunity costs of domestic labour and welfare. *Economica*, *58*(229), 107–121.

Guha-Khasnobis, B., & Kanbur, R. (Eds). (2006). *Linking the formal and informal economy: Concepts and policies.* Oxford: Oxford University Press.

Guha-Khasnobis, B., Kanbur, R., & Ostrom, E. (2006). Beyond formality and informality. In B. Guha-Khasnobis, R. Kanbur, & E. Ostrom (Eds), *Linking the formal and informal economy: Concepts and policies* (pp. 75–92). Working Paper No. 4. Ithaca, NY: Cornell University, Department of Applied Economics and Management.

Gupta, N. (2016). Decline of cultivators and growth of agricultural labourers in India from 2001 to 2011. *International Journal of Rural Management*, *12*(2), 179–198.

Haggblade, S. (2007). Alternative perceptions of the rural nonfarm economy. In S. Haggblade, P. B. R. Hazell, & T. Reardon (Eds), *Transforming the rural nonfarm economy: Opportunities and threats in the developing world* (pp. 25–54). IFPRI.

Haggblade, S., Hazell, P. B., & Reardon, T. (2002). Strategies for stimulating poverty-alleviating growth in the rural nonfarm economy in developing countries (IFPRI Environment and Production Technology Division (EPTD) Discussion Paper No. 92). IFPRI. Retrieved 22 June 2025, from https://ageconsearch.umn.edu/record/16092/?v=pdf.

Haggblade, S., Hazell, P. B. R., & Reardon, T. (2008). *Transforming the rural nonfarm economy: Opportunities and threats in the developing world.* Oxford: Oxford University Press.

Haggblade, S., Hazell, P., & Reardon, T. (2010). The rural non-farm economy: Prospects for growth and poverty reduction. *World Development*, *38*(10), 1429–1441.

Harris, J. R., & Todaro, M. P. (1970). Migration, unemployment and development: A two-sector analysis. *American Economic Review*, *60*(1), 126–142.

Harriss, J. (2020). The implications of 'stunted structural transformation' for rural India: *How lives change: Palanpur, India and development economics*, by Himanshu, Peter Lanjouw and Nicholas Stern, Oxford University Press, 2018.

Revue canadienne d'études du développement/Canadian Journal of Development Studies, 42(4), 580–589.

Harriss-White, B. (2013). West Bengal's rural commercial capital. *International Critical Thought, 3*(1), 20–42.

Harriss-White, B. (2023). Awkward classes and India's rural development. *Indian Economic Journal*, 71(1), 56–77.

Harriss-White, B., Olsen, W., Vera-Sanso, P., & Suresh, V. (2013). Multiple shocks and slum household economies in South India. *Economy and Society, 42*(3), 398–429.

Harvey, D. (2003). Accumulation by dispossession. In *The new imperialism* (pp. 137–182). Oxford: Oxford University Press.

Hazell, P. B., & Haggblade, S. (1990). *Rural–urban growth linkages in India* (Vol. 430). World Bank Publications.

Himanshu, Lanjouw, P., & Stern, N. (2018). *How lives change: Palanpur, India, and development economics.* Oxford: Oxford University Press.

Himanshu. (2019, 28 March). India's farm crisis: Decades-old and with deep roots. *The India Forum.* Retrieved 13 March 2025, from https://www.theindiaforum.in/article/farm-crisis-runs-deep-higher-msps-and-cash-handouts-are-not-enough.

Hitayezu, P., Okello, J. J., & Obel-Gor, C. (2014). Farm households' participation in rural non-farm employment in post-war Rwanda: Drivers and policy implications. *Development Southern Africa, 31*(3), 452–474.

Hoda, A. (2018, July). Land use and land acquisition laws in India (Indian Council for Research on International Economic Relations (ICRIER) Working Paper No. 361). ICRIER. Retrieved 22 June 2025, from https://icrier.org/pdf/Working_Paper_361.pdf.

Hohberg, M., & Lay, J. (2015). The impact of minimum wages on informal and formal labor market outcomes: Evidence from Indonesia. *Institute of Labor Economics (IZA) Journal of Labor & Development, 4*, 1–25.

Howe, G., & McKay, A. (2007). Combining quantitative and qualitative methods in assessing chronic poverty: The case of Rwanda. *World Development, 35*(2), 197–211.

Hymer, S., & Resnick, S. (1969). A model of an agrarian economy with nonagricultural activities. *American Economic Review, 59*(4), 493–506.

ILO (International Labour Organization). (2015). Indonesia: Trends in wages and productivity, January 2015. ILO. Retrieved 22 June 2025, from https://www.ilo.org/sites/default/files/wcmsp5/groups/public/@asia/@ro-bangkok/@ilo-jakarta/documents/publication/wcms_343144.pdf.

ILO. (2018). *Women and men in the informal economy: A statistical picture.* Geneva: ILO. Retrieved 22 December 2024, from https://www.ilo.org/sites/default/files/2024-04/Women_men_informal_economy_statistical_picture.pdf.

ILO. (2020, 20 April). COVID-19 and the world of work. *Updated Estimates and Analysis, 27.* Retrieved 22 June 2025, from https://www.assiv.it/wp-content/uploads/2020/04/ILO.pdf.

Invest India. (2024, 30 September). A decade of economic transformation with 'Make in India'. Retrieved 21 June 2025, from https://www.investindia.gov.in/blogs/decade-economic-transformation-make-india.

Iqbal, M. A., Rizwan, M., Abbas, A., Makhdum, M. S. A., Kousar, R., Nazam, M., . . . & Nadeem, N. (2021). A quest for livelihood sustainability? Patterns, motives and determinants of non-farm income diversification among agricultural households in Punjab, Pakistan. *Sustainability*, *13*(16), 9084.

Issah, I., Khan, T. Y., & Sasaki, K. (2005). Do migrants react to infrastructure difference between urban and rural areas? Development of an extended Harris–Todaro model. In *Review of Urban & Regional Development Studies: Journal of the Applied Regional Science Conference* (Vol. 17, No. 1, pp. 68–88). Oxford; and Boston, MA: Blackwell Publishing, Inc.

Jabbar, A., Wei, L., Zhang, J., Liu, J., Wang, Y., Wu, Q., & Peng, J. (2023). Exploring the contributions of non-farm income diversification for improving soil and water conservation practices and reducing rural poverty in rain-fed areas of Punjab, Pakistan. *Frontiers in Sustainable Food Systems*, *7*, 1179919.

Jatav, M. (2010). Casualisation of workforce in rural non-farm sector of India: A regional level analysis across industries. *Indian Journal of Labour Economics*, *53*(3), 501–516.

Jatav, M., & Sen, S. (2013). Drivers of non-farm employment in rural India: Evidence from the 2009–10 NSSO Round. *Economic and Political Weekly*, *48*(26/27), 14–21.

Jayne, T. S., Chamberlin, J., & Headey, D. D. (2014a). Land pressures, the evolution of farming systems, and development strategies in Africa: A synthesis. *Food Policy*, *48*, 1–17.

Jayne, T. S., Chapoto, A., Sitko, N., Nkonde, C., Muyanga, M., & Chamberlin, J. (2014b). Is the scramble for land in Africa foreclosing a smallholder agricultural expansion strategy? *Journal of International Affairs*, *67*(2), 35–53.

Jha, P. (2019). Labour, capital and state in neoliberal India: Some reflections on recent developments. In A. K. Mehta & A. Shepherd (Eds), *Perspectives on neoliberalism, labour and globalization in India: Essays in honour of Lalit K. Deshpande* (pp. 99–121). Springer.

Kalaiyarasan, A. (2022, 6 June). Stunted structural transformation in the Indian economy. Center for the Advanced Study of India, University of Pennsylvania. Retrieved 21 June 2025, from https://casi.sas.upenn.edu/iit/kalaiyarasana.

Kalecki, M. (1934/1971). On foreign trade and 'domestic exports'. *In Selected essays on the dynamics of the capitalist economy*. Cambridge: Cambridge University Press.

Kalecki, M. (1955/1993). The problem of financing economic development. In J. Osiatyński (Ed.), *Collected works of Michał Kalecki* (Vol. 5, pp. 45–60). Oxford: Clarendon Press.

Kalra, A., & Stecklow, S. (2021, 13 October). Amazon copied products and rigged search results to promote its own brands, documents show. *Reuters*. https://www.reuters.com/investigates/special-report/amazon-india-rigging.

Kanbur, R. (2009). Conceptualising informality: Regulation and enforcement (IZA Discussion Paper No. 4186). IZA. Retrieved 22 June 2025, from https://www.econstor.eu/bitstream/10419/35431/1/602117542.pdf.

Kanwal, N., Khan, M. A., & Zheng, Z. (2016). Analyzing the determinants of non-farm income diversification of farm households in Peshawar district of Pakistan. *Timisoara Journal of Economics and Business*, *9*(1), 33–48.

Kar, S., & Marjit, S. (2001). Informal sector in general equilibrium: Welfare effects of trade policy reforms. *International Review of Economics & Finance*, *10*(3), 289–300.

Kathuria, V., Raj, S. N. R., & Sen, K. (2013). The effects of economic reforms on manufacturing dualism: Evidence from India. *Journal of Comparative Economics, 41*(4), 1240–1262.

Kazmi, S. M. A., Imran, S. M., Nasim, I., & Ayub, M. (2023). Impact of non-farm activities on income: A case of rural areas of district Bahawalpur. *International Research Alliance for Sustainable Development (IRASD) Journal of Economics, 5*(1), 120–126.

Kemal, M. A. (2007). A fresh assessment of underground economy and tax evasion in Pakistan: Causes, consequences and linkages with the formal economy (Working Paper No. 2007:13). Pakistan Institute of Development Economics.

Kesar, S. (2023). Economic transition, dualism and informality in India: Nature and patterns of household-level transitions. *Review of Development Economics, 27*(4), 2438–2469.

Kesar, S., & Bhattacharya, S. (2020). Dualism and structural transformation: The informal manufacturing sector in India. *European Journal of Development Research,* 32(3), 560–586.

Khan, F., & Mansoor, K. (2020, 11 May). COVID-19 impact: Informal economy workers excluded from most govt measures, be it cash transfers or tax benefits. *Firstpost.* Retrieved 22 June 2025, from https://www.firstpost.com/business/covid-19-impact-informal-economy-workers-excluded-from-most-govt-measures-be-it-cash-transfers-or-tax-benefits-8354051.html.

Kowalski, J., Lipcan, A., McIntosh, K., Smida, R., Sørensen, S. J., Seff, I., & Jolliffe, D. (2016). Nonfarm enterprises in rural Ethiopia: Improving livelihoods by generating income and smoothing consumption? *Ethiopian Journal of Economics, 25*(2), 171–204.

Kundu, A., & Chakrabarti, S. (2008). Some micro-economic aspects of informal sector enterprises: Field-based evidence from West Bengal. *Artha Vijnana, 50*(3), 209–238.

Kundu, A., & Chakrabarti, S. (2010). Non-agricultural Informal sector in India: Impacts of agrarian conditions. *Indian Journal of Labour Economics, 53*(2), 199–224.

Kundu, A., Bhattacharjee, M., Datta, P. K., Sadhu, K., & Chakrabarti, S. (2021). The pandemic and the informal sector of India: Probable impacts and strategic intervention. In R. Bhattacharyya, A. G. Dastidar & S. Sikdar (Eds.), *The COVID-19 pandemic, India and the world* (pp. 289–308). Routledge India.

La Porta, R., & Shleifer, A. (2014). Informality and development. *Journal of Economic Perspectives, 28*(3), 109–126.

Lagakos, D. (2020). Urban–rural gaps in the developing world: Does internal migration offer opportunities? *Journal of Economic Perspectives, 34*(3), 174–192.

Lanjouw, J. O., & Lanjouw, P. (2001). The rural non-farm sector: Issues and evidence from developing countries. *Agricultural Economics, 26*(1), 1–23.

Lee Jr, J. E. (1965). Allocating farm resources between farm and nonfarm uses. *American Journal of Agricultural Economics, 47*(1), 83–92.

Lee, J. W., & Wie, D. (2015). Technological change, skill demand, and wage inequality: Evidence from Indonesia. *World Development, 67*, 238–250.

Leinbach, T. R. (Ed.). (2003). *The Indonesian rural economy: Mobility, work and enterprise* (Vol. 245). Institute of Southeast Asian Studies.

Lerche, J. (2013). The agrarian question in neoliberal India: Agrarian transition bypassed? *Journal of Agrarian Change, 13*(3), 382–404.

Lerche, J. (2021). The farm laws struggle 2020–2021: Class–caste alliances and bypassed agrarian transition in neoliberal India. *Journal of Peasant Studies, 48*(7), 1380–1396.

Lewis, W. A. (1954). Economic development with unlimited supplies of labour. *The Manchester School, 22*(2), 139–191.

Loayza, N., & Rigolini, J. (2006). *Informality trends and cycles* (Vol. 4078). World Bank Publications.

Lowder, S. K., Skoet, J., & Singh, S. (2014, April). What do we really know about the number and distribution of farms and family farms in the world? Background paper for The State of Food and Agriculture 2014. FAO. Retrieved 22 June 2025, from https://openknowledge.fao.org/server/api/core/bitstreams/f508c32d-cfdf-44ad-b792-865a957fdb59/content.

Lowder, S. K., Skoet, J., & Raney, T. (2016). The number, size, and distribution of farms, smallholder farms, and family farms worldwide. *World Development, 87*, 16–29.

Maloney, W. F. (2003). Informal self-employment: Poverty trap or decent alternative? In G. S. Fields & G. Pfeffermann (Eds.), *Pathways out of poverty* (pp. 65–82). Dordrecht: Springer.

Maloney, W. F. (2004). Informality revisited. *World Development, 32*(7), 1159–1178.

Marchetta., F. (2013). Migration and nonfarm activities as income diversification strategies: The case of Northern Ghana. *Canadian Journal of Development Studies, 34(1)*, 1–21.

Marjit, S. (2003). Economic reform and informal wage—a general equilibrium analysis. *Journal of Development Economics, 72*(1), 371–378.

Marjit, S., & Kar, S. (2011). *The outsiders: Economic reform and informal labour in a developing economy*. Oxford: Oxford University Press.

McMichael, P. (2008). Peasants make their own history, but not just as they please. *Journal of Agrarian Change, 8*(2–3), 205–228.

Mehta, B. S., & Kumar, A. (2020, 22 April). Covid-19 lockdown impact: Estimating the job losses in India's informal economy. *Swarajyamag*. Retrieved 12 March 2025, from https://swarajyamag.com/economy/covid-19-lockdown-impact-estimating-the-job-losses-in-indias-informal-economy.

Mellor, J. W., & Lele, U. J. (1973). Growth linkages of the new foodgrain technologies. *Indian Journal of Agricultural Economics, 28*(1), 35–55.

Milanovic, B. L. (2013, 20 November). Global income inequality (GII) 1988–2002. Ref. WLD_2002_GII_v01_M. Retrieved 5 December 2021, from https://microdata.worldbank.org/index.php/catalog/1784/get-microdata.

Milanovik, J. W. (n.d.). One Nation One Market. Retrieved 21 June 2025, from https://www.narendramodi.in/mobile/one-nation-one-market.

Moene, K. O. (1988). A reformulation of the Harris–Todaro mechanism with endogenous wages. *Economics Letters*, 27(4), 387–390.

Mookherjee, D., & White, J. (2011). Urban–regional dualism in India: An exploration of developmental indicators across urban size classes. *Asian Geographer, 28*(1), 21–31.

Moser, C. O. (1978). Informal sector or petty commodity production: Dualism or dependence in urban development? *World Development*, *6*(9–10), 1041–1064.

Mosley, P. (2017). *Fiscal policy and the natural resources curse: How to escape from the poverty trap*. Routledge.

Mughal, K. S., & Schneider, F. G. (2020). How informal sector affects the formal economy in Pakistan? A lesson for developing countries. *South Asian Journal of Macroeconomics and Public Finance*, *9*(1), 7–21.

Mukherjee, A., & Chakrabarti, S. (2016). *Development economics: A critical perspective*. PHI Learning Pvt. Ltd.

Mukherjee, A., Saha, N., Datta, P. K., & Chakrabarti, S. (2019). Informal sector: Progression or Persistence?. In S. Bandyopadhyay & M. Dutta (Eds.), *Opportunities and challenges in development: Essays for Sarmila Banerjee* (p. 117).

Mulia, R., Simelton, E., Nguyen, T. Q., & Jirström, M. (2021). Non-farm activities and impacts beyond the economy of rural households in Vietnam: A review and link to policies. *Sustainability*, *13*(18), 10182.

Mulyaningsih, T., Adhitya, D., & Rosalia, A. C. T. (2021). Education, skills and labour market outcome in Indonesia: An instrumental variable approach. *Economic Journal of Emerging Markets*, *13*(2), 168–177.

Munck, R. (2013). The precariat: A view from the South. *Third World Quarterly*, *34*(5), 747–762.

Nadkarni, M. V. (2018). Crisis in Indian agriculture: Can it be overcome? *Economic and Political Weekly*, *53*(17), 28–34.

Nadkarni, M. V. (2022). The viability crisis and institutional challenges before Indian agriculture. In S. R. Hashim, R. Mukherji, & B. Mishra (Eds.), *Perspectives on inclusive policies for development in India: In honour of Prof. R. Radhakrishna* (pp. 385–394). Singapore: Springer Nature Singapore.

Narendra Modi. (n.d.). One Nation One Market. Retrieved 21 June 2025, from https://www.narendramodi.in/mobile/one-nation-one-market.

Navaratne, W. M. U. (2000). Contribution of small tanks to upkeep the village community. Food Security and Small Tank Systems in Sri Lanka; National Science Foundation: Colombo, Sri Lanka.

Nazir, A., Li, G., Inayat, S., Iqbal, M. A., Humayoon, A., & Akhtar, S. (2018). Determinants for income diversification by farm households in Pakistan. *Journal of Animal & Plant Sciences*, *28*(4), 1163–1173.

Neglo, K. A. W., Gebrekidan, T., & Lyu, K. (2021). The role of agriculture and non-farm economy in addressing food insecurity in Ethiopia: A review. *Sustainability*, *13*(7), 3874.

News18. (2024, 1 April). Nearly 60,000 hectares of forest land diverted for commercial use in three years, Centre tells Parliament. *News18*. Retrieved 22 June 2025, from https://www.news18.com/india/nearly-60000-hectares-of-forest-land-diverted-for-commercial-use-in-three-years-centre-tells-parliament-9273308.html.

Nguyen, H. T. T., Pham, X. H., & Kondo, T. (2021). The impact of non-farm activities on agricultural investment in Vietnam: The difference made by credit constraints levels. *Studies in Agricultural Economics*, *123*(3), 141–152.

Nilsson, P. (2019). Spatial spillovers and households' involvement in the non-farm sector: Evidence from rural Rwanda. *Regional Studies*, *53*(5), 731–740.

Nkegbe, P. K., Abdelkrim, A., Abu, B. M., Ustarz, Y., Alhassan, H., Setsoafia, E. D., & Abdul-Wahab, S. (2019). Encouraging non-farm work to increase agricultural commercialization in Ghana (Partnerships for Economic Policy (PEP) Policy Brief No. 189). PEP.

Niroula, G. S., & Thapa, G. B. (2005). Impacts and causes of land fragmentation, and lessons learned from land consolidation in South Asia. *Land Use Policy, 22*(4), 358–372.

NSSO (National Sample Survey Office). (2019). Situation assessment of agricultural households and land and livestock holdings of households in rural India (NSS Report No. 587). Ministry of Statistics and Programme Implementation, Government of India.

Nun, J. (2000). The end of work and the 'marginal mass' thesis. *Latin American Perspectives, 27*(1), 6–32.

Osumanu, I. K., & Ayamdoo, E. A. (2022). Has the growth of cities in Ghana anything to do with reduction in farm size and food production in peri-urban areas? A study of Bolgatanga Municipality. *Land Use Policy, 112*, 105843.

Otsuka, K., Liu, Y., & Yamauchi, F. (2016). The future of small farms in Asia. *Development Policy Review, 34*(3), 441–461.

Oviedo, A. M. (2009). Economic informality: Causes, costs, and policies: A literature survey of international experience. Background paper prepared for Country Economic Memorandum (CEM)–Informality: Causes, Consequences, Policies, 361711–1277211666558.

Pandey, B., & Seto, K. C. (2015). Urbanization and agricultural land loss in India: Comparing satellite estimates with census data. *Journal of Environmental Management, 148*, 53–66.

Patnaik, P. (2008). The accumulation process in the period of globalisation. *Economic and Political Weekly, 43*(26/27) 108–113.

Patnaik, P. (2016). Globalisation, inequality and economic crisis. *Studies in People's History, 3*(1), 71–81.

Patnaik, P. (2017, 5 October). The class content of the Goods and Services Tax. *International Development Economics Associates (IDEAs) blog*. Retrieved 12 March 2025, from https://www.networkideas.org/news-analysis/2017/10/class-content-goods-services-tax.

Pattayat, S. S., & Parida, J. K. (2024). Drivers of rural non-farm sector employment in India, 1983–2019. *South Asia Economic Journal, 25*(1), 45–73.

Pham, T. L., Le, N. T., Ho, N. N. P., & Le, T. C. (2024). Consumption inequality between farm and non-farm households in rural Vietnam. *Journal of Asian Business and Economic Studies, 31*(4), 290–306.

Portes, A. (1989). Latin American urbanization during the years of the crisis. *Latin American Research Review, 24*(3), 7–44.

Portes, A., & Jensen, L. (1989). The enclave and the entrants: Patterns of ethnic enterprise in Miami before and after Mariel. *American Sociological Review, 54*(6), 929–949.

Raj, S. N. R., & Sen, K. (2016). Moving out of the bottom of the economy? Constraints to firm transition in the Indian informal manufacturing sector. *IZA Journal of Labor & Development, 5*(1), 1–20.

Rajeev, M., & Bhattacharjee, M. (2017). Augmenting small farmers' income through rural non-farm sector in India: Role of information and institutions. In V. Xaxa, D. Saha, & R. Singha (Eds.), *Work, institutions and sustainable livelihood: Issues and challenges of transformation* (pp. 73–99). Singapore: Springer.

Rajeev, M., & Bhattacharjee, M. (2018, July). Farm non-farm linkage and role of non-farm sector for rural development (Policy Brief No. 20). Institute for Social and Economic Change. Retrieved 12 March 2025, from https://www.isec.ac.in/wp-content/uploads/2023/07/PB-20-Farm-Non-Farm-Policy_final.pdf.

Rakshit, M. (Ed.). (1989). *Studies in the macroeconomics of developing countries.* Delhi: Oxford University Press.

Rakshit, S. (2014). Output, surpluses and 'stressed commerce': A study on farm viability and agrarian transition in West Bengal, India, in the new millennium. *Journal of Peasant Studies, 41*(3), 343–363.

Ralston, L. R., Tiwari, S., Al Faizin, R. E., Borden, M. G., Mosquera, J. A., Cartwright Ramon, J. A., . . . & Utami, A. F. (2020). *No one left behind: Rural poverty in Indonesia.* Washington D.C.: World Bank.

Ranis, G., & Fei, J. C. (1961). A theory of economic development. *American Economic Review, 51*(4), 533–565.

Ranis, G., & Stewart, F. (1993). Rural nonagricultural activities in development: Theory and application. *Journal of Development Economics, 40*(1), 75–101.

Ranis, G., & Stewart, F. (1999). V-goods and the role of the urban informal sector in development. *Economic Development and Cultural Change, 47*(2), 259–288.

Ray, Debraj (1998) *Development Economics.* Princeton, NJ: Princeton University Press.

Reardon, T. (1997). Using evidence of household income diversification to inform study of the rural nonfarm labor market in Africa. *World Development, 25*(5), 735–747.

Reardon, T., Stamoulis, K., Balisacan, A., Cruz, M. E., Berdegué, J., & Banks, B. (1998). Rural non-farm income in developing countries. *The State of Food and Agriculture, 1998*, 283–356.

Reardon, T., Berdegué, J., Barrett, C. B., & Stamoulis, K. (2006). Household income diversification into rural nonfarm activities. In S. Haggblade, P. B. R. Hazell, & T. Reardon (Eds), *Transforming the rural nonfarm economy: Opportunities and threats in the developing world* (pp. 115–140). Baltimore, Maryland: Johns Hopkins University Press.

Reddy, D. N., Reddy, A. A., Nagaraj, N., & Bantilan, C. (2014). Rural non-farm employment and rural transformation in India (Working Paper Series No.57). International Crops Research Institute for the Semi-Arid Tropics (ICRISAT). Retrieved 12 March 2025, from https://oar.icrisat.org/10392/1/Rural%20Non-Farm%20Employment%20and%20Rural%20Transformation%20in%20India.pdf.

Retief, F. P., & Cilliers, L. (1998). The epidemic of Athens, 430–426 BC. *South African Medical Journal, 88*(1), 50–53.

Review of Agrarian Studies. (2020). COVID-19 and the rural non-farm sector. *Review of Agrarian Studies, 10*(1). Retrieved 22 June 2025, from http://ras.org.in/covid_19_and_the_rural_non_farm_sector.

Rigg, J. (1997). *Southeast Asia: The human landscape of modernization and development.* London: Routledge.

Rijkers, B., & Costa, R. (2012). Gender and rural non-farm entrepreneurship. *World Development, 40*(12), 2411–2426.

Rijkers, B., Söderbom, M., & Teal, F. (2008). Rural non-farm enterprises in Ethiopia: Challenges and prospects. In *Rural Europe in the global agro-food system.* Copenhagen.

Rodrik, D. (2013). Unconditional convergence in manufacturing. *Quarterly Journal of Economics, 128*(1), 165–204.

Rodrik, D. (2018). An African growth miracle? *Journal of African Economies,* 27(1), 10–27.

Rosser, A. (2004, March). Why did Indonesia overcome the resource curse? (Institute of Development Studies (IDS) Working Paper No. 222). IDS. Retrieved 14 March 2025, from https://opendocs.ids.ac.uk/articles/report/Why_did_Indonesia_overcome_the_resource_curse_/26477479?file=48231289.

Roychowdhury, S. (2018). Welfare without work or wages: A contradiction. *Economic and Political Weekly, 53*(35), 53–60.

Ruppert Bulmer, E. (2020). Sri Lanka jobs diagnostic (Jobs Series No. 21). World Bank. Retrieved 22 June 2025, from https://documents1.worldbank.org/curated/en/973321591596940034/pdf/Sri-Lanka-Jobs-Diagnostic.pdf.

Sadhu, K., & Chakrabarti, S. (2021). Neo-dualism: Accumulation, distress, and proliferation of a fissured informality. *Review of Radical Political Economics, 53*(4), 694–724.

Sala-i-Martin, X., & Subramanian, A. (2013). Addressing the natural resource curse: An illustration from Nigeria. *Journal of African Economies, 22*(4), 570–615.

Sanyal, K. (2007). *Rethinking capitalist development: Primitive accumulation, governmentality and post-colonial capitalism.* Routledge India.

Sanyal, K., & Bhattacharyya, R. (2009). Beyond the factory: Globalisation, Informalisation of production and the new locations of labour. *Economic and Political Weekly, 44*(22), 35–44.

Schmidt, E., Mugabo, S., & Rosenbach, G. (2024). Rural income diversification in Rwanda: Opportunities and challenges (IFPRI Working Paper No. 13). IFPRI. Retrieved 22 June 2025, from https://cgspace.cgiar.org/server/api/core/bitstreams/28c8a5d4-59fb-4ad9-ab02-7aa2be3f18c3/content.

Sen, A. (1983). Development: Which way now? *Economic Journal, 93*(372), 745–762.

Sen, K. (2012, 5 January). Economic reforms have not reduced dualism in Indian manufacturing. *Economic Times.* Retrieved 21 June 2025, from https://economictimes.indiatimes.com/economic-reforms-have-not-reduced-dualism-in-indian-manufacturing/articleshow/11370473.cms?.

Sen, K. (2024). Broken ladders? Labour market inequality in Indonesia and India. *Bulletin of Indonesian Economic Studies, 60*(2), 161–191.

Senadza, B. (2012). Non-farm income diversification in rural Ghana: Patterns and determinants. *African Development Review, 24*(3), 233–244.

Sharma, A. K., & Rai, S. K. (2024). COVID-19 and sectoral employment in India: Impact and implications. *Indian Journal of Labour Economics, 67*(1), 177–196.

Sharma, H. R., & Malik, S. H. (2021). Land distribution structure, marginalisation of holdings and dimensions of viability crisis in Indian Agriculture: A state level analysis. *Indian Journal of Agricultural Economics, 76*(2), 207–224.

Singh, I., Squire, L., & Strauss, J. (1986). A survey of agricultural household models: Recent findings and policy implications. *World Bank Economic Review, 1*(1), 149–179.

Standing, G. (2011). *The precariat: The new dangerous class.* London, UK: Bloomsbury Academic.

Standing, G. (2014). Understanding the precariat through labour and work. *Development and Change, 45*(5), 963–980.

Sudaryanto, T. (2020, 16 Ocotber). Indonesian agricultural labor policy: Issues and challenges. *Food and Fertilizer Technology Center (FFTC) Agricultural Policy Platform (FFTC-Asia Pacific (AP))*. Retrieved 28 March 2025, from https://ap.fftc.org.tw/article/2592.

Taufique, M., & Hoque, A. (2017). Tribal labour out migration in Malda district of West Bengal: A spatial analysis. *International Journal of Scientific Research and Development, 5*(02), 845–849.

Tesgera, W. D., Beyene, A. B., & Wakjira, T. K. (2024). Does non-farm employment increase rural households' consumption in western Ethiopia? Empirical evidence from the Horo Guduru Wollega Zone. *Heliyon, 10*(7), e29500.

Thakur, G. M., & Guha, S. (2019). Petty services, profit-led growth and rural–urban migration in a developing economy. *Metroeconomica, 70*(1), 144–171.

The Economic Times. (2014, 12 November). Government plans to create unified national market. *The Economic Times.* Retrieved 21 June 2025, from https://economictimes.indiatimes.com/news/economy/policy/government-plans-to-create-unified-national-market/articleshow/45116293.cms?from=mdr.

The Economic Times. (2015, 28 October). GST key reform for creating a single market in India: World Bank. *The Economic Times.* Retrieved 21 June 2025, from https://economictimes.indiatimes.com/news/economy/policy/gst-key-reform-for-creating-single-market-in-india-world-bank/articleshow/49568864.cms.

The Economic Times. (2021, 29 December). E-commerce hiring up 28 pc in 2021; 2022 likely to be even more promising: TeamLease. *The Economic Times.* Retrieved 12 March 2025, from https://economictimes.indiatimes.com/jobs/e-commerce-hiring-up-28-pc-in-2021-2022-likely-to-be-even-more-promising-teamlease/articleshow/88568712.cms.

The Hindu Business Line. (2015, 30 December). Agriculture market reforms are a must. *The Hindu Business Line.* Retrieved 21 June 2025, from https://www.thehindubusinessline.com/opinion/agriculture-market-reforms-are-a-must/article10007561.ece/amp.

Tuyishime, C., Pernechele, V., Bizimana, C., & Semwaga, O. (2020). *Rwanda food and agriculture policy monitoring review 2020.* FAO of the United Nations. Retrieved 12 March 2025, from https://www.fao.org/agrifood-economics/publications/detail/en/c/1370434.

UNDP (United Nations Development Programme. (2006). *Human development report 2006: Beyond scarcity—Power, poverty and the global water crisis.* UNDP. Retrieved 21 June 2025, from https://www.undp.org/libya/publications/

human-development-report-2006-beyond-scarcity-power-poverty-and-global-water-crisis.

Van Vu, H. (2020). The effect of education on poverty in rural Vietnam. *International Journal of Innovation, Creativity and Change, 13*(7), 906–917.

Weerahewa, J., Kanthilanka, H., Farquharson, J. R., Thrikawala, S., Ramilan, T., & Dayananda, D. (2021). An analysis of labour use pattern in Thirappane village tank cascade system in Sri Lanka: Determinants and potential effects of off-farm employment. *Sri Lankan Journal of Agricultural Economics, 22*(1), 77–101.

Wise, T. A. (2015). The great land giveaway in Mozambique. *Dollars & Sense.* Retrieved October 13, 2025, from https://www.dollarsandsense.org/the-great-land-giveaway-in-mozambique/.

World Bank. (n.d.). India overview: Development news, research, data. World Bank. Retrieved 21 March 2025, from https://www.worldbank.org/en/country/india/overview#1.

World Bank. (2003). Natural resources: When blessings become curses (Country Note H). World Bank. Retrieved 12 March 2025, from http://www1.worldbank.org/prem/lessons1990s/chaps/Ctrynote7_AreNaturalResources.pdf.

World Bank. (2007). Agriculture for development: World development report 2008. World Bank. Retrieved 12 March 2025, from https://openknowledge.worldbank.org/handle/10986/5990.

World Bank. (2009). World development report 2009: Reshaping economic geography. World Bank. Retrieved 12 March 2025, from https://openknowledge.worldbank.org/server/api/core/bitstreams/19d4154e-b830-560d-bb24-0d6a9210d5c7/content.

World Bank. (2018). India development update, March 2018: India's growth story. World Bank. Retrieved 12 March 2025, from https://documents.worldbank.org/en/publication/documents-reports/documentdetail/729671522172750342/india-development-update-march-2018-indias-growth-story.

World Bank. (2020a). Informality, job quality, and welfare in Sri Lanka (Report No. 34399). World Bank. Retrieved 12 March 2025, from https://openknowledge.worldbank.org/server/api/core/bitstreams/21abf1e1-1b5b-568d-8851-33fd10285824/content.

World Bank. (2020b). COVID-19 crisis through a migration lens (Migration and Development Brief No. 32). World Bank. Retrieved 12 March 2025, from https://openknowledge.worldbank.org/handle/10986/33634.

World Bank. (2021). Economic effects of COVID-19: Rapid surveys of rural households in India. World Bank. Retrieved 12 March 2025, from https://pubdocs.worldbank.org/en/645971613651626018/Economic-Effects-of-COVID19-Rapid-Rural-Surveys.pdf.

World Bank. (2024). World development indicators. Retrieved 20 March 2025, from https://databank.worldbank.org/source/world-development-indicators.

World Bank Group. (2021, 1 October). The rural nonfarm sector and livelihood strategies in Sri Lanka: Background report to Sri Lanka poverty assessment. World Bank. Retrieved 14 March 2025, from https://documents.worldbank.org/en/publication/documents-reports/documentdetail/210021634313271639/the-rural-nonfarm-sector-and-livelihood-strategies-in-sri-lanka-background-report-to-sri-lanka-poverty-assessmen.

World Economic Forum. (2021, 4 February). COVID-19 has caused a huge amount of lost working hours. Retrieved 20 March 2025, from https://www.weforum.org/stories/2021/02/covid-employment-global-job-loss.

World Resources Institute. (n.d.). Current urbanization in the Global South: Realities (in transformations for equitable & sustainable cities). Retrieved 21 March 2025, from https://publications.wri.org/transformations-equitable-sustainable-cities/current-urbanization-global-south-realities#2.1-urbanization-shifting-to-low-and-middle-income-countries.

Yadu, C. R., & Mehra, S. (2023, 10 April). Structural transformation: Then and now. Developing Economics. Retrieved 21 March 2025, from https://developingeconomics.org/2023/04/10/structural-transformation-then-and-now/#:~:text=Structural%20and%20demographic%20features&text=The%20issues%20of%20high%20population,transformation%20along%20the%20expected%20lines.

Yamauchi, F. (2016). Rising real wages, mechanization and growing advantage of large farms: Evidence from Indonesia. *Food Policy*, *58*, 62–69.

Yaried, A. A., Abate, K. A., & Atinkut, H. B. (2024). A leisure or livelihood strategy? Understanding nonfarm activities and income effects in rural Ethiopia. *Journal of Social and Economic Development*, 1–21.

Zellner, A. & Theil, H. (1962). Three stage least squares: Simultaneous estimation of simultaneous equations. *Econometrica*, *30*, 54–78.

Zerai, B., & Gebreegziabher, Z. (2011). Effect of nonfarm income on household food security in eastern Tigrai, Ethiopia: An entitlement approach. *Food Science and Quality Management*, *1*(10), 1–23.

Author Index

For the benefit of digital users, indexed terms that span two pages (e.g., 52–53) may, on occasion, appear on only one of those pages.

Tables and figures are indicated by an italic *t* and *f* following the page number.

Subject Index

For the benefit of digital users, indexed terms that span two pages (e.g., 52–53) may, on occasion, appear on only one of those pages.

Tables and figures are indicated by an italic *t* and *f* following the page number.